terest in alleviating this social ill, analyzes its depth and complexity, and explains why poverty is a vicious cycle that tends to be self-perpetuating. In the preface, Gunnar Myrdal argues that a welfare state is needed to cope with the dimensions of this problem.

Poverty, as a breeder of ignorance and crime, as social injustice, as a by-product of technological advances, or simply as a waste of human resources, is an issue that bears direct consequences for all of us. Mr. Seligman and a distinguished group of contributors have performed a valuable service in presenting original and incisive discussions of the economics and politics of poverty.

ABOUT THE EDITORS

BEN B. SELIGMAN is Professor of Economics and Director, Labor Relations and Research Center, University of Massachusetts. He is the author of *Main Currents in Modern Economics* and *Most Notorious Victory: Man in an Age of Automation*, both published by The Free Press. His articles on economics and public issues appear frequently in *Dissent*, *Commentary*, *New Leader*, and other journals.

GUNNAR MYRDAL, Professor of International Economics at the Institute for International Economic Studies, Stockholm, has written many books, among them *An American Dilemma* (with Richard Sterner and Arnold Rose).

THE FREE PRESS
A DIVISION OF THE MACMILLAN COMPANY
866 Third Avenue, New York 10022

Poverty as a Public Issue

Poverty
as a Public Issue

EDITED, WITH AN INTRODUCTION BY

Ben B. Seligman

Preface by Gunnar Myrdal

Fp

The Free Press, New York
Collier-Macmillan Limited, London

Preface

A dramatic change in American attitudes toward the social problem is under way. The nation is finally—and rather suddenly—becoming prepared to accept the welfare state. This implies an intellectual as well as a moral catharsis for that majority of Americans who are prosperous and secure. They cannot conceal from themselves any longer that there is in the United States a large "underclass" of poor and destitute people in the urban and rural slums who are largely cut off from the life and aspirations of the nation. They are brought to see the serious and dangerous consequences of poverty amidst plenty, not only for those people who are poverty-stricken, and their children, but for the progress and welfare of the nation as a whole. They are compelled to give up a whole system of irrational conceptions that had been built up in order to protect their indifference. Broad policy measures which a few years ago would have seemed to be radical and unacceptable are now rapidly becoming part of practical policy. The swelling flood of statistical investigations devoted to the poverty problem, conferences, seminars, books and articles, speeches, and policy declarations, give expression to this catharsis at the same time as they spur it on.

There are many other social changes that work in the same direction, and so become integrated in the movement toward the acceptance of the welfare state. The Negro rebellion within the past two years or so is one of them. It brought Congress last year to accept a civil-rights law more radical than anybody could have dreamed it would accept only three years ago. As this is written, the President feels it to be an urgent matter to announce a federal law with teeth in it to protect the Negroes' right to vote, and only last-ditch diehards are talking about a filibuster.

Even more important is the fact that it is now commonly recognized that equal rights are not enough to give real equality to a group that for so long has been treated as comprising second-class citizens. Very much more needs to be done than abolishing segregation and discrimination by legislation—in the fields of housing, employment, education, health, and so on. But Negroes do not make up more than a third or a fourth of those who are poverty-stricken. Moreover, for technical reasons alone, policies in these fields cannot be dealt with as merely Negro problems. Finally, such a segregation of policies cannot meet the Negroes' demand for equal treatment. And so we are back to the general problem of how to abolish poverty in America.

For the Negroes this implies the necessity to feel solidarity with all other disadvantaged groups, which is not an easy demand, because they often meet resentment from exactly those groups who have been their competitors. It means also that Negroes must acquire the wisdom to align themselves with all the progressive forces in the United States. They have, for instance, the greatest interest in supporting all those who strive for changing the American economy into a full-employment economy. As long as many white workers are unemployed or dread the risk of unemployment, all efforts to stamp out discrimination in the labor market cannot have more than rather futile effects.

At the same time, other sections of the population must share the responsibility of developing a solidarity which accommodates the aspirations of the Negro and all other disadvantaged groups. For socially balanced and secure progress toward a welfare state, the American people require a stronger and more progressive trade-union movement. Ironically, there are wide sections of the business community who are more prepared to accept the welfare state, or significant aspects of it, than some sectors of the labor leadership. They have at last learned from such liberal economists as Alvin Hansen, John Kenneth Galbraith, and others, that anything less is a drag on their own self-interest.

Another important change lies in the rise of the annual increase in Gross National Product from 2.5 per cent in the Eisenhower era to 5 per cent in the Kennedy-Johnson era. This change has been brought about by deliberately conceived policies. However, the growth rate is still not high enough. More than 1 per cent has to be subtracted in comparison with other rich countries with a lower population increase. Reckoned per head, there was almost total economic stagnation during the 1952–1960 period.

We know also that in the latter years the unemployment rate has gone down only from a little above 6 to under 5 per cent—not counting those who are not seeking jobs because they have lost confidence in their ability to get jobs, and those who are "underemployed" in the sense that their productivity and incomes are abnormally low. Because, moreover, the labor force will from now on increase half a time faster than up till now, the United States needs a considerably more rapid economic growth for the years to come in order to make a real dent in unemployment and, indeed, in order not to see the unemployment rate start to rise again.

A rapid and steady economic growth, raising the demand for labor and decreasing unemployment, must necessarily be a first precondition for success in the War on Poverty. But as part of the great intellectual and moral catharsis, it is now becoming generally recognized that much more than economic growth is needed in order to win this war. By education, training, and retraining, the quality of the labor supply must be raised to meet a changed labor demand. At the same time there is need for adjusting the labor demand to fit the labor supply more closely, which is an additional reason for speeding up various types of construction work that are badly needed for their own sake—as well as in the fields of transportation, low-cost housing and city renewal generally.

There must also be a more effective income redistribution in the interest of the aged, the sick, the disabled, and, in particular, the children. It is especially worth remarking at this point that if one-fifth of the nation is counted as poor or at the poverty level—one-quarter of the children are in that situation! Indeed, the whole Social Security system needs to be overhauled. It is still too much like the out-of-date pattern of the times of Bismarck and Lloyd George— when social welfare policy was considered *"eine Arbeiter-frage"*—which, in practice, means that the most needy are often left for discriminatory public and private charity. The United States can very well afford to give every citizen what he needs in health facilities and a pension when he reaches a certain age; this would also mean a tremendous simplification and rationalization of administration.

We are increasingly coming to recognize as part of this great catharsis that not only social security policies but almost all other policies—agricultural policies, taxation policies, housing policies, minimum-wage legislation, and so forth—have followed the perverse tendency to aid the not-so-poor, while leaving a bottom layer of very poor unaided. The War on Poverty will therefore have to be fought on many fronts and will in the end have to imply not only an enlargement but a redirection of all economic and social policies. In financial terms, it will soon amount to very much greater public expenditure than is still generally appreciated. But, the gradual increase of public expenditure will sustain demand and economic growth.

Nobody should expect this "unconditional War on Poverty," which was planned by the late President Kennedy and declared by President Johnson, to be a brief encounter. Even if courageously fought, it will take the best efforts of the nation for many years and even decades. Plans have to be carefully worked out and gradually set into effect. Hospitals and schools have to be built; doctors, nurses, and teachers have to be trained; and teachers of the teachers. Cities have to be rebuilt. The catharsis will result in new visions, and these visions will come out clearer and stretch farther, the more the efforts are intensified and prove their wholesome results for not only the poor but the whole nation.

To further that catharsis, discussions of the kind represented by the papers in this volume are most appropriate. The more the American public evaluates and analyzes the nature of poverty, the better will it be able to achieve the consensus so necessary to the solution of its social problems.

GUNNAR MYRDAL
PROFESSOR OF INTERNATIONAL ECONOMICS
INSTITUTE FOR INTERNATIONAL ECONOMIC STUDIES

Stockholm, March 1965

Contributors

Elinor Graham wrote her papers while a student at the Institute for Policy Studies. She majored in political science at Antioch College and is now working with a political-action group in eastern Kentucky.

Zona Fairbanks Hostetler was graduated from Harvard Law School in 1960. Her paper is based on several years of experience as a volunteer legal-aid attorney handling cases for indigent persons.

Earl E. Huyck is a Program Analysis Officer of the staff of the Assistant Secretary for Legislation, United States Department of Health, Education, and Welfare.

Gardiner C. Means is a well-known economist whose long career spans service under the New Deal. His major contribution to economics has been the theory of administered prices. Dr. Means is the author, among other works, of *Pricing Power and the Public Interest* (1962).

Herman P. Miller is special assistant to the Director of the U.S. Census Bureau. Author of *Rich Man, Poor Man* (1964), and many articles on income and poverty, he has taught at the American University and the University of California at Los Angeles.

S. M. Miller is professor of sociology at Syracuse University and Senior Research Associate at the Youth Development Center of the University. Formerly on the faculty at Brooklyn College he has written widely on the social problems of the poor.

Gunnar Myrdal is professor of international economics at Stockholm University. He is the author of the monumental study of race relations in the United States, *An American Dilemma* (1944) and numerous other books on economic and social problems. The most recent is *Challenge to Affluence* (1963), an analysis of unemployment in America.

Mollie Orshansky is with the Long Range Research Branch, Division of Research and Statistics, Social Security Administration. She is the author of numerous articles and reports on Social Security, child care, and problems of poverty.

W. J. Page, Jr. is Field Administration Representative, Office of the Secretary of Health, Education, and Welfare.

Martin Rein is associate professor of social work and social research at Bryn Mawr College. He has authored numerous articles on social planning, poverty, and social welfare, including "The Social Service Crisis" and "Dependency."

Walter E. Riddick is a research associate with the United Planning Organization in Washington, D. C. He received his education in psychology at Howard University and Columbia University and has coauthored several studies in geriatrics and juvenile delinquency.

Ben B. Seligman is Director of the Labor Relations and Research Center and professor of economics at the University of Massachusetts. He is also an Associate Fellow of the Institute for Policy Studies. Author of *Main Currents in Modern Economics* (1962), he has written on economic problems for *Commentary, Dissent, Challenge*, and other journals.

Harold L. Sheppard is Staff Social Scientist with the W. E. Upjohn Institute for Employment Research in Washington, D. C. Formerly assistant administrator for the Area Redevelopment Administration, he has written extensively on problems of aging and labor displacement stemming from plant shutdown.

Charles V. Willie is associate professor of sociology at Syracuse University and senior research associate at the university's Youth Development Center. His article on the Cardozo area was written while research director of the Washington Action for Youth.

Harold Wolozin is associate professor of economics at The American University and consultant to the Ford Foundation. He has specialized in the evaluation of standards and criteria for public programs.

Contents

Poverty as a Public Issue

Introduction[1]

BEN B. SELIGMAN

Quite recently, a noted economist of liberal persuasion tried to remind me that America had always experienced some measure of poverty and unemployment. Hence, was the implication, we ought to take consolation in the fact that the "numbers"—he meant the statistics on employment and income—revealed how much better off we were today than 30 years ago. I agreed that it was difficult to become indignant over poverty in an affluent society: such a response was more appropriate to the 1930's. The proper feeling now, I replied, was disgust. How else was one to react when a society could push its Gross National Product to $630 billion and at the same time tolerate within its midst abysmally low levels of income for some 30 to 40 million of its inhabitants?

Now, the attitude of my colleague was not smug or complacent. He was merely hopeful that we were in fact solving the problem of poverty. But were we? Except for a handful of social scientists and journalists, most Americans had deluded themselves, as they rushed across turnpikes and freeways, in believing that there were no more poor around, or if there were, these benighted few represented isolated instances that could be treated by the case method, whatever that might be. Such a view had been quite common in the postwar era. In the late 1940's a now eminent sociologist assured me that income-distribution patterns had been so altered that we were rapidly becoming middle class in respect to income figures as well as to aspiration. My offer to test his hypothesis by a visit to some nearby slums was not accepted. Somewhat later I became embroiled in a colloquy in the pages of *Commentary* (Sept. 1951) with William D. Grampp, a fairly conservative economist, who, utilizing some Federal Reserve Board data, had argued that inequality was being eliminated from the American scene. This, it seemed to me, was not only a premature observation, but an evasion of a persistent problem. Moreover, the business decline in 1949, a rather modest one, had accentuated the disproportion as compared to the previous year.

The debate remained inconclusive. The prosperous years of the fifties, with their burgeoning suburbias, pushed the poor further back into the hills or left them isolated in crowded city slums, while at the same time they were erased from our national consciousness. As we were celebrating a new class with television and tail-fin autos, we forgot that an old poor was living in quiet desperation in the rural slums of Appalachia and in the Negro ghettos of the city. We forgot too that technology was beginning to add to the poor in the coal towns of Pennsylvania. We forgot that silent yet dramatic changes accompanying prosperity in our economy were leaving behind a residue of poverty that might one day call into question the sensibilities of the larger society.

During these years a small number of writers, whose awareness of the realities of income and poverty was perhaps keener than most, kept reminding us that we had by no means solved all the social and economic problems of the day. One of these was Gabriel Kolko, whose *Wealth and Power in America* (1962), a self-conscious but serious work, attempted to demonstrate that the statistics on income failed to tell all there was to say about poverty. Unfortunately, it was marred by overanxious interpretations of the relevant data, as when Kolko argued that 23 per cent of those earning less than $1000 a year owned a car, as compared to 95 per cent of those earning more than $10,000. Dwight Macdonald later observed in a strikingly perceptive piece in *The New Yorker* (January 19, 1963) that the real point was just the opposite ". . . as any citizen of Iran, Ghana, Yemen or the U.S.S.R. would appreciate—not that the rich have cars but that almost a quarter of the extremely poor do." But Macdonald let another point escape him: in a technological society a car may be no luxury, for to earn something, one frequently needs better transportation than an ancient auto held together with baling wire.

Another difficulty with Kolko's book was his insistence that the distribution of income in the United States had remained substantially the same since 1910, a palpable misstatement of the facts. Further, as Herman P. Miller demonstrated in his book, *Rich Man, Poor Man* (1964), the data for 1910–1937, on which Kolko had relied, were considered so inaccurate that they were deleted by a panel of experts from the official *Historical Statistics of the U. S.* The critical point about income distribution, as Miller notes in his book, is that it has remained virtually unchanged since 1944. Hence, it would seem that income figures per se, while relevant, do not adequately demonstrate the nature of poverty. One needs to examine the quality of life, especially by contrast with the standards and expectations generated in modern society.

This was precisely the task that Michael Harrington set for himself in his *The Other America* (1962), a work that unquestionably helped arouse the recent furor over poverty. Harrington sharply reminds those preoccupied by the wonders of affluence that beneath it all there is a heavy layer of deprivation. The poor, says he, suffer from no temporary aberration but are subjected rather to a persistent and degrading suppression of their living standards and whatever humanity they once possessed. Moreover, America's poor, are strange and estranged, for they are invisible. As I wrote in a review of Harrington's book: "The average traveler on speedy turnpikes does not see the rundown company town where permanently unemployed loiter on street corners and in bars. Suburbanites at shopping centers no longer glimpse the poverty of downtown."

Harrington's great service was to reveal this hidden subculture of American society—one in which values exist that statistics cannot possibly describe. It is a culture that perpetuates itself in an endlessly desperate circle; it is a culture beyond the reach of the welfare state and its inhabitants are lonely, insecure, fatalistic, without pleasure. All this Harrington discovered by visits to flea-bitten employment agencies supplying dishwashers to restaurants; by talking with workers cast adrift by automated industry; by helping the Catholic Workers' group in their remarkable mission on New York's Bowery; by serving as a social worker in St. Louis.

Many of the poor are the unseen work force of the city. These are the employed poor: the restaurant workers, hospital employees, clerks in small shops, janitors, and menial jobholders. Unprotected by most social legislation they are unskilled and poorly educated, and more often than not are brutalized by unscrupulous employers and racketeer unions. They are also the displaced mineworkers kept in idleness forever by John L. Lewis' desperate deals with the coal operators. They are migrant farm workers, "hillbillies" hidden by the foliage of Appalachia. They are small farmers, the last of America's yeomanry. They are Negroes, long-time inhabitants of the poverty subculture, at work, if at all, mainly in the lowest and poorest paying jobs. They are the aged, of whom there are now more than ever before, and whom we merely tolerate and store away in institutions and roominghouses to die.

Of course, there has been improvement since the days of the Great Depression. No one in his right mind would assert that starvation is rampant in America. But as Dwight Macdonald says, the continuation of poverty in the midst of plenty denies the proposition that every citizen has a right to be part of our society; if that right is denied, "it impov-erishes us all." True, nobody starves in an absolute sense, but who can measure the starvation, Macdonald has asked, that places many of the poor in a long vestibule to death?

Macdonald's extraordinary piece was read by many persons who had overlooked the Harrington book or had been frightened off by Kolko's appalling prose. One such reader was Ted Sorensen, special assistant to President John F. Kennedy. According to Washington legend, Sorensen was so moved—or perhaps so astute—that he at once urged his chief to read the *New Yorker* article. Thus was born the War on Poverty, or at least its beginnings. On February 14, 1963, President Kennedy proposed a national youth service akin to the Peace Corps that was working so well overseas. Through the months that followed public discussion and congres-sional talk revolved about the notion of a Domestic Service Corps. Obviously, this was a limited approach, and aware of the political atmosphere on the Hill, the Kennedy Adminis-tration, always concerned with the politically possible, moved with characteristic caution. When Lyndon Johnson was required by an assassin's rifle to take over the reins of power, it seemed doubtful that much would be done. But in March 1964, hearings on a broader bill started in the House of Representatives. Suddenly, "poverty" became fashionable: Adam Clayton Powell, chairman of the House Committee on Education and Labor opened the hearings with a flourish and a press release. The Administration spoke not only of youth, but of the aged, fatherless, Negroes, rural poor, and industrially dispossessed. It proposed to spend a billion dol-lars in skirmishing along the poverty front.

As is underscored by several of the authors in the sym-posium that follows, the government's modest proposal rep-resented but a beginning, although perhaps a significant one. Harrington delights in telling the story of his first visit to Sargent Shriver after the latter had been designated chief of the War on Poverty. Shriver asked Harrington what he thought of the assignment. Said Harrington, "It's nickels and dimes in the poverty problem." Shriver stared at him. "Mr.

Harrington," he replied, "perhaps you've spent a billion dollars before, but this is my first time around." One supposes the point to be well taken, at least for a program whose administrators must face up to the particular problem to which it is addressed for the first time. Yet Harrington's wry response cannot be gainsaid, for public assistance alone accounts for some $5–$6 billion, while OASDI and unemployment insurance require about $18 billion of outlays. One can hardly expect that a billion dollars a year will cure wounds for which band-aid treatment has cost more than twenty times that much.

Some members of the affluent society, especially those who might have experienced rough times in their youth, or those whose parents were poor immigrants, are apt to be somewhat bemused by the recent concern over poverty. No one, they say, legislated a war on poverty for Irish, Italian, or Jewish immigrants at the turn of the century. Faced by a hostile environment that was nevertheless filled with opportunity, these ethnic groups overcame their bewilderment, seized the main chance, and climbed the ladder of success. If there are poor people around us today, then it must be due to defects of character, lack of will, or an unwillingness to undertake risk.

What is not acknowledged, however, is that poverty today has a new shape, a physiognomy substantially different from that which existed 50 or 60 years ago. The older poverty was an accompaniment to the unfolding of industrial expansion. Not much more pleasant than the situation facing today's 30 million dispossessed, it was at least surrounded by a layer of hope. Not only were there burgeoning industries to absorb the newcomer—steel, railroads, textiles, clothing—but the economy's need for sheer muscle power obviated any prospective demand for great skill or education. Job opportunities were plentiful, but even more important, there was a kind of internal ladder of opportunity allowing a young man to climb, for example, all the way from floorsweeper to skilled machinist in not too many years. In any case, there were enough such instances to lend a measure of reality to the American promise.

There are some writers who insist that the promise indeed has been fulfilled. For such persons the existence of poverty in the United States is a tale told by dyspeptic social scientists who have allowed themselves to be blinded by propaganda and false statistics. They quickly attack those who decry the presence of poverty in an affluent society, offering supposedly sophisticated data and casually concluding that there are too few poor to make the problem really troublesome: in any case, they say, "voluntary cooperation in charity, no less than in economic production, can be and is guided by an invisible hand." Such are the words of Rose D. Friedman who, in a pamphlet on poverty written for the American Enterprise Institute, concludes that only 10 per cent of the populace should be classified as "poor." Mrs. Friedman's sole standard is an income level at which a diet adequate in nutrition is made available to the consumer, a standard defined in money terms at $2200 per annum. Anything above that is "not-poor." She excludes from this caloric criterion any consideration of clothing needs, shelter, or other requirements that make an individual a viable member of society. Thus she asks: how many yards of cloth are basic to decency? How many square feet of space constitute adequate shelter? Evidently, for Mrs. Friedman, it is enough that shelter protect one from the elements: it does not seem to have occurred to her that a tar papered shack in Appalachia achieves that purpose also —after a fashion. The consequence is that efforts to define shelter or clothing standards are deemed by her to be totally subjective and therefore not part of any scientific evaluation of poverty. Worse still, Mrs. Friedman assumes *a priori* that families with adequate nutrition have adequate clothing and housing. As a result, her pure caloric standard reveals poverty to be negligible in the United States today. But such a definition equates poverty with hunger or starvation, and since the latter doesn't exist, *ipso facto* there is no poverty.

The syllogism is attractively simple and totally egregious. The most charitable thing that might be said about such an analysis is that as a clear case of conservative economics, it has as much connection with the realities of poverty as its political counterpart has with the realities of world affairs.

What are some of the economic elements involved in American poverty? As Dr. Willie suggests in his paper, low wages and unemployment are obvious factors. Despite the improved employment numbers to which my economist friend persists in alluding, production jobs in manufacturing industries declined between 1953 and 1964 by 960,000. Of all the major manufacturing sectors, only fabricated metals showed a gain during this period—of 6000 jobs. The recent recovery in some factory jobs by no means has made up the losses sustained since 1953. Clearly, some rather striking and dramatic changes in the manpower profile of the nation were occurring under our very noses, and many of them were being imposed by a new technology. True, total employment has been increasing, but the postwar explosion in population was the "exogenous" factor, as the theoretician has it, that provided the motive power. The expansion of the population was indeed job-creating; together with the larger consumer market which it supplied, the vast growth in output, almost 50 per cent in real dollars between 1953 and 1964, provided the necessary fillip. If there had been no job gain at all in these years, we should be in a perilous condition. Yet one wonders as to its adequacy, for most of the job advance has come in those soft-goods lines that have not yet been caught up in the new technology, and in government and service occupations— beauty shops, hospitals, teaching.

What the data imply is an enormous shift of the *employed* work force out of manufacturing into services. This hardly means that a displaced auto worker becomes a government clerk: obviously he has neither the training nor the inclination for that sort of work. We are now discovering that his new job, after months of search, is apt to be a poorer one in a repair shop or gasoline station. If the worker persists in looking for something to which he has given the years of his life, he may very well remain unemployed. Meanwhile most of the new entrants into the work force— at the rate of 1.5 million a year—find no jobs or go to work part time at low pay, generally in the service trades.

Consequently, the economy tends to create a "frozen," unusable industrial reserve army with no palpable relation to the affluent, functioning segments of the society. One may estimate the hard-core unemployment attributable to such structural change, that is, stemming from alterations in production functions or capital-labor coefficients, or whatever it is the theoretical economist wishes to call them— changes that are inherent in technology—at approximately 1.3 million persons. But this is merely the visible portion of technology's toll. To these souls one must add, as does Leon Keyserling, a million or more workers who have dropped out of the labor force because they got tired looking for jobs and are therefore not counted in the official censuses, and a million in full-time equivalents for those working part-time.

If we are to search for the causes of much of the poverty we now have we need to go little further than these phenomena. Automation in industry appears to be a powerful contributing factor. Numerical controls operated by computers carve metal pieces with greater precision than a skilled mechanic can; process-control computers guide production from the mixture of a raw-material batch to the finished product ready to be loaded onto a freight car; printing is being converted from a craft into an industry by phototypesetting and computer methods that do all the justifying and hyphenation of copy. In industry after industry, advanced mechanization and automation are substituting machines for men. With increasing automation, control over a machine itself is exercised by a machine, and industrial measurement is done electronically. The outcome is a movement out of the skilled occupations into the semiskilled, accompanied by unemployment of the unskilled, who if lucky, can drift into the odds and ends of the service trades.

Surprisingly enough, or perhaps not so surprisingly, many economists, still subscribing to the archaic notion of Say's Law—to wit, that every supply creates its own demand, contend that unemployment and poverty, especially among youth, would evaporate if only wage rates were reduced. The assumption is that labor would then become more competitive with the machine. The argument is not unrelated to the explicit hostility among many professional economists to minimum-wage laws; such legislation, it is said, has prevented concerns from employing as many workers as they might otherwise have done. One economist, then resident in a great western university, even suggested to me that juvenile delinquency would be solved if only supermarket operators were allowed to pay something like half the statutory minimum!

Aside from the moral obtuseness these arguments reflect, there is no warrant in economic theory or fact for such contentions. To paraphrase Lord Keynes, economists as well as politicians and practical men are enthralled by ancient scribblers. For one thing, a perusal of recent empirical studies, such as the C. A. Pearce, *et al.*, analysis, *Economic Effects of Minimum Wages in New York State*, would reveal no "disemployment" stemming from a minimum wage. To apply archaic theory to policy would simply depress earnings in industries where they are already low. Second, Lord Keynes' teaching stressed the urgency of adequate levels of purchasing power, something that not a few economists appear to have forgotten.

A further argument in the arsenal of the conventional wisdom, again stemming from Say's Law, is the proposition that increasing real wages represents a barrier to economic development. A proper analysis, however, would acknowledge that increases in real wages, given our rules of the economic game, are occasioned by the competition of growing industries for resources. Such an effect was observed almost three-quarters of a century ago by Knut Wicksell, the famous Swedish economist, who had remarked that expansion must take into account increased real wages. For so long as earnings are sustained by growth or shifts to new techniques there should be no objection by entrepreneurs to improved wage standards. In fact, most discussions of this question—the relation of real wages to capital accumulation—assume perfect competition and a homogeneous production function; under conditions of monopolistic or imperfect competition, the relationship poses even less of a problem. Provision necessarily must be made for a larger amount of "subsistence" goods, that is, for real wages, unless the entire added accumulation is to be applied exclusively to capital purposes. Indeed, this cannot be the situation in an economy in which decisions on savings and investment are made by different persons. Investment without any absorption at all by wages of at least a portion of the capital accumulation can occur only when the saver and investor are identical—as in a command economy with strict central planning.

And, as we have indicated, account must be taken of the level of effective demand. For when prices and wages are sticky, with the latter at low levels, it is possible for each firm to gain individually from low real wages in terms of its own output, but all would soon suffer from the limited market for commodities which such a policy would enforce. If prices and wages are flexible, a condition that ordinary theory deems to be so desirable, and if population were to increase more rapidly than investment, then all that will have been achieved is a pool of unemployed, while the real wage may at best remain unchanged. Maintaining the same rate of investment will not create more employment. When prices are sticky and wages flexible, the situation would be even worse, since both demand and investment would stagnate. Of course, if investment were to grow and the real wage along with it, then the economy might achieve a state of nirvana, but in any case, the possibility of a bleaker prospect cannot be denied. The crux of the situation, consequently, is that real wages must move in consonance with productivity to provide enough demand to absorb the larger output stemming from the investment of capital. Moreover, if population keeps growing, then expansion of production must be even greater simply to absorb the additional bodies entering the labor force. And, to compound the difficulty, additional investment may not contribute much to maintaining the requisite balance because capital-saving is now a significant feature of newly installed equipment. That is, surplus savings unmatched by investment or consumption can develop and upset the delicate balance of the equations. In essence, underconsumption and the conditions of poverty that follow in its wake, so long depreciated in standard economic theory, is an ever-present ghost at the banquet table.

Thus, real wages must keep pace with productivity if a market for goods is to be maintained and capital accumulation is to continue to provide capacity for growth. This is especially necessary if jobs are to be provided under conditions of innovation. The economy might still exhibit a sense of exhilaration, even if real wages were lagging, but the truth is that trouble would be in the making. It therefore seems evident, both from the standpoint of theory and fact, that a modern economy requires a high level of real wages rather than a low one. With the latter, conditions are bound to develop such that marketability of goods and capital accumulation would both grind to a halt.

Historically, capital was substituted for labor because of the latter's relative scarcity. This, at least, was the experience of the nineteenth century. Theoretically, the availability of surplus labor ought to have exerted some restraining influences on such substitutions, for when labor competes for jobs, especially in a fluid labor market, the "capitalist" presumably has less impetus to mechanize. In effect, labor competes against machines. However, given an advanced technology, such competition can occur only between machines and *usable* labor.

Meanwhile, the Wicksell effect, operating through the real wage, tends over the long run to absorb a portion of capital accumulation in that sector of the economy employing the usable work force. In order to maintain a predetermined ratio of profit to capital accumulation, it would be necessary for the "capitalist" to mechanize even further, which in turn would make some of the skilled redundant. This all-important ratio, of profit to capital accumulation, may be maintained by resorting to capital-saving investment; in fact, this is often preferable, since such a process makes the application of accumulation to investment more extensive, thereby yielding an even greater volume of profit. But what all this suggests is that the "coefficients" implicit in the production function are not invariable. They shift with alterations in the underlying technology and do affect the ratio of capital to labor.

This seems to be the crux of the problem today: the surplus labor pool that is being accumulated is less and less usable with existing techniques and cannot really compete with machines. One cannot dip into the pool, since the relevant labor force must have certain skills and education. As E. Gilpatrick has argued, the more mechanized an industry, the more fixed the specific labor skills required per unit of capital or per unit of output and the less can one skill be substituted for another. Moreover, because specialized training and education are increasingly necessary to perform existing jobs, the less likely are skills to be transferred from one job to another. The worker who reads with difficulty is virtually unemployable once laid off. Further, in the absence of use, skills deteriorate, creating a continuing barrier between the displaced and the employed. The consequence is that the pool of unskilled becomes a stagnant one; untapped by society because it has no function, it becomes a conglomerate collection of economically and socially useless persons. Here, perhaps, is an economic explanation of the persistent unemployment and poverty of our time.

The contributions that follow stem from a seminar on poverty conducted at the Institute for Policy Studies in Washington, D.C. from January to June, 1964. Virtually all of the papers were first presented at these sessions. When they had been gathered and edited for publication, it was

realized that some lacunae still remained; it was therefore
decided to supplement the delivered papers by soliciting
additional articles to fill the gaps. The latter are those by
Zona F. Hostetler ("Poverty and the Law"); S. M. Miller
and M. Rein ("The War on Poverty") and Harold Wolozin
("Poverty and the Criteria for Public Expenditures"). In
addition, the article on Appalachia by Page and Huyck,
which first appeared elsewhere, has been added.

A word on the "seminarians": the object of the seminar
was to reach persons involved in local as well as federal
activities relating to the poverty issue. While individuals in
the President's Task Force on Poverty were too preoccupied
with guiding a bill through Congress and establishing the
necessary administrative structures to be able to attend, the
seminar did attract individuals from such operating agencies as the Washington Action for Youth, the United Planning Organization, and the District of Columbia Department
of Recreation. In addition, there were representatives from
the Department of Health, Education, and Welfare, the
Department of Labor, the Housing and Home Finance
Agency, and the Department of Commerce. Several private
research organizations also participated. Representatives
from a number of labor unions and universities completed
the roster.

The "seminarians" were impressed by Dr. Herman P.
Miller's analysis of changes in the concept of poverty from
the mid-nineteenth century to the present, and by the contrast between New Deal and contemporary approaches to the
"impoverished." Nevertheless, issue was taken with some
of the cultural and economic implications of Miller's remarks. The point in question was the extent to which the
possession of material goods defines poverty. It was argued
that a telephone or radio or TV were not luxuries, but often
represented functional necessities, especially for elderly people who are physically isolated. Notions of subsistence have
changed and will continue to be modified, and thus the
category of material goods without which a person may
be considered deprived, will necessarily broaden.

The significance of Dr. Miller's statistics on the numbers of families with incomes of $3000 or less who actually owned cars, houses and other forms of tangible property was also questioned. Long-term mortgages and the "buying-on-time" craze may involve considerable debt, yet hardly represents full ownership. One would need data, it was said, on overdue payments, reclaimed items, and equity as opposed to market values in order to arrive at a more reasonable estimate of what the poor do and do not "own." Further, a number of the participants were disturbed by efforts to arrive at any economic or statistical measure of poverty. The problem, if one is to accept that term at all, is spiritual and cultural, and one for which the larger society and its basic, persistent values are largely to blame. Similarly, participants cautioned against being too critical of the consumption habits of the poor, for in too many respects they simply emulate the behavior of the middle classes. While the latter have enough income to take care of subsistence and health needs, as well as frivolous items, the poor do not have enough for either, much less for both types of expenditure.

There was concern over Dr. Miller's comments on the permanency of poverty. Was there any evidence other than impressions that the immigrants of fifty years ago had aspiration and hope in addition to their economic poverty, while the present poor lack aspiration and tend to pass on their impoverished economic and spiritual state from one generation to another? It was finally agreed that in dealing with such evasive variables as group characteristics, changing economic and social conditions, aspiration levels, and generational or endemic poverty, there was much room for conjecture and that the amount of "hard" data was limited.

Thus the discussion continued in rather lively fashion. One seminarian, head of a major local social-welfare program, confessed to being tired of the debate over modifying or extending public-assistance programs. In his view, this approach was no longer appropriate. Present conditions, said he, required the creation of new ways for people to work, to be and feel useful, and to receive a legitimate return for their work. Others replied that it was precisely the shortage of suitable jobs, the inadequate wage scales of many, and continuing automation that required maintenance of public-assistance programs, and indeed, required the abandonment of the notion that a person deserves a livable income only in return for work. The suggestion that people be employed to build hospitals, schools, and highways, said some of the participants, reminded them of New Deal WPA and PWA efforts, and did not hold much promise of a dramatic break from contemporary methods of production and employment.

Obviously, some clarification was needed at this point: the speaker's attack on public-assistance programs was not to minimize their function, but to highlight the ways in which these are administered and have served to demean recipients rather than to help them out of their dependent position. Most of the participants agreed. In particular, it was noted that some of the compromises written into social security and welfare legislation were due largely to the ingrained American reluctance to give away anything "for nothing." If America is sorely in need of new job opportunities and training techniques, it is equally in need of revised notions about work.

While acknowledging that the idea of "work" needed redefining, others were concerned that the lot of those who are now employed be improved. In addition to the many unskilled workers not yet covered by minimum-wage requirements, there are an unknown number of workers who may never earn much more than the minimum wage. Studies of wage rate movements are deceptive, it was said, and inconclusive, for they reveal little on the lifetime earning levels of different groups of people. Recent evidence suggested that people who start out in low-paying jobs tend to remain at comparable job levels and not to move in the proverbial "rags-to-riches" direction. There was some question as to whether further increases and extended coverage of minimum-wage levels would do much to relieve poverty:

what would be the effects on investment, on employment, on family living standards, and prices?

When Dr. Means presented his thesis on the aggregate demand solution, some fear was expressed that inflationary forces might stimulate rapid price increases even if there were no necessary economic causes. Dr. Means replied that effective government action, and especially pressure on the business community, would prevent that sort of "irrational" inflation. Nevertheless, some participants thought that Dr. Means had underestimated the extent to which price increases in consumer goods and services would get out of hand in case aggregate demand should suddenly increase by 5 to 6 per cent.

Exception was also taken to Dr. Means's argument that new jobs would be created largely by upgrading those now employed and bringing in new, unskilled or untrained workers. It was argued that if past experience were any guide, then the tendency would be to supplement the existing labor supply with capital and technological improvements, rather than to increase the overall number of employed. If such factor substitution continued, as it has in the past decade, then it would be difficult to see how further increases in aggregate demand would enhance job opportunities. Means remained convinced that new laborers would be drawn into a plant even if pressures to increase wages of existing workers had to be met.

Had Dr. Means overlooked the problem of a time lag between a sudden increase in disposable income and the availability of additional services or consumer products, it was asked? Wasn't he too optimistic about preventing sudden inflation? Similarly, if 35 to 40 per cent of Means's projected demand increases were to go into the service industries, inflationary pressures would be very high, and increased job opportunities would not be nearly so great as Dr. Means had hoped.

Another participant wondered if Dr. Means had not made too many free-market assumptions. After the deliberate action by the government to increase aggregate demand, was there not assumed a more or less automatic process of upgrading existing workers and adding new ones? Had some of the problems attendant upon structural changes been neglected—for example, the increased costs of educating people to fill higher job positions? The point at which structural changes accompany changes in aggregate demand is one where, it was said, the "aggregate demand theorists" and the "structuralists" ought to cooperate; there is need for greater understanding of which structural changes are natural, which intentional, and which possible.

A persistent theme throughout the various discussions was the critical importance of the sociopsychological and not merely the economic dimension of the poverty problem. This was especially evident in Dr. Sheppard's incisive and perceptive contribution. Originally presented as a single paper at the seminar, Dr. Sheppard's analysis is here offered as three distinct chapters—on poverty among youth, aged, and Negroes. During the discussions, Dr. Sheppard insisted that known statistical data on the aged leave unanswered critical questions regarding their social and economic status. Tabulations on income and assets, he said, tend to confuse descriptive statements with normative propositions and frequently lead to the presumption that older persons in fact live as they should: that is, it is all too frequently assumed that needs and expectations suddenly lessen when an individual crosses the age 65 threshold. Several of the participants wondered whether a time or "longitudinal" analysis would indicate that poor older persons had always been poor, or whether they entered upon the poverty condition only in old age. Dr. Sheppard argued too that the aged were entitled to a share of their earlier contributions to the economy and society: he wondered whether direct cash subsidies to the aged might not be a feasible way of dealing with the problem. This was questioned by another seminarian (my economist friend so fascinated by numbers!) on the grounds of theoretical welfare economics of an almost pure Paretian character: would not a subsidy program for one group in society, he asked, diminish the welfare of some other group?

Objection was raised to Dr. Sheppard's exploration of the feasibility of providing income to youth when no jobs might be available. Here the issue revolved about the curious double standards developing in our society: the worth of an individual depends upon work, yet no work is provided to many youths. Moreover, the sort of preparation for work that once existed—either in a family enterprise or through farm chores—is no longer available. The entrance to work is devoid of early experience, yet employers demand of youths that they shall have acquired some experience. Inevitably, the Ad Hoc Committee's Report on the Triple Revolution proposing annual guaranteed incomes entered the debate. Some would accept the TR's prescriptions for the elderly, but not for other groups in the society; others were concerned that a guaranteed minimum income, regardless of whether a person were employed or not, might reinforce "nonworking" as a way of life; and still others were utterly skeptical of minimum-income-guarantee programs.

However, it is time to let the reader judge for himself.[2]

NOTES

1. Several paragraphs on technology were taken from a study on automation now in preparation.
2. Needless to say, the views of the various authors are their own and are not to be attributed to any of the organizations with which they are affiliated.

The Dimensions
of Poverty

HERMAN P. MILLER

The Concept of Poverty

Definitions of poverty change and our attitudes toward the poor are altered accordingly. In the thirties you were not stigmatized for being poor. Poverty was blamed on the times and the system. Today, poverty and failure are blamed on the individual. Poor farmers are told to get off the farm; residents of depressed areas are advised to move elsewhere; the uneducated and the untrained are sent back to school. During the depression the poor were helped by giving them more money. Today, we want to make them "better people." Why the change? Just what is poverty and who are the poor?

Poverty is hard to define and even harder to measure. All would agree with Webster that poverty is the "quality or state of being poor or indigent"; but like all defintions that are not controversial, it is also not very meaningful. It is only when Webster attempts to elucidate his meaning and equates poverty with "need, destitution . . . and inadequacy" that the nature of the problem comes into focus. These three words are the key to much of the confusion that exists about poverty. They all pertain to the boundaries that separate the poor from everyone else, but the similarity ends there. For it is the failure to recognize the differences among the terms that has led to thinking in terms of a poverty *line* rather than a poverty *band*. This failure is also responsible for much of the disagreement about the numbers of poor in the United States, not only at present, but dating back to the last century.

In 1883, William Graham Sumner stated "that there was no possible definition of a poor man. He deplored the use of the phrase because he deemed it dangerously elastic and covering a host of social fallacies."[1] Robert Hunter, a contemporary of Sumner's, took issue with him and argued that poverty could be defined and measured. Hunter and others defined a poor man as "any person who, for whatever reason, was unable to provide himself and his dependents with a decent standard of living. They maintained that it was possible to determine the components of a decent living and also to compute the income required to obtain it. According to their definition, therefore, the poor were simply those members of society whose incomes fell below the established minimum."[2]

— Most modern economists who have thought about this problem have adopted Hunter's point of view relating income to needs; yet, they have defined the level of need in remarkably different ways. Galbraith, for example, considers people as "poverty-stricken when their income, even if adequate for survival, falls markedly behind that of the community."[3] Implicitly, he defines this group as families and individuals with incomes under $1000 in 1955.[4] Several years later, Leon Keyserling placed the poverty line at $4000 for a family of two or more persons and $2000 for unrelated individuals.[5] On this basis he estimated that about one-fifth of the nation

—38 million Americans—lived in poverty in 1960. Building
on Keyserling's estimate, Gunnar Myrdal[6] concluded that
more than 12½ million Americans, or nearly 7 per cent of
the population, live in utter destitution, which he defined
as less than $2000 a year for families of two or more per-
sons and $1000 a year for unrelated individuals.

The problem of defining poverty in an abundant society
is nowhere more apparent than in the pages of a recent
issue of *The New Leader* magazine. One of its regular contributors, Irving Kristol, argues that it is hard to associate
poverty in America "with a heartless *ancien régime*" when
14 per cent of the families with incomes under $3000 buy
a new car each year.[7] He attributes this statistic to a study
conducted by the Survey Research Center of the University
of Michigan in 1960. In reply to this allegation, Paul Jacobs
defends new-car purchases by the poor on the ground that
"in most of the United States a car is an absolute necessity
for either working or seeking work."[8] It just so happens that
the 14 per cent figure is utterly wrong. The survey cited by
Kristol actually shows that less than 2 per cent of the low-
income families bought new cars in 1960; but that is beside
the point. The significant fact is that if the purchase of new
cars by a large proportion of the poor can be justified on
the basis of need, then there is indeed no end to needs.

It is obvious from these few examples that wide variations exist in the designation of the poverty band. Many
other examples could be cited to show that the number of
poor is greater than or less than the foregoing figures imply.
They would only be elaborations of the same basic point,
namely, that there is a strong element of subjectivity in any
definition of poverty.

Income is used in most poverty measures as a proxy
variable for consumption. It is presumed that families with
incomes below the level required to maintain an adequate
or minimum budget are in poverty because they are unable
to have the goods that are considered necessary in our
society. This relationship between income and consumption

is undoubtedly correct in the great majority of cases; yet, there is some evidence that many things that are not always thought of as necessities are available to low-income families. The available census data on the subject are grossly inadequate, but they do provide some foundation for analysis. The figures in Table 1 show the quality of housing,

Table 1—Adequacy of Housing, for Nonfarm Renter Primary Families with Income in 1959 Under $4000, by Presence of Television and Telephone in the Home and Color, for the United States and Central Cities of Urbanized Areas

(in thousands)

Subject	Total	WITH TELEVISION		WITH NO TELEVISION	
		With Tele-phone	With No Tele-phone	With Tele-phone	With No Tele-phone
UNITED STATES					
All nonfarm renter primary families with income under $4,000	5732	2471	1966	339	957
Apparently adequate housing	3108	1796	883	195	234
Apparently inadequate housing	2624	675	1083	143	723
White	4229	2007	1407	261	555
Apparently adequate housing	2638	1561	724	168	185
Apparently inadequate housing	1591	446	683	92	370
Nonwhite	1503	464	559	78	402
Apparently adequate housing	470	235	159	27	49
Apparently inadequate housing	1033	229	400	51	353
CENTRAL CITIES OF URBANIZED AREAS					
All nonfarm renter primary families with income under $4,000	2452	1229	801	150	272
Apparently adequate housing	1550	918	429	92	111
Apparently inadequate housing	902	311	372	58	161
White	1618	879	492	99	148
Apparently adequate housing	1173	722	305	70	76
Apparently inadequate housing	445	157	187	29	72
Nonwhite	834	350	309	51	124
Apparently adequate housing	377	196	124	22	35
Apparently inadequate housing	457	154	185	29	89

SOURCE: U.S. Census of Population: 1960, PC(2)-4A, Families, table 32.
NOTE: Apparently adequate housing defined as units with direct access, kitchen or cooking equipment for exclusive use of occupants, not dilapidated, flush toilet and bath for exclusive use, hot piped water, and less than 1.01 persons per room. Units lacking one or more of these characteristics were classified as apparently inadequate.

television ownership, and availability of a telephone for white and nonwhite families with incomes under $4000 living in rented apartments in central cities of urbanized areas. A $3000 income cutoff would have been more appropriate for consistency with the definition of poverty used by the Council of Economic Advisers, but figures for that level were not available. "Apparently adequate" housing is defined as an apartment with direct access, kitchen and cooking equipment for exclusive use, not dilapidated, with flush toilet and bath for exclusive use, hot piped water, and less than 1.01 persons per room. A family was classified as "with" a telephone if it had access to one for receiving calls. It was not necessary for the phone to be in the dwelling unit.

If lack of adequate housing and the absence of a telephone and television set are treated as symptoms of "grinding poverty," we can see from this table that only 5 per cent of the white families and 10 per cent of the nonwhites were in this status. On the other hand, nearly 50 per cent of the white families and 25 per cent of the nonwhites were considered in poverty, despite the fact that they had apparently adequate housing, a television set, and access to a telephone.

Table 2—Adequacy of Housing, Tenure of Home, Value of Property, and Gross Rent as Per Cent of Family Income, by Presence of Television and Telephone in the Home, for Nonfarm Primary Families with Income in 1959 Under $4000, for the United States

(in thousands)

Subject	Total	WITH TELEVISION		WITH NO TELEVISION	
		With Telephone	With No Telephone	With Telephone	With No Telephone
TOTAL					
All nonfarm primary families with income under $4,000	11831	6448	3167	744	1472
Owner families	6098	3977	1201	405	515
In one-unit, no-business properties	4998	3350	931	334	382
Value of property:					
Under $7,500	2515	1291	685	202	337
$7,500 to $14,900	1812	1455	212	106	39
$15,000 and over	671	604	34	26	6

Table 2—(Cont'd)

Subject	Total	WITH TELEVISION		WITH NO TELEVISION	
		With Tele-phone	With No Tele-phone	With Tele-phone	With No Tele-phone
In property with 2 or more units or with business	1100	627	270	71	133
Renter families	5732	2471	1966	339	957
Gross rent as per cent of income:					
Under 20 per cent	1792	615	661	102	415
20 to 29 per cent	1462	676	517	79	190
30 per cent or more	2477	1180	788	158	351
APPARENTLY ADEQUATE HOUSING[1]					
All nonfarm primary families with income under $4,000	7466	5154	1492	463	357
Owner families	4358	3358	609	268	123
In one-unit, no-business properties	3653	2855	474	227	97
Value of property:					
Under $7,500	1363	918	272	109	64
$7,500 to $14,900	1647	1352	173	94	28
$15,000 and over	643	585	29	24	5
In property with 2 or more units or with business	705	503	135	41	26
Renter families	3108	1796	883	195	234
Gross rent as per cent of income:					
Under 20 per cent	665	374	192	45	54
20 to 29 per cent	873	503	262	49	59
30 per cent or more	1569	919	429	101	120
APPARENTLY INADEQUATE HOUSING[2]					
All nonfarm primary families with income under $4,000	4364	1294	1674	281	1115
Owner families	1740	619	592	137	392
In one-unit, no-business properties	1346	494	458	107	287
Value of property:					
Under $7,500	1153	372	414	93	274
$7,500 to $14,900	165	103	39	12	11
$15,000 and over	28	19	5	2	2
In property with 2 or more units or with business	394	125	134	30	105
Renter families	2624	675	1082	144	723
Gross rent as per cent of income:					
Under 20 per cent	1127	241	469	56	361
20 to 29 per cent	588	172	255	30	131
30 per cent or more	909	262	359	57	231

SOURCE: *U.S. Census of Population: 1960,* PC(2)-4A, *Families,* table 32.
  1. Units with direct access, kitchen or cooking equipment for exclusive use of occupants, not dilapidated, flush toilet and bath for exclusive use, hot piped water, and less than 1.01 persons per room.
  2. Units lacking one or more of the characteristics specified for adequate housing.

A more detailed view of the relationship between low income, quality and price of housing, access to telephone, and television ownership is shown in Table 2 for all non-farm families, classified by tenure, value of home, and rent-income ratio. About one-half of the families in this table are homeowners. Their circumstances appear to be far better than those of renters. Note that about 13 per cent of the private-family homes occupied by these families are valued over $15,000. Very few of these families could be called poor under any reasonable definition. An additional one-third of the homes are valued between $7500 and $15,000. A closer examination of the circumstances of these families might remove many from the poverty class. Perhaps the major fact revealed by this table is that one-half of the home-owners and one-third of the renters live in apparently adequate homes, own a television set, and have access to a telephone. In the case of the single-unit dwellings, the telephone is undoubtedly in the home in virtually all cases. Evidence of "grinding poverty," using this very restricted definition, is found among only about 6 per cent of the homeowners and 13 per cent of the renters.

The term poverty connotes hunger, but this is not what we generally mean when we talk about poverty in America. The foregoing figures suggest this conclusion, but there is other evidence as well. Tunica County, Mississippi, is the poorest county in our poorest state. About eight out of every ten families in this county are poor by national standards; yet, 52 per cent own television sets, 46 per cent own automobiles, and 37 per cent own washing machines. These families may be deprived of hope and poor in spirit, but their material possessions, though low by American standards, would be the envy of the great majority of mankind in the world today. We are told that when the Russians showed the film *The Grapes of Wrath* to depict the miserable conditions of farm workers in America, the thing that most impressed the audiences was that the Okies owned automobiles. Will Rogers hit the nail on the head when he said years ago that this is the only country that ever went to the poorhouse in an automobile.

There are dangers in associating poverty with the absence of certain material possessions like adequate housing, a TV set, a washing machine, or even an automobile. Ignoring for the moment the very real possibility that our measuring device is much too gross, it is very likely that for some poor families material possessions may be merely relics of an earlier affluence. (Others among the poor may obtain such items as hand-me-downs from more prosperous friends or relatives, as gifts from children, or even by the very expensive process of paying a penny down and a penny forever. Far from being a symptom of affluence, the ownership of the automobile or the television set may be a cause of poverty because it is purchased in lieu of a good diet, medical care, education, or other goods that would yield a much greater return in terms of increasing productivity.)

Poverty in its truest sense is more than mere want; it is want mixed with a lack of aspiration, and this is very difficult to measure in any quantitative sense. The immigrants who came to this country in the early part of this century were poor, but their poverty was mixed with hope. They escaped from political oppression and religious persecution to a new world where there was freedom, and they had the hope that their children would share in it one day also. Many of the poor today have "adequate" homes, television sets, telephones, and other appurtenances of the "good life," but they have no hope either for themselves or their children. This is one of the factors that makes the problem today worse, in a certain sense, than it was in the past.

The current national attack on poverty is not being conducted in the narrow sense of raising the levels of living of the poor, as was the case in the thirties. One reason for the change is that we now have Social Security, Aid to Dependent Children, Old-Age Assistance, and other income-maintenance programs which were nonexistent at the outset of the New Deal. The feeling now seems to be that something new must be done to change the attributes of the poor —ignorance, incompetence, shortsightedness, apathy, despair. The matter was summed up very neatly in an article by Christopher Jencks in *The New Republic* as follows: "What has been launched," says Jencks "is not just a war on poverty but a war on the poor, aiming to change them beyond all recognition. The aim is not just to provide them with a lower-middle class standard of living, but also with the lower-middle class virtues such as they are."[9] This is indeed a very ambitious undertaking, and there are many who will question our ability to succeed, not only because we are planning to spend merely $1 billion, but because we have a very limited understanding of the nature of the problem. We must also remember that even if minimum levels of living are raised so that all families have adequate housing and an adequate diet, those who receive the minimum may still feel deprived, especially if they have limited opportunities to rise about that level.

Profile of the Poor

A detailed picture of some of the demographic characteristics of poor families and some basic facts regarding their geographic distribution is provided in Tables 3–5. The term "poor" may be applied to these tables, in the same sense as in the report of the Council of Economic Advisers, for families with incomes under $3000. (Refinements of this definition will be presented below. This may change the picture considerably, but it may be advisable to establish some of the relationships before we consider the refinements.)

Attention must be called to the great diversity that exists among the poor. Poverty is not just a Negro problem, a rural problem, a southern problem, or an unemployment problem. It is all of these and then more. Unemployment is undoubt-

Table 3—Families with Incomes Under $3000 by Color, Residence, and Type of Family, for the United States: 1959

Residence and Type of Family	NUMBER (thousands)			PER CENT DISTRIBUTION		
	Total	White	Nonwhite	Total	White	Nonwhite
UNITED STATES						
Total	9650	7615	2035	100.0	100.0	100.0
Male head under 65	5071	3948	1123	52.5	51.8	55.2
Female head under 65	1626	1065	561	16.8	14.0	27.6
Head 65 and over	2953	2602	351	30.6	34.2	17.2
URBAN						
Total	5227	3950	1277	54.2	51.9	62.8
Male head under 65	2336	1704	632	24.2	22.4	31.1
Female head under 65	1216	768	448	12.6	10.1	22.0
Head 65 and over	1675	1478	197	17.4	19.4	9.7
RURAL NONFARM						
Total	2853	2329	524	29.6	30.6	25.7
Male head under 65	1602	1283	319	16.6	16.8	15.7
Female head under 65	345	253	92	3.6	3.3	4.5
Head 65 and over	906	793	113	9.4	10.4	5.6
RURAL FARM						
Total	1570	1336	234	16.3	17.5	11.5
Male head under 65	1133	961	172	11.7	12.6	8.5
Female head under 65	65	44	21	0.7	0.6	1.0
Head 65 and over	372	331	41	3.9	4.3	2.0

SOURCE: U.S. Census of Population: 1960, Detailed Characteristics, United States Summary, PC(1)-1D, table 224.

edly an important cause of poverty. Yet note that 31 per cent of the poor are aged and 17 per cent represent broken families; their poverty has little to do with unemployment. Together, these two groups account for nearly half the poor. Here again caution must be exercised, since the picture is changed when a more adequate measure is used. The aged decrease considerably in importance when the income measure is adjusted for size of family and age of head of household.

Negroes account for about one-fifth of the poor. Many associate Negro poverty with urban slums in large northern cities. But observe that three-fourths of the poor Negro families live in the south, and only half of these reside in urban areas. Negro poverty in the north follows the stereotype of urban congestion; in the south it is still largely

Table 4—White Families with Incomes Under $3000 by Region, Residence, and Type of Family: 1959

Residence and Type of Family	NUMBER (thousands)			PER CENT DISTRIBUTION		
	Total	South	North and West	Total	South	North and West
ALL FAMILIES						
Total	7615	3013	4602	100.0	100.0	100.0
Male head under 65	3948	1800	2148	51.8	59.7	46.7
Female head under 65	1065	372	693	14.0	12.3	15.1
Head 65 and over	2602	841	1761	34.2	27.9	38.3
URBAN						
Total	3950	1230	2720	51.9	40.8	59.1
Male head under 65	1704	645	1059	22.4	21.4	23.0
Female head under 65	768	224	544	10.1	7.4	11.8
Head 65 and over	1478	361	1117	19.4	12.0	24.3
RURAL NONFARM						
Total	2329	1176	1153	30.6	39.0	25.1
Male head under 65	1283	725	558	16.8	24.1	12.1
Female head under 65	253	123	130	3.3	4.1	2.8
Head 65 and over	793	328	465	10.4	10.9	10.1
RURAL FARM						
Total	1336	607	729	17.5	20.1	15.8
Male head under 65	961	430	531	12.6	14.3	11.5
Female head under 65	44	25	19	0.6	0.8	0.4
Head 65 and over	331	152	179	4.3	5.0	3.9

SOURCE: U.S. Census of Population: 1960, *Detailed Characteristics, United States Summary,* PC(1)-1D, table 266.

associated with rural slums. Among northern whites, poverty is to a very large extent associated with old age. About two-fifths of the northern families with low incomes are headed by a person over sixty-five years of age. Among southern whites poverty is more closely associated with rural slums. About three-fifths of the poor families in this region reside in rural areas.

The most distinctive characteristic of the low-income group is their low productivity, due primarily to the fact that a large proportion are headed by persons who cannot command a high income because of age, or lack of training or work experience. The aged are a case in point. They form the single largest block at the bottom. Since most of them are in retirement and depend on social security or other

Table 5—Nonwhite Families with Incomes Under $3000 by Region, Residence, and Type of Family: 1959

Residence and Type of Family	NUMBER (thousands)			PER CENT DISTRIBUTION		
	Total	South	North and West	Total	South	North and West
ALL FAMILIES						
Total	2035	1458	577	100.0	100.0	100.0
Male head under 65	1123	853	270	55.2	58.5	46.8
Female head under 65	561	334	227	27.6	22.9	39.3
Head 65 and over	351	271	80	17.2	18.6	13.9
URBAN						
Total	1277	764	513	62.8	52.4	88.9
Male head under 65	632	404	228	31.1	27.7	39.5
Female head under 65	448	232	216	22.0	15.9	37.4
Head 65 and over	197	128	69	9.7	8.8	12.0
RURAL NONFARM						
Total	524	471	53	25.7	32.3	9.2
Male head under 65	319	285	34	15.7	19.5	5.9
Female head under 65	92	83	9	4.5	5.7	1.6
Head 65 and over	113	103	10	5.6	7.1	1.7
RURAL FARM						
Total	234	223	11	11.5	15.3	1.9
Male head under 65	172	164	8	8.5	11.2	1.4
Female head under 65	21	19	2	1.0	1.3	0.3
Head 65 and over	41	40	1	2.0	2.7	0.2

SOURCE: U.S. Census of Population: 1960, *Detailed Characteristics, United States Summary,* PC(1)-1D, table 266.

pensions, it is to be expected that their incomes will lag behind those of the working population. While pensions and payments have gone up, they have not risen sufficiently to keep the incomes of the aged on a par with the rest of the population. Younger men can always take on a second job when they feel that they are falling behind—and millions do. They also can send their wives out to work--and millions do that too. The aged have no such option, and so they tend to fall behind in a booming economy.

The economic problems of broken families are not too dissimilar from those of the aged. These families are the product of divorce, desertion, illegitimacy, or the death of a husband. In a very large proportion of these cases, there are young children present in the home, and so the mothers are unable to work because they must stay home to take care of them. Of course, even when they work, many are employed in low-paying jobs because of lack of training, skill, or work experience; or they can only work part-time because of family responsibilities.

The third major group at the bottom are the nonwhites, the great majority of whom are Negroes. Overall, they represent only about 10 per cent of the total number of families, but they form 21 per cent of the bottom income group. Much has been written and said about the plight of the Negro. Their overrepresentation in the bottom income groups should surprise no one. There are undoubtedly many factors that keep the Negro perpetually at the bottom, but, there can be little doubt that racial discrimination is a key cause. Some time ago the Council of Economic Advisers estimated the economic loss to the nation resulting from racial discrimination in employment. It showed that if the education and training of the Negro population were fully utilized by the elimination of racial barriers in employment, our national product might rise by as much as 2½ per cent per year. In 1961, this would have placed $13 billion more in the hands of people who are now concentrated in the bottom income groups. These wasted skills amounted to one-fourth of the total we spent for national defense that year. The monetary loss in income is, of course, only a small part of the total cost that results from discrimination. When we add the costs of higher crime rates, poor health, lack of urban renewal, and many other problems that stem directly or indirectly from discrimination, the amount becomes astronomical.

Of all the problems in this broad area, it seems to me that the amelioration of poverty in old age is the one most amenable to solution, assuming we have the will to do so. All it takes to solve the economic problems of the aged is money. In the case of the aged, we need not be worried about undesirable side effects, such as the stimulation of fertility or the encouragement of idleness. It would be possible to provide every elderly couple with a minimum income of $3000 and every elderly individual with a minimum income of $1500 at a total annual cost of $5 billion per year. I do not suggest that this be done immediately, since $5 billion is a considerable sum, even in the context of a $100-billion-a-year budget. But surely it is time to start thinking seriously about ways and means of alleviating poverty in old age. The most fruitful approach would seem to be through the Social Security System. An increase in the tax rate, the tax base, or both, should make it possible, after a period of time, to increase social security pensions considerably. This, of course, would mean an increase in taxes and it would limit current spending. But, we cannot continue to pay out nearly all of what we make on current consumption and have adequate savings for old age at the same time. Despite the relatively full employment of the past 25 years, most of the families entering old age today are below the poverty line in terms of both current income and accumulated saving. The experience of the past two prosperous decades should teach us that we will not individually set aside an adequate part of our current income to provide for retirement. Therefore, if we really desire to reach our objective, we should plan to have this done automatically through the Social Security System.

Designation of the Poverty Line

The magnitude of poverty and the characteristics of the poor depend to a large extent on the location of the poverty line. Rural families, the aged, and parents without partners will be predominant among the poor if a low poverty line is used. Rural families have lower incomes than city workers even when income "in kind" is taken into account; but their "needs" are also less and they pay less for what they buy. These factors are often not taken into account in national studies. Broken and aged families are clustered near the bottom of the income-distribution scale because they depend

largely on transfer payments which are low relative to earnings. As the poverty line is moved closer to the middle of the
distribution scale, there is a greater tendency to include
husband-wife families headed by underemployed or unskilled workers. It is this fact which primarily accounts for
the increase in the aged among the poor from 20 per cent
in 1947 to 34 per cent in 1962 and for the increase in the
proportion of families with female heads from 16 per cent
to 25 per cent. In 1947, an income of $3000 (in 1962
purchasing power) represented the thirty-third percentile,
whereas in 1962 the same income represented the twentieth percentile. Since the poverty line in 1947 was much
closer to the middle of the distribution scale, the aged and
the broken families represented far smaller fractions of the
poor. It is significant that, if poverty is defined as the lowest
fifth of the distribution, the characteristics of the poor have
not changed at all during the past 15 years.

Although the poverty line in the United States shows
distinct upward mobility, there is strong resistance to the
designation of a given segment of the income distribution,
such as the lowest fifth, as the poor for comparisons over
time. Irving Kristol, for example, states that "if one defines
the poverty line as that which places one-fifth of the nation
below it, then one-fifth of the nation will always be below
the poverty line."[10] In commenting on this observation by
Kristol, author Michael Harrington observed that "this is,
of course, absolutely true; it is also absolutely irrelevant
since no one, either implicitly or explicitly, has defined
poverty in this fashion."[11] Yet, consider the following evidence:

Item: In summarizing the results of a three-year study of
poverty sponsored by the Twentieth Century Fund, Oscar
Ornati concluded that between 1947 and 1960 there was
some reduction in the proportion of families living at or
below subsistence levels, but that there was no change in
the proportion living in poverty just above bare subsistence.
He states: "In 1947, by 1947 standards, 27 per cent of all

people lived below levels of minimum adequacy and in 1960 by 1960 standards they amounted to 26 per cent. The 1947 proportion living below minimum comfort was 39 per cent while in 1960 it was 40 per cent."[12] In other words, if these two standards of poverty are used, it would be appropriate to conclude that a fixed proportion of the population lived in poverty in both periods.

Item: In 1949 when the Joint Economic Committee made the first congressional investigation of low-income families, the poverty line was set at $2000 for a family of two or more persons. The lowest fifth would have been found at the $1600 level. The use of the higher level was purely arbitrary and entirely related to the discrete intervals in which the data were tabulated: that is, it was a statistical convenience. Price increases since that time should have raised the level to about $2500 in 1962. But the poverty line actually used in 1962 was $3000, the dollar value representing the bottom fifth of the distribution. Here again the poverty line coincided with a dollar value for which tabulated census data were readily available. The rise in the poverty line from $2500 (that is, the 1947 figure adusted for price changes) to $3000 represents an increase of about 20 per cent in 13 years—a growth rate of about 1½ per cent per year.

Item: Evidence of the rise in the poverty line is provided by a Bureau of Labor Statistics study which shows that the cost of a "modest but adequate level of living" (excluding taxes) for a working-class family of four persons in New York City was about $4000 in 1947 and about $5200 in 1959 (both figures in terms of 1961 purchasing power). In other words, the modest but adequate level of living rose by 28 per cent in New York City in this twelve-year period —a growth rate of about 2 per cent per year.

When does poverty end in a society that has such flexible standards? Probably never. So long as there is more, people will demand more. And that is a good thing, too. A society whose average family income, adjusted for price changes, grows at the rate of 2½ per cent per year would soon run out of domestic markets if the "needs" of the bottom income groups were fixed. Old-timers may harken back to the "good old days" when people were happy without electricity, flush toilets, automobiles, and television sets. However, they must also realize that once it becomes possible for all to have these "luxuries," they will be demanded and will quickly assume the status of "needs." For this reason, it is unrealistic in an expanding democratic society to think in terms of a fixed poverty line.

Perhaps all of this is just another way of saying that poverty is an emotionally charged word that can trip us up if we are not careful. There is no *objective* definition of a poor man. The standards of poverty are culturally determined. These may be defined arbitrarily for a given time and place, but they vary from place to place and they differ from time to time for a given place. Dorothy Brady has stated wisely that "when faced directly with the problem of determining [poverty] for a given time and place, the theorist will deny the possibility of a unique answer and the propagandist will settle for one of many solutions if the result suits his purposes."

A word before concluding this section on the choice of a $3000 poverty line by the Council of Economic Advisers. As in other studies, the choice was arbitrary but it was camouflaged with a rationale which I suspect was developed after the deed was done. The procedure was probably similar to that used in titling an abstract painting. The *Economic Report* states that various market basket studies "provide support for using as a boundary a family whose annual money income from all sources was $3000." The only study actually cited is a report by Mollie Orshansky of the Department of Health, Education, and Welfare, *Children of the Poor*, which classifies a family as poor if its annual income is less than three times the cost of an inexpensive, adequate diet. Two different classes of poverty are recognized: (1) families that spend over one-third of their income for an adequate "low-cost" diet; and (2) those that spend over one-third of their income for an adequate "economy" diet, defined as four-fifths of the cost of the "low-cost" diet. According to these criteria, a nonfarm family of four would have been classified as poor in 1962 under the "low-cost" diet criterion with an income of less than $3955; and it would have been called poor under the "economy" diet criterion with an income under $3165. No allowance was made for the fact that the cost of this diet would have been less for smaller families and more for larger ones.

In all fairness to the Council of Economic Advisers, it should be pointed out that they were fully aware of the limitations of an arbitrary poverty line and of the failure to consider family size, age of head, geographic location, and other factors that influence needs and costs. The council felt that a beginning had to be undertaken and, even though a case could be made for using an income limit that was above or below $3000, "the analysis of the sources of poverty, and of the programs needed to cope with it, would remain substantially unchanged." This judgment is undoubtedly true for the antipoverty program that was recently submitted to Congress. It is subject to serious limitations, however, if it is considered as a general proposition.

The use of a single poverty line for families of all sizes does not make much sense from a statistical standpoint. It can be defended only on the grounds that adequate data on the needs and incomes of families classified by size of family and other characteristics were not available. The Council may have also felt that the simple definition of poverty had the virtue of being readily understood by the general public without seriously distorting the results. Some justification for this view is provided by an earlier study prepared by Professor Robert Lampman for the Joint Economic Committee (*The Low-Income Population and Economic Growth*), which suggested that the use of a single poverty line for all families (without regard to size) produced the same number of low-income families as a variable poverty line adjusted for size of family. New tabulations from the 1960 census (see

Table 6) suggest that the use of a single poverty line tends to overstate the amount of poverty. The number of persons in urban low-income families is reduced by 11 per cent when the poverty line is changed from a flat $3000 for all families

Table 6—Urban Families with Incomes Under $3000 Adjusted for Family Size and Age of Head, by Size of Family, Number of Persons in Families, and Color of Head: 1959

(Numbers in thousands. For adjustment procedure see report cited in source.)

Size of Family and Number of Persons in Families	UNADJUSTED			ADJUSTED		
	Total	White	Nonwhite	Total	White	Nonwhite
Families	5216	3942	1274	3802	2666	1136
Size of family:						
2 persons	2831	2354	477	1432	1138	295
3 persons	985	727	258	701	501	200
4 persons	583	408	174	519	358	160
5 persons	353	225	128	437	289	148
6 persons or more	464	228	237	713	380	333
Persons in families	15916	11077	4839	14149	9081	5068
Number of persons:						
In 2 person families	5663	4709	955	2865	2276	589
In 3 person families	2954	2180	774	2102	1504	599
In 4 person families	2331	1633	697	2075	1433	642
In 5 person families	1765	1126	639	2187	1445	741
In 6 or more person families	3203	1429	1774	4920	2423	2497
Per Cent Distribution						
Families	100.0	100.0	100.0	100.0	100.0	100.0
Size of family:						
2 persons	54.3	59.7	37.4	37.7	42.7	26.0
3 persons	18.9	18.4	20.3	18.4	18.8	17.6
4 persons	11.2	10.4	13.7	13.7	13.4	14.1
5 persons	6.8	5.7	10.0	11.5	10.8	13.0
6 persons or more	8.9	5.8	18.6	18.8	14.3	29.3
Persons in families	100.0	100.0	100.0	100.0	100.0	100.0
Number of persons:						
In 2 person families	35.6	42.5	19.7	20.2	25.1	11.6
In 3 person families	18.6	19.7	16.0	14.9	16.6	11.8
In 4 person families	14.6	14.7	14.4	14.7	15.8	12.7
In 5 person families	11.1	10.2	13.2	15.5	15.9	14.6
In 6 or more person families	20.1	12.9	36.7	34.8	26.7	49.3

SOURCE: U.S. Census of Population: 1960, Sources and Structure of Family Income, PC(2)-4C, table 4.

of two or more persons to a variable standard centered on $3000 for a four-person family headed by a middle-aged person, but ranging from $1800 for a young couple to $4200 for a couple with four or more children. Perhaps the major shortcoming of the procedure used in the *Economic Report* is that it distorts the characteristics of the poor. The use of a flat $3000 poverty line tends to overstate the number of aged among the poor, because the aged have smaller-than-average families, fewer-than-average earners, and lower-than-average incomes as a result. In the 1960 census tabulation cited above, 32 per cent of the poor-family heads were aged, using the flat $3000 poverty line, as compared with 21 per cent obtained with a variable poverty line. The more refined procedure produces many more children and many fewer oldsters among the poor.

Toward a Minimum Estimate of Poverty

As noted at the outset, it is more fruitful to think of poverty then in terms of a band cutting through the lower segment of the income curve rather than as a line. It is not clear just what part of the low-income band is covered by the concept used by the Council of Economic Advisers; however, it seems unlikely that the estimated 35 million persons classified as poor under that definition represents a minimum estimate of poverty for the United States. In this section, an attempt will be made to provide a measure based on the number of persons whose family incomes are below the amounts needed to qualify for public-assistance payments in each state. This definition is based on the assumption, which some may call naïve, that a person is "needy" if his income is so low as to make him eligible to apply for financial aid in his local community. The standards vary from place to place, partly because some can afford to pay more than others. It is no more reasonable to assume that the "yardstick for need" should be the same in a rich state like New York and a poor one like Mississippi than it is to assume that poverty in Mississippi should be defined in the same way as in the Congo. Also, it will be found in using this definition that some states have little poverty because they provide assistance to all families that qualify for aid, whereas other states will have much poverty because they do not provide assistance to families that fall below the standards they have set. This definition could easily become a tautology if the states attempted to bring all needy families up to the standard; but this is far from the case at the present time. Indeed, it will be shown that under the above definition, about one person out of every eight in the United States is "needy."

Other problems of definition and measurement will emerge as the method is described and the procedures are explored. The findings are not presented as a "final solution" to the problem of measuring poverty, because there is no final solution. These are only faltering first steps which, it is hoped, may provide a basis for further work.

Yardstick for Need[13]

There are four public-assistance programs in the United States that have been established as part of the Social Security Act: Old-Age Assistance, Aid to Families with Dependent Children, Aid to the Blind, and Aid to the Permanently and Totally Disabled. The primary objectives of these programs are to provide needy persons with incomes that will "enable them to secure the necessities of life and medical and remedial care and services."[14] The laws governing the public-assistance programs authorize federal grants-in-aid to states for their assistance programs. However, the states are given the responsibility for establishing their own definitions of need. In most states, the assistance act defines a "needy" individual as one who has insufficient income or other resources to maintain a standard of living compatible with "decency and health." In addition to meeting the income requirements specified by the state, the individual must meet all of the other standards specified by law in order to receive assistance. The "decency and health" standard has generally been interpreted to mean *minimum subsistence,* which includes certain *basic* needs such as food, clothing, personal incidentals, medicine chest supplies, household supplies, shelter, and utilities; and various *special needs* that may be related to health problems, employment, and school attendance. The state welfare agencies determine the amount of goods and services that are considered essential. The monthly cost of these items becomes the standard or the yardstick by which the total amount to be paid is determined. The cost of the standard varies considerably from state to state. For example, in 1961, the total monthly amounts set for basic needs in the program for Aid to Families with Dependent Children (AFDC), for a family composed of a mother aged thirty-five, with a boy aged fourteen and two girls aged nine and four, ranged among the states from a low of $124 to a high of $295.

Of course, not all states provide the income, or additions to income, that are required to meet the standards. Some states have maximum amounts they will pay; others have limits on the amount they will provide for rent or other needs. Moreover, some states may set their requirements rather low and meet them completely, whereas others may set comparatively high standards and meet only a portion of them. Such variations produce differences among states in the extent to which "needs" are actually met, regardless of standards.

Consequently, there is no easy way in which to summarize the actual levels of living that are contemplated under individual state standards. The fact that these are designed to provide minimum subsistence levels of living conveys the impression that families with incomes below the standard would not enjoy many luxuries. A rough indication of levels of living that might be possible in states with some of the higher standards in 1961 is provided by the following example cited in the pamphlet, *Yardstick for Need.* The standard for one state in the AFDC program for the family of four composed of mother, one boy, and two girls, and aged as previously described, was as follows:

Food	$100
Clothing	30
Personal incidentals	6
Medicine chest supplies ...	2
Household supplies	7
Shelter[1]	40
Utilities[2]	25
School supplies	5
	$215

Less mother's monthly net income from part-time employment	50
Payment	$165

1. Rent.
2. Fuel, electricity, water.

In this illustration, the standard required for such a family calls for a monthly income of $215. The state would deduct the mother's monthly net income of $50, earned from part-time employment. Therefore, the amount of the monthly payment to the family would be $165. With the $50 earned income, this family would have $215 a month to spend for family living. Here is how the money might be spent in a given month:

Food	$80
Clothing	25
Personal incidentals	10
Household supplies	9
Shelter[1]	50
Utilities[2]	25
School supplies	6
Life insurance	5
Church	1
Sunday paper	1
Transportation	3
	$215

1. Rent.
2. Fuel, electricity, water.

This family's expenditure of $80 per month for food
(about 67 cents a day per person) would provide cheap cuts
of meat three times a week and eggs twice a week. Each
person would have one cup of milk a day. Green and yellow
vegetables might be served twice a week. Fats, dried beans,
and cereal would have to be used frequently.

The expenditure for personal incidentals might include
a home permanent for the mother that month, haircuts for
the children, and four bars of soap. In other months, these
items might not be bought. The $9 spent for household
supplies would include one towel, one sheet, dishes, some
cooking utensils, washing powder, bleach, and scouring
powder.

Income Needs by Size of Family

The preceding section described in a general way the
standards used to determine income needs under the public-
assistance programs in the United States. Note, of course,
must be taken of the wide geographic dispersion in the range
of standards. The absolute figures for continental United
States (excluding Alaska and Hawaii) range from a low of
$1255 for Arkansas to a high of $2213 for the state of
Washington. A relatively small part of the dispersion
(15 to 20 per cent at most) is caused by differences in the
cost of living. Most of the dispersion, however, represents
differences in actual content. The states with the lowest requirements, which by and large are also the poorest states,
tend to provide only the barest essentials, and generally
assign a relatively large proportion of the requirements to
food. About 65 per cent was assigned to food in the west
south central states, 58 per cent in the south Atlantic, and
57 per cent in the east south central region. In contrast,
slightly under half of the requirements were for food in New
England, the middle Atlantic, and the east north central
states. The proportion was lowest in the Pacific and the
west north central states, where only 45 per cent was
assigned to this item.[15]

There is a rather close association between the income level of the state and its income requirements. As a general rule the states with the lowest incomes are among those with the lowest requirements, and those with the highest incomes are among those with the highest requirements. The ratio of requirements to median family income, however, tends to vary inversely with income level. In high-income states like New York, New Jersey, Pennsylvania, Illinois, and California, requirements represent about one-third of median family income. In the lower-income states, such as Arkansas, Alabama, and Kentucky, requirements represent about 40 per cent of income. The fact that requirements represent a larger proportion of income levels in the poorer states may account for the proportionately greater number of families with unmet needs in these states. Over one-fourth of the AFDC families in states like Arkansas, Alabama, and Kentucky had incomes from all sources (including AFDC) that were below the requirements.[16] In Alabama and Mississippi this proportion was over 50 per cent. In contrast, none of the AFDC families in states like New York, New Jersey, and Illinois had unmet needs.

Families and Individuals with Substandard Incomes

Income data collected in the 1960 census provide the critical link for estimating the number of families and individuals with incomes below the foregoing requirements. The census data provide a distribution of families of different sizes by income levels for each state. By calculating the number of families in each size group with incomes below the requirements and summarizing the results, an estimate may be obtained for the state as a whole of the number of families and individuals with substandard incomes. Since the number of persons in these families is also known, such calculations can provide an estimate of the number of persons in families with substandard incomes. The following is an illustration of how the figures in these tables were obtained for New York State.

Column 1 shows the cost standards for basic needs for families of different sizes in New York State. These figures were taken from Table 1. Column 2 shows the number of families in each size of family group with incomes below the cost standards. These estimates were derived from *U.S. Census of Population: 1960*, Vol. I, Part 34, Tables 141 and 142. Column 3 shows the number of persons in families with substandard incomes.

The data show that nearly 10 million families and unrelated individuals had substandard incomes as defined above. Within this group, unrelated individuals (5.3 million) slightly outnumbered families of two or more persons (4.5 million). In terms of persons rather than family groups,

Table 7—Method of Obtaining Data for New York State

| Size of Family | Cost Standard | NUMBER WITH INCOMES BELOW COST STANDARD | |
		Families	Persons in Families
1 person	$1269	519,693	519,693
2 persons	1463	137,349	274,698
3 persons	1769	51,144	153,432
4 persons	2154	39,104	156,416
5 persons	2501	27,526	137,630
6 persons	2883	19,276	115,656
7 or more persons	3523	26,731	213,848
Total	—	820,823	1,571,373

$$\frac{\text{Substandard families and individuals}}{\text{All families and individuals}} = \frac{820,823}{5,755,393} = 14.3\%$$

$$\frac{\text{Persons in substandard families}}{\text{All persons in household}} = \frac{1,571,373}{16,513,182} = 9.5\%$$

this low-income population contained 23½ million persons, about 18 million of whom lived in family groups. Because of the relatively low incomes in the south, a large proportion of these people were concentrated in this region. Slightly over 10 million people, representing 44 per cent of all people in families with substandard incomes, lived in the south. The comparable figure for the north central states was slightly over 6 million people, representing about 26 per cent of the total. The west contained 3 million persons in families with substandard incomes (13 per cent of the total), and the northeastern states had nearly 4 million (17 per cent of the total).

When one examines the number of families and unrelated individuals with substandard incomes expressed as a proportion of all families and unrelated individuals, it is found that 17 per cent of all families and individuals had substandard incomes. The largest incidence of substandard incomes was in the south, where 21 per cent of all families and individuals were in this category. In the other regions the proportion varied within a narrow range from 14 per cent in the northeast to 17 per cent in the north central states.

If the rates are viewed in terms of all persons in households rather than family units, then about 13 per cent of all persons in the United States were in families with substandard incomes. The proportion in the south (19 per cent) was twice as great as in the northeast (9 per cent). The north central region and the west had about the same proportion as the national average (13 per cent). As might be expected, the largest proportions were found in the poorest regions of the country. The east south central states led the nation in this respect, with one person out of every four residing in a family with substandard income.

The proportion of families with substandard incomes was largest in the farm states. This tendency is in part related to the fact that only information on money income was collected in the census. Such a restriction tends to understate the effective purchasing power of farm families, although it is undoubtedly true that these families have lower incomes than the rest of the population, even when income "in kind" is taken into account. Nevertheless, the level and geographic dispersion of poverty is reduced considerably when the analysis is restricted to the urban population. Overall, about 9 per cent of the urban families had substandard incomes (as compared with 12 per cent of *all* families). The south was somewhat above the national average, with 12 per cent, whereas the figures for the other three regions were almost identical with the national average.

Statistical Gaps in the Measurement of Poverty: The Poverty Line

Little has been done to specify the meaning of poverty. Each study establishes its own poverty line and all apologize for the inadequacy of the measures that are used. Poverty cannot be objectively defined; but it should be possible to go beyond the intuitive judgments that are now used. Nearly 20 years ago, the Bureau of Labor Statistics developed the concept of a City Worker Family Budget which provided the standard for a "modest but adequate" level of living for urban families. A similar standard is needed for families closer to the poverty line. From the descriptions I have seen, it appears that the "minimum adequate" budget now being considered by BLS would fill this important gap. The new budget would be minimum in the sense that downward adjustments would be made in the content and/or manner of living of the "modest but adequate" standard when this is possible without compromising the family's physical health or social acceptability.

Longitudinal Studies

Most of what is now known about the characteristics of low-income families comes from single interviews with samples of households. Although these data are useful in delineating the broad dimensions of the problem, they fail to answer most of the questions that really need to be answered. What proportion of the people who are now poor were reared in poor families? How much poverty is transmitted from one generation to the next, and for what reasons—unstable family life, lack of motivation, lack of opportunity? These are not the kinds of questions that can be answered in "hit and run" interviews. They require questioning in depth over a period of time, record checks, testing, and many other techniques that are not now used in census surveys. Serious consideration should be given to the creation of a panel of families, heavily weighted in the low- and middle-income groups, in which periodic interviews, perhaps every quarter, are conducted over a period of several years.

Annual Surveys of Poverty

As part of its regular operations, the Bureau of the Census identifies each year a representative national sample of about 6000 families with incomes under $3000. Although some social and economic characteristics of these families are published regularly in the Bureau's reports each year, there is much more that can be done. Several years ago, for example, a reinterview survey was conducted with all families in the sample headed by an elderly person. Detailed information was obtained on living arrangements, assets, help received from relatives, and many other subjects. There is no reason why similar surveys could not be conducted with the entire low-income group. The surveys could be varied from year to year, or more than one survey could be conducted each year. In this way, useful information about many of the vexing analytical problems associated with poverty could be obtained at relatively little cost.

Improved Statistics for Appalachia

High on my list of statistical gaps that should be filled is the provision of current social and economic data for Appalachia. The name of this region has become almost synonymous with poverty in America. A vast new program is on the verge of being started in Appalachia, and sound planning calls for the creation of a statistical intelligence system that will keep us informed of the progress.

The measurement of change in Appalachia calls for

objective periodic reports covering the entire region, and comparisons with the rest of the country. The 1960 census provides a wealth of benchmark information for the past. It will, however, soon be obsolete for describing the changes that are taking place. Administrators, businessmen, and planners in Appalachia will need regular up-to-date indicators of change and conditions; otherwise, they run the risk of having to base their decisions on limited information, scattered visits in the area, and intermittent and obviously inconsistent partial investigations. In order to provide the information that is needed, I would propose the early establishment of a population survey of Appalachia comparable in content and methodology to the nationwide Current Population Survey. Such a survey could provide current information on the levels of income, employment, unemployment, and underemployment, as well as information about the living conditions and characteristics of the workers. Information on other aspects of life in the region could be secured through a regular household survey based on a scientifically designed sample of the population of the area. If such a survey were in being, it would be possible to launch urgent special surveys on an areawide or localized basis in a relatively short time. Similarly, samples of selected portions of the population could be readily developed for intensive study as needed. But even more than this can and should be done.

The Current Population Survey measures the impact of economic change on the people. Other surveys are needed to measure the impact of federal expenditures on the economy of the area. I am told that for a modest sum—less than $500,000—it would be possible to provide annual data for the region based on the Survey of Manufactures, the Current Business Survey, and a Census of Governments. The inclusion of these measures on an annual basis would permit the preparation of a comprehensive annual social and economic report for the region. With the establishment of the proper benchmarks based on recent censuses, we could begin to measure, for the first time perhaps, the direct impact that large-scale federal expenditures have on the major social and economic aspects of life in one area.

Mid-Decade Census

Many government statisticians, some very highly placed, seem to think that the statistical data program for local areas that sufficed for a $100-billion economy is also adequate for a $600-billion economy which is in the process of adjusting to an electronic revolution, a Negro revolution, and, hopefully, a vast reduction in defense spending. I think they are wrong. Many people assume that the problem areas of 1960 are the problem areas today, and that they will continue to be the problem areas in 1970. This view is fallacious. The 1960 census produced many surprises, even for some of our most sophisticated analysts. There is no reason to believe that the process of change stopped 10 years ago. Without a mid-decade census we are as likely to be as unprepared for the 1970 census findings as we were in 1960.

NOTES

1. William Graham Sumner, *What the Social Classes Owe to Each Other* (New York: Harper & Bros., 1883); discussed in Robert H. Bremner, *From the Depths: The Discovery of Poverty in the United States* (New York: New York Univ. Press, 1956), p. 152.

2. *Ibid.*, pp. 152–3.

3. John K. Galbraith, *The Affluent Society* (Boston: Houghton Mifflin, 1958), Mentor edition, p. 251.

4. *Ibid.*, p. 251.

5. Leon H. Keyserling, *Poverty and Deprivation in the U.S.* (Washington, D.C.: Conference on Economic Progress, 1962), pp. 14 and 16.

6. Gunnar Myrdal, *Challenge to Affluence* (New York: Pantheon Books, 1963), p. 46.

7. Irving Kristol, "The Lower Fifth," *The New Leader*, Feb. 17, 1964.

8. Paul Jacobs, "Our Permanent Paupers," *The New Leader*, March 30, 1964.

9. Christopher Jencks, "Johnson vs. Poverty," *The New Republic*, March 28, 1964.

10. Irving Kristol, "The Lower Fifth," *The New Leader*, Feb. 17, 1964.

11. Michael Harrington, "A Glib Fallacy," *The New Leader*, March 30, 1964.

12. Oscar Ornati, *Poverty in America* (Washington, D.C.: National Policy Committee on Pockets of Poverty, March 1964), (Mimeographed).

13. This title is borrowed with apologies from the excellent pamphlet by Gladys O. White, *Yardstick for Need* (1963), published by the Bureau of Family Services of the Department of Health, Education, and Welfare.

14. Department of Health, Education, and Welfare, *Public Assistance Under the Social Security Act*, July 1961, p. 3.

15. U.S. Department of Health, Education, and Welfare, *Characteristics of Families Receiving Aid to Families with Dependent Children*, Nov.–Dec. 1961, Table 44.

16. *Ibid.*, Table 38.

Consumption, Work, and Poverty[1]

MOLLIE ORSHANSKY

A revolution of expectations has taken place in this country as well as abroad. There is now a conviction that everyone has the right to share in the good things of life. Yet there are still many who must watch America's parade of progress from the sidelines, as they wait for their turn—a turn that does not come. The legacy of poverty awaiting many of our children is the same as that handed down to their parents, but in a time when the boon of prosperity is more general, the taste of poverty is more bitter.

Now, however, the nation is committed to a battle against poverty. And as part of planning the how, there is the task of identifying the whom. The initiation of corrective measures need not wait upon final determination of the most suitable criterion of poverty, but the interim standard adopted and the characteristics of the population thus described will be important in evaluating the effectiveness of the steps taken.

There is not, and indeed in a rapidly changing pluralistic society there cannot be, one standard universally accepted and uniformly applicable according to which it can be decided who is poor. Almost inevitably, a single criterion applied across the board must either leave out of the count some who should be there or include some who, all things considered, ought not to be classed as indigent. There can be, however, agreement on some of the considerations to be taken into account in arriving at a standard. And if it is not possible to state unequivocally "how much is enough," it should be possible to assert with confidence, how much, on an average, is too little. Whatever the level at which we peg the concept of "too little," the measure of income used should reflect at least roughly an equivalent level of living for individuals and families of different size and composition.

We thus need a profile of poverty based on a particular income standard that makes allowance for the different needs of families with varying numbers of adults and children to support. We must recognize, too, that a family on a farm normally is able to manage on somewhat less cash income than a family living in a city. For example, a family of father, mother, two young children, and no other relatives is assumed on the average to need a minimum of $1860 today if living on a farm and $3100 elsewhere. Although such cutoff points have their place when the economic well-being of the population at large is being assessed, they do not necessarily apply with equal validity to each individual family in its own special setting.

The standard itself is admittedly arbitrary, but not unreasonable. It is based essentially on the amount of income remaining after allowance for an adequate diet at minimum cost. Under the criteria adopted, it is estimated that in 1963 a total of 7.2 million families and 5 million individuals living alone or with nonrelatives (exclusive of persons in institutions) lacked the wherewithal to live at anywhere near a tolerable level. Literally, for the 34½ million persons involved, 15 million of them children under age eighteen and 5.2 million sixty-five or older, everyday living implied choosing between an adequate diet of the most economical sort and some other necessity, because there was not money enough to have both.

There are others in need not included in this count. Were one to add in the hidden poor, the 1.7 million elderly, and the 1.1 million members of subfamilies—including 600,000 children—whose own income does not permit independent living at a minimum standard, but who escape poverty by living in a household with relatives whose combined income is adequate for all, the number of poor rises to nearly 37.5 million persons.

The aggregate income available to the 7.2 million families and 5 million individuals in 1963 was only 60 per cent as much as they needed, or about $11½ billion less than their estimated minimum requirements.

The Poverty Profile

From data reported to the Bureau of the Census in March 1964, it can be inferred that one in seven of all families of two or more and almost half of all persons living alone or with nonrelatives had incomes too low in 1963 to enable them to eat even the minimal diet that could be expected to provide adequate nutrition and still have enough left over to pay for all other living essentials. Such a judgment is predicated on the assumption that, at current prices and current standards, an average family of four can achieve an adequate diet on about 70 cents a day per person for all food, and an additional $1.40 for all other items— from housing and medical care to clothing and carfare.[2] For those dependent on a regular pay check, such a budget would mean, for the family of four, total family earnings of $60 a week.

By almost any realistic definition, individuals and families with such income—who include more than a fifth of all our children—must be counted among our undoubted poor. A somewhat less conservative, but by no means generous standard, calling for about 90 cents a day for food per person and a total weekly income of $77, would add 8.8 million adults and 6.8 million children to the roster. There is thus a total of 50 million persons—of whom 22 million are young children—who live within the bleak circle of poverty or at least hover around its edge. In these terms, though progress has been made, there are still from a fifth to a fourth of our citizens whose situation reminds us that all is not yet well in America.

Who are these people who tug at the national conscience? Are they all social casualties, visited by personal misfortune, like the woman left alone to raise a family? Are they persons who find little opportunity to earn their living, like the aged and the unemployed? Or are they perhaps mainly Negroes and members of other minority groups, living out the destiny of their years of discrimination? These groups, to be sure, are among the poorest of the poor, but they are not alone.

The population groups most vulnerable to the risk of inadequate income have long been identified and of late much publicized, but they make up only a small part of all the nation's poor. Families headed by a woman are subject to a risk of poverty three times that of units headed by a man, but they represent only a fourth of all persons in families classed as poor. Indeed, almost three-fourths of the poor families have a man as the head. Children growing up without a father must get along on less than they need far more often than children living with both parents. In fact, two-thirds of them are in families with inadequate income. But two-thirds of all the children in the families called poor do live in a home with a man at the head.

Many of our aged have inadequate incomes, but almost four-fifths of the poor families have someone under age sixty-five at the head. Even among persons who live alone, as do so many aged women, nearly half of all individuals classified as poor have not yet reached old age. Nonwhite families suffer a poverty risk three times as great as white families do, but seven out of ten poor families are white.

And finally, in our work-oriented society, those who cannot or do not work must expect to be poorer than those who do. Yet more than half of all poor families report that the head currently has a job. Moreover, half of these employed family heads, representing almost 30 per cent of all the families called poor, have been holding down a full-time job for a whole year. In fact, of the 7.2 million poor families in 1963, one in every six (1.3 million) is the family of a white male worker who worked full time throughout the year. This is the kind of family that in our present society has the best chance of escaping poverty.

All told, of the 15 million children under age eighteen counted as poor, about 5¾ million were in the family of a man or woman who had a full-time job all during 1963.

Defining the Poverty Line

Poverty has many facets, not all reducible to money. Even in such terms alone, it will not be possible to obtain unanimous consent to a list of goods and services that make up the *sine qua non* and the dollars it takes to buy them. The difficulty is compounded in a country such as ours, which has long since passed the stage of struggling for sheer survival.

In many parts of the world, the overriding concern for the majority of the populace every day is still "Can I live?" For the United States as a society, it is no longer whether, but how. Although by the levels of living prevailing elsewhere, some of the poor in this country might be well-to-do, no one here today would settle for mere subsistence as the just due for himself or his neighbor, and even the poorest may claim more than bread. Yet as yesterday's luxuries become tomorrow's necessities, who can define for today how much is enough? And in a society that equates economic well-being with earnings, what is the floor for those whose earning capacity is limited or absent altogether, as it is for aged persons and children?

Available Standards for Food Adequacy

Despite the nation's technological and social advance, or perhaps because of it, there is no generally accepted standard of adequacy for essentials of living except food. Even for food, social conscience and custom dictate that there be not only sufficient quantity but sufficient variety to meet recommended nutritional goals and conform to customary eating patterns. Calories alone will not be enough.

Food plans prepared by the Department of Agriculture have for more than 30 years served as a guide for estimating costs of food needed by families of different composition. The plans represent a translation of the criteria of nutritional adequacy set forth by the National Research Council into quantities and types of foods compatible with the preference of United States families, as revealed in food-consumption studies. Plans are developed at varying levels of cost to suit the needs of families with different amounts to spend. All the plans, if strictly followed, can provide an acceptable and adequate diet, but—generally speaking—the lower the level of cost, the more restricted the kinds and qualities of food must be, and the more the skill in marketing and food preparation that is required.[3]

Each plan specifies the required weekly quantities of foods in particular food groups for individuals of varying age and sex. The department regularly publishes cost estimates at United States average prices based on the assumption that all meals are prepared at home from foods purchased at retail. Because no allowance is made for using any food from the home farm or garden, the cost estimates are not applicable without some adjustment to farm families, although the quantities presumably could be.

The low-cost plan, adapted to the food patterns of families in the lowest third of the income range, for many years has been used by welfare agencies as a basis for food allotments for needy families and others who wished to keep food costs down. Often, however, the actual food allowance for families receiving public assistance was less than that in the low-cost plan. Although spending as much as this food plan recommends by no means guarantees that diets will be adequate, families spending less are more likely to have diets falling below the recommended allowances for some important nutrients.

Recently, the Department of Agriculture began to issue an "economy" food plan, costing only 75 to 80 per cent as much as the basic low-cost plan, for "temporary or emergency use when funds are low." In January 1964, this plan suggested foods costing $4.60 a week per person, an average of only 22 cents a meal per person in a four-person family.[4] For some family members, such as men and teenage boys, the cost was higher; for others—young children and women, for example—it was less. The food plan as such includes no additional allowance for meals eaten out or other food eaten away from home. Meals eaten by family members at school or on the job, whether purchased or carried from home, must still come out of the same household food allowance.

The food costs for individuals according to this economy plan, at January 1964 prices, were used as the point of departure for determining the minimum total income requirement for families of different types. An additional set of poverty income points was computed, using the low-cost plan with its average per-capita weekly cost of $5.90.

The Income-Food Expenditure Relationship

Even when the food costs are computed, the task of translating them into total income requirements still remains. It has been long accepted for individuals as for nations that the proportion of income allocated to the "necessaries," and in particular to food, is an indicator of economic well-being. A declining percentage has been associated with prosperity and higher income, and the rising percentage associated with lower income has been taken as an indicator of stringency.

The fact that larger households tend to spend a larger share of their income for food has not been so readily recognized as an indicator of economic pressure because of the assumed economy of scale. Yet, on the whole, larger families are less likely to have diets that satisfy the recommended allowances in essential nutrients. The dearth of data on expenditures of families classified by both size and income has made it difficult to assay the situation, and the fact that the age and sex distribution of the members also changes as families increase in size has obscured the picture further.

In its 1955 study of household food consumption, the Department of Agriculture found that the diets of almost a fourth of the two-person households, but about half of the households with six or more members, had less than the recommended amounts of calcium—a nutrient found mainly in milk products. Similarly, large households were twice as likely as the small households to have diets lacking in ascorbic acid and two-and-a-half times as likely to be short in protein. The latter situation is particularly striking because, though lack of protein is far less common in this country than deficiency in other nutrients, it is more telling: diets too low in protein are more likely than other diets to have deficiencies in other essential nutrients also.[5]

It thus appears that what passes for "economy of scale" in the large family may in part reflect a lowering of dietary standards enforced by insufficient funds. Support for this thesis may be gained from the fact, illustrated later in this chapter, that families with large numbers of children do indeed have lower incomes than smaller families. Moreover, analysis of recent consumption data suggests that large families, given the opportunity, prefer to devote no larger a share of their income to food than do smaller families with the same per-capita income.

The Agriculture Department evaluated family food consumption and dietary adequacy in a 1955 survey week and reported for all families of two or more—farm and nonfarm—an expenditure for food approximating one-third of money income after taxes.[6] Two-person nonfarm families used about 27 per cent of their income for food, and families with three or more persons about 35 per cent. A later study made in 1960–1961 by the BLS found for urban families that nearly a fourth of the family's income (after taxes) went for food. There is less variation by size of family than might have been anticipated, ranging between 22 per cent and 28 per cent, as Table 1 indicates.

Table 1—Comparison of Family Food Consumption and Dietary Adequacy in 1955 and 1960–1961 Surveys

	USDA 1955, NONFARM[1]		BLS 1960–1961, URBAN[2]	
Family Size	Average Per-Capita Income	Per Cent Spent for Food	Average Per-Capita Income	Per Cent Spent for Food
1	([3])	([3])	$2967	23
2 or more, total	$1328	33	1886	22
2	2036	27	2750	22
3	1603	31	2302	22
4	1299	35	1854	24
5	1067	36	1512	26
6	837	40 ⎫	1034	28
7 or more	616	46 ⎭		

1. Derived from U.S. Department of Agriculture, Household Food Consumption Survey Report, 1955, Report No. 1, December 1956.
2. Derived from Consumer Expenditures and Income, Supplement 3, Part A, to BLS Report No. 237-38, July 1964.
3. Because of the housekeeping eligibility requirements for this study, the single individuals included are not representative of all persons living alone.

The data suggest that the declining income per person in the larger families may have been responsible for the different rate of spending as well as possibly more efficient utilization of food. Indeed, on more critical examination of the income-size distributions, it would appear that, given the same per-capita income, the spending patterns appear to converge considerably. Urban families in 1960–1961, for example, spending on the average approximately every third of their available dollars for food, are estimated to have had incomes of approximately $1000 per person when there were two in the family, $900 when there were three, $910 when there were four, $915 for five, and $800 for six or more.

Some of the difference in the results of the two studies cited may be attributed to differences in methodology. The questions employed by the BLS to obtain the data on annual food outlays usually have yielded lower average expenditures than the more detailed item-by-item checklist of foods used in a week that serves as a questionnaire for the Agriculture Department. Moreover, since the latter studies are limited to families who have ten or more meals at home during the survey week, they leave out some high food-spenders represented in the BLS figures. On the other hand, the decreases undoubtedly reflect in part the general improvement in real income achieved by the nation as a whole in the six years elapsed between the two studies.

For the present analysis, the earlier relationship was adopted as the basis for defining poverty—that is, an income less than three times the cost of the economy food plan (or alternatively the low-cost plan)—for families of three or more persons. For families with two members the ratio of 27 per cent observed in that study was applied partly because it is generally acknowledged that a straight per-capita-income measure does not allow for the relatively larger fixed costs that small households face. Moreover, the more recent consumption curves themselves indicate that the one- or two-person families, who as a group are less homogeneous in composition, seem to be "out of line" with larger families with respect to the spending pattern.

For one-person units, for whom the consumption data are hard to interpret because of the heavy representation of aged individuals not shown separately, the income cutoff at the low-cost level was taken at 72 per cent of the estimated $2480 for a couple, following BLS recent practice.[7] For the economy level, the income cutoff was assumed at 80 per cent of the couple's requirement, on the premise that the lower the income the more difficult it would be for one person to cut expenses such as housing and utilities below the minimum for a couple.[8]

As stated earlier, for each family size, several poverty income points were developed in relation to the sex of the head and different combinations of adults and children. When weighted together in accordance with the distribution of families of these types in the current population, they yield a set of assumed food expenditures and income that can be compared with the income of families of the same size who spend that amount per person for food, as estimated roughly from the 1960–1961 consumption study.

Table 2—Study of Poverty Income Points in Relationship to Family Distribution in the Current Population

Family Size	SSA POVERTY INDEX— ECONOMY LEVEL (NONFARM) Per-Capita Food Expense	Income	BLS 1960–1961 Average (Urban)[1]— Estimated Income Corresponding to Economy Food Expenditure
1	([2])	$1540	([2])
2	$240	1990	$1560
3	270	2440	2475
4	260	3130	3120
5	245	3685	3600
6	230	4135	4020
7 or more	210	5090	([2])

1. Derived from BLS Report No. 237-38, July 1964.
2. Not estimated.

The low-cost food plan criterion, derived correspondingly, can be taken as a rough measure of the results that would obtain if the income-food ratios in the BLS study were accepted as the guideline and applied to the lower food standard. Inasmuch as the economy plan for many families requires roughly three-fourths as much to buy as does the low-cost plan, multiplying the purchase requirement in the low-cost food plan by three yields approximately the same income point as multiplying the economy plan cost by four.

The Farm-Nonfarm Adjustment

One additional adjustment was made to allow in some degree for the lesser needs of farm families for cash income. Farm families today buy much of their food, in contrast to the situation 40 or 50 years ago when they depended almost entirely on their own production. Yet it was still true in 1955 that about 40 per cent of the food items consumed by all farm families—valued at prices paid by any families who did buy them—came from their home farm or garden. On the other hand, the food purchased represented—as it did for nonfarm families—a third of total cash income for the year after deductions for operating expenses.[9]

Farm families generally can count not only some of their food but most of their housing as part of the farm operation. Thus, it was assumed that a farm family would need 40 per cent less net cash than a nonfarm family of the same size and composition.

The Resultant Standard

The poverty lines thus developed served to classify a representative Bureau of the Census population sample as of March 1964 for comparison of characteristics of poor and nonpoor units in terms of 1963 money income.[10] That is, for the farm and nonfarm population separately, unrelated individuals were classified by age and sex, and families by sex of head, total number of members, and number of related children under age eighteen. The income of each unit was then compared with the appropriate minimum. The households thus classified as poor and nonpoor were then analyzed for characteristics other than income.[11]

With the information on how the population is divided into units by size and number of children, it is possible to condense the 248 separate criteria into an abbreviated set for families of different size. The income cutoff points set in the economy food plan for nonfarm units would range from $1580 for a single person under age sixty-five to $5090 for a family averaging eight members—that is, seven or more persons. At the low cost level, the corresponding income range runs from $1885 to $6395. A nonfarm family of husband, wife, and two young children would need $3100 or $3980.

When applied to the census income distributions the cutoff points were related to income before income taxes, although they were derived on an after-tax basis. At the economy level the incomes are so low that for most families of more than two persons and for aged unrelated individuals no tax would be required. By contrast, the BLS "modest but adequate" budget for a similar family of four in autumn 1959 in 20 large cities ranged from $5000 to $6000 before taxes and from $5400 and $6600 after taxes.[12]

How Adequate Is the Standard?

The measure of poverty thus developed is arbitrary. Few could call it too high; many might find it too low. Assuming the homemaker is a good manager and has the time and skill to shop wisely, she must prepare nutritious, palatable meals on a budget that for herself, a husband, and two young children—an average family—would come to about 70 cents a day per person.

For a meal all four of them ate together, she could spend on the average only 95 cents, and to stay within her budget she could allow no more a day than a pound of meat, poultry, or fish altogether, barely enough for one small serving for each family member at one of the three meals. Eggs could fill out her family fare only to a limited degree because the plan allows less than two dozen a week for all uses in cooking and at table—not even one to a person a day. And any food extras, such as milk at school for the children, or the coffee her husband might buy to supplement the lunch he carries to work, have to come out of the same food money or compete with the limited funds available for rent, clothing, medical care, and all other expenses. Studies indicate that, on the average, family members eating a meal away from home spend twice as much as the homemaker would spend for preparing one for them at home. The 20 to 25 cents allowed for a meal at home in the economy plan would not buy much even in the way of supplementation.

There is some evidence that families with very low income, particularly large families, cut their food bills below the economy-plan level—a level at which a nutritionally good diet, though possible, is hard to achieve. Indeed, a study of beneficiaries of old age-age, survivors, and disability insurance—limited to one- or two-person families— found that only about 10 per cent of those spending less than the low-cost plan (priced about a third higher than the economy plan) had meals furnishing the full recommended amounts of essential nutrients. Not more than 40 per cent had even as much as two-thirds the amounts recommended. Only when food expenditures were as high as those in the low-cost plan, or better, did 90 per cent of the diets include two-thirds of the recommended allowance of the nutrients, and 60 per cent meet them in full.[13] Few housewives with greater resources—income and other—than most poor families have at their disposal could do better. Many might not do as well.

Varying the Reference Point

Much of the recent discussion of the poor has centered about an *ad hoc* definition adopted in 1963. Under this definition a family of two persons or more with income of less than $3000, and one person alone with less than $1500, were considered poor. At the time, a more refined poverty income test was believed to be desirable. The hope was expressed that, although the statistical magnitude of the problem would undoubtedly be altered by a different measure, "the analysis of the sources of poverty, and of the programs needed to cope with it, would remain substantially unchanged."[14] Since programs are selected on other than purely statistical considerations, this part of the statement is unchallenged. But at least the relative importance of various phases of the poverty question does depend on the criterion used.

The present analysis pivots about a standard of roughly $3130 for a family of four persons (all types combined) and $1540 for an unrelated individual—a level in itself not materially different from the earlier one. The standard assumes in addition that families with fewer than four persons will, on the average, require less and that larger families will need more, despite the fact that in actuality they do not always have incomes which correspond. The resulting count of the poor therefore includes fewer small families and more large ones, many of them with children. Moreover, the preceding standard treats farm and nonfarm families alike, but the one discussed here assumes a lower cash requirement for families receiving some food and housing without direct outlay, as part of a farming operation. Accordingly, farm families, despite their low cash income, have a somewhat smaller representation in the current count of the poor for 1963 than in the earlier statistic.

The gross number of the population counted as poor will reflect, in the main, the level of living used as the basis. In this respect the old definition and the present one are much alike: 28½ million persons in families would be called poor today because their families have incomes less than $3000; 29¾ million persons in families would be poor because their family income is considered too low in relation to the number it must support. What is more telling, however, is the composition of the groups selected, for in considerable measure they are not the same.

To the extent that families differing in composition tend also to differ in income, the power of the poverty line to approximate an equivalent measure of need determines how accurately the selected group reflects the economic well-being of families of different composition. It may be that the consistency of the measure of economic well-being applied to different types of families is even more important than the level itself.

Though one may question the merits of a food-income relationship alone as a poverty index, it probably does serve as an interim guide to equivalent levels of living among families in different situations. Additional variables could improve it, as, for example, allowance for geographic variables of community size and region, and indeed further study of the income-consumption patterns themselves. Even as it stands, however, this index is undoubtedly a better leveler than a single income applied across the board.

Comparison of different measures of poverty suggests that the flat sum of $3000 for a family and $1500 for an individual would indicate that 33.4 million persons were living in poverty in 1963. One in seven of them would be a farm resident, and one in three a child under age eighteen. Modification of this scale to allow $1500 for the first person and $500 for every additional family member raises the number of the poor to 34.5 million, and the per cent who are children to more than 40, but the ratio of one in seven on a farm remains unchanged. Under the economy-plan definition, the most complex and differentiated of the standards, there are 34.6 million poor—almost the same number as under the $500-per-person modification of the single $3000 standard—but the number of poor children, who now represent 43 per cent of the population living in poverty, is a million greater. As would be expected, the proportion of the poor who live on farms is considerably lower, or only 1 in 11.

Of particular significance is the incidence of poverty among different kinds of families. The uniform $3000 test, which designated 9.3 million families as poor in 1962, by 1963 counted 8.8 million, or about 1 in 5. By contrast, in

1963 the economy-plan standard would tag only 1 in 7 families as poor, or 7.2 million all told. Although half the families poor by the $3000 income test include no more than two members, two-person units represent only a third of the families poor according to the economy-level definition. In corresponding fashion, only one in eight of the families with less than $3000 had four or more children, but among those poor according to the economy level every fourth family had at least four children. Families with an aged head represented more than a third of all the families with less than $3000 but only a fifth of those with incomes below the economy plan standard.

Clearly, a profile of the poor that includes large numbers of farm families and aged couples may raise different questions and evoke different answers than when the group is characterized by relatively more young nonfarm families—many of them with several children. Nonwhite families, generally larger than white families, account for about 2 million of the poor units by either definition. Because the total number of families counted among the poor by the economy standard is smaller, however, the nonwhite families make up a larger part of them.

Because the measure of poverty for nonfarm unrelated individuals is almost the same under the economy level definition as under the earlier one—the one-person households seldom live on a farm—the characteristics of the 4.9 million persons called poor by the two criteria are almost identical.

The Income Deficit

Before elaborating further on who is poor and who is not, it may be well to assess the magnitude of the poverty complex in dollar terms. Just how much less than the aggregate estimated need is the actual income of the poor? Does it fall short by much or by little?

In the very rough terms that the selected income standard permits, it can be estimated that the 34.6 million persons identified as poor needed an aggregate money income of $28.8 billion in 1963 to cover their basic requirements. Their current income actually totaled about $17.3 billion, or only 60 per cent of their estimated needs. Some of the deficit could have been—and no doubt was—offset by use of savings. By and large, however, it has been well documented that the low-income persons who could benefit most from such additions to their meager resources are least likely to have the advantage of them. And it is not usually the poor who have the rich relatives.

Unquestionably the income of the poor included the $4.7 billion paid under public-assistance programs from federal, state, and local funds during 1963. In December of that year such payments were going to a total of 7½ million recipients (or a fifth of the poor). Not all persons who are poor receive assistance, but all persons receiving assistance are unquestionably poor. It cannot be said for sure how many of the poor were benefiting from other public income-support programs, such as old-age, survivors, and disability insurance, unemployment insurance, veterans' payments, and the like.

Of the total deficit, about $5 billion represented the unmet needs of families headed by a woman. About three-fifths of the total ($6.6 billion) represented the shortage in income of families with children under age eighteen and about 60 per cent of this shortage was in the income of families with a man at the head. It is estimated that $600 million represented the deficit of poor persons on farms.

Even among the needy, there are some who are worse off than others, and in dollar terms the families consisting of a mother and young children must rank among the poorest. Such families as a group had less than half the money they needed, and the greater the number of children the greater the unmet need: poor families with a female head and five or more children, including altogether about 1,650,000 children, as a group were living on income less by 59 per cent than their minimum requirement. Of the total family units of this type in the population—that is, of all families with female head and five or more children— 9 out of 10 were poor. As the following figures show, for both male and female units, those families with the highest poverty rate—the families with several children—tended also to include the poorest poor. Unrelated individuals, including a large number of aged persons, also have both high rates of poverty and substantial income deficits.

Table 3—Comparison of Poverty Rates

| | MALE HEAD | | FEMALE HEAD | |
| | Incidence of Poverty at the Economy Level | Income of the Poor as Proportion of Required Income | Incidence of Poverty at the Economy Level | Income of the Poor as Proportion of Required Income |
Type of Unit				
	(in percentages)			
Total	14	64	46	53
Unrelated individual	34	57	50	58
Family	12	65	40	49
With no children	12	64	19	62
With children	12	65	55	47
1 or 2	8	68	42	53
3 or 4	14	66	72	45
5 or more	36	62	92	41

Children and Poverty

Of all the persons in family units with income below the economy level (that is, disregarding for the moment persons living alone), half were children under age eighteen. These 15 million youngsters represented more than 1 in 5 of all children living in families. Because poor families sometimes find it necessary to "double up" in order to cut down their living expenses, about 9 per cent of the children in the poor families were designated as "related" rather than "own" children. In other words, they were not the children of the head of the family, but the children of other relatives making their home with the family. Among the poor families with a woman at the head, one-seventh of the children were "related" rather than "own," and nearly a third of these related children were part of a subfamily consisting of a mother and children. Among poor families with a male head, 6 per cent of the children in the households were children of a relative of the head.

A considerable number of subfamilies that include children are poor—a third of those with a father present, and nearly three-fourths of those with only a mother. But from 50 per cent to 60 per cent of the subfamilies with inadequate income manage to escape poverty by living with relatives. Counting as poor the children in subfamilies whose own income is inadequate, but who live as part of a larger family with a combined income above the poverty level, would add 580,000 to the number of children whose parents are too poor to support them even at the economy level. Together with their parents, these children represent a group of 1.1 million persons under age sixty-five not included in the current count of the poor, although they would be if they had to rely solely on their own income.

In contrast to this total of 15.6 million needy children, in December 1963 only 3.1 million children were receiving assistance in the form of aid to families with dependent children (AFDC), the public program designed especially for them. Because some families stay on assistance less than a full year, roughly 4.5 million children received assistance during 1963.

Many children receive benefits from other public programs, such as old-age, survivors, and disability insurance, and veterans' programs. It is not known at this writing how many of them are numbered among the poor or how many are in families with total income from all sources below the public assistance standards for their state.

Children in poor families with a man at the head are less likely than others to receive help. Such children number more than 10 million, but today the number of children with a father in the home who receive assistance in the form of aid to families with dependent children is less than 1 million, a ratio of not even 1 in 10.

Many of the families with children receiving public assistance undoubtedly are among the poorest of the poor, because even by the limited standards of assistance of their own states—almost all of which allow less than the economy level of income—nearly half the recipients have some unmet need. For a fourth of the families, according to a recent study, the unmet need came to as much as $30 a month or more.[15]

As would be expected, the larger the family, the more likely it is to include children. Indeed, among families of five or more, almost all have some children, and three-fourths have at least three. The fewer adults in the family, the less opportunity there will be for additional earnings.

It is readily apparent from 1963 data for income and family size that no matter what the family size, the income decreases with increasing number of children at a rate that is not likely to be offset by the fact that children have lower-income needs. Accordingly, not only do poverty rates among families vary with family size, but among families of a given size the chances of being poor vary in accordance with the number of children under age eighteen. The per-

Table 4—Differences in Poverty Rates with Respect to Family Size

Total Number of Family Members	CHILDREN UNDER AGE EIGHTEEN						
	0	1	2	3	4	5	6 or More
Families with male head:							
3	6	8	(^{1})	–	–	–	–
4	3	6	7	(^{1})	–	–	–
5	2	9	9	11	(^{1})	–	–
6	(^{1})	(^{1})	4	14	16	(^{1})	–
7 or more	(^{1})	(^{1})	(^{1})	10	22	30	42
Families with female head:							
2^2	14	47	–	–	–	–	–
3	9	21	54	–	–	–	–
4	(^{1})	18	43	73	–	–	–

1. Percentages not shown for base less than 100,000.
2. Head under age sixty-five.

centages above show the incidence of poverty—as defined
by the Social Security Administration criterion at the economy level—among nonfarm families with specified numbers
of children. The sorry plight of the families with female
head and children is also evident. It needs no poverty line
to explain why two-thirds of the children in such families
must be considered poor. One report cited evidence that
women in families without a husband present had had more
children than in those where the husband was still present.[16]
Some families with children and a female head may well,
at an earlier stage, have been members of a large household
with a male head and inadequate income.

Finally, since the data both on income and on incidence
of poverty relate to the number now in the family, there is
an understatement of the relationship between large families and low income: Some of the families currently listed
as having only one or two children undoubtedly will have
more in the future or have others who are now past age
eighteen and may no longer be in the home. It is not likely
that family income adjustments are made in equal measure.
If anything, income may decline rather than increase as
the family grows, because it will be more difficult for the
mother to work, and many families can escape poverty only
by having the wife as well as the head in the labor force.

Work and Poverty

The greater overall vulnerability of families headed by
a woman is evidenced by the fact that such families, who
number only 1 in 10 of all families in the country, account
for nearly 1 in 3 of the nation's poor. Although the inadequate income of poor families with a female head may be
attributed to the fact that few of these women are employed,
this is not the reason among the families headed by a man.
A majority of the men are working, but at jobs that do not
pay enough to provide for their family needs. Moreover, of
those not at work, most report themselves as out of the labor

force altogether rather than unemployed. Yet the rate of unemployment reported by the poor was more than three times that among the heads of families above the poverty level.

The employment status of family heads in March 1964, when the income data were collected, was recorded as shown in Table 5. Despite the fact that unemployment generally is more prevalent among the nonwhite population than the white, among families whose income marked them as poor there was no difference as to race in the total proportion of the men currently looking for work. Among white

Table 5—Employment Status of Family Heads (March 1964)

Employment Status of Head, March 1964	MALE HEAD		FEMALE HEAD	
	Poor Family	Nonpoor Family	Poor Family	Nonpoor Family
Total	100	100	100	100
In labor force	67	88	33	60
Employed	60	85	29	57
Unemployed	6	3	4	3
Not in labor force	33	12	67	40

and nonwhite male heads alike, 6 per cent said they were out of a job. Indeed, since fewer among the white heads of families who are poor were in the labor force than was true among nonwhite heads of poor families, the rate of unemployment among those actually available for work was noticeably higher for the former group. What is more significant is that 73 per cent of the nonwhite male heads of poor families were currently employed, and more than half of them—42 per cent of all the poor—had been employed full time throughout 1963. Among male heads in white families with incomes below the economy level, only 56 per cent were currently working, and no more than a third had been year-round full-time workers in 1963.

Unemployment for nonwhite workers is undeniably serious. But the concentration of nonwhite men in low-paying jobs at which any worker—white or nonwhite—is apt to earn too little to support a large family may be even more crucial in consigning their families to poverty at a rate three times that of their white fellow citizens. In point of fact, the family of a nonwhite male is somewhat worse off in relation to that of a white male when both are working than when both are not, as the figures in Table 6 suggest.

Table 6—Employment Status of Family Heads (March 1964)

Employment Status of Head, March 1964	PER CENT OF FAMILIES WITH MALE HEAD WITH INCOME BELOW THE ECONOMY LEVEL	
	White	Nonwhite
All families	10	34
Not in labor force	25	50
Unemployed	22	47
Employed	7	31
Year-round, full-time in 1963	5	23

This difference does not come as a complete surprise. Earlier analysis of the income life cycle of the nonwhite man suggested that it is only when he and his white counterpart exchange their weekly pay envelope for a check from a public income-maintenance program that they begin to approach economic equality.[17] For most white families, retirement or other type of withdrawal from the labor force brings with it a marked decline in income. Some nonwhite families, however, are then actually not much worse off than when working.

Since it was the annual income for 1963 that determined whether the family would be ranked as poor, the work experience of the head in 1963 is even more relevant to the poverty profile than the employment status at the time of the Current Population Survey.

Among the male heads, only 1 in 3 of those in poor families was a full-time worker all during the year, compared with 3 in 4 of the heads in nonpoor families. Among the female heads, as would be expected, the proportion working full time was much smaller—a tenth among poor families and not a full four-tenths among the nonpoor. All told, the poor families headed by a man fully employed throughout 1963 included 5.2 million children under age eighteen, and those headed by a fully employed woman worker had half a million. Thus 2 in 5 of all the children growing up in poverty were in a family of a worker with a regular full-time job.

It is difficult to say which is the more striking statistic: that 6 per cent of the families headed by a male year-round full-time worker were nevertheless poor, or that 25 per cent of the families with a male head who did not have a full-time job all year were poor. That a man risks poverty for his family when he does not or cannot work all the time might be anticipated, but to end the year with so inadequate an income even when he has worked all week every week must make his efforts seem hopeless.

Yet, with the minimum wage law guaranteeing an annual income of only $2600, and many workers entitled to not even this amount, it should not be too surprising that

Table 7—Families in Poverty (1963)

Type of Family	All Families	Male Head	Female Head
		(in millions)	
Total number of poor families	7.2	5.2	2.0
With head a year-round, full-time worker	2.0	1.8	0.2
White	1.4	1.3	0.1
Nonwhite	0.6	0.5	0.1
Other	5.2	3.4	1.8
White	2.7	2.6	1.1
Nonwhite	1.5	0.8	0.7

in 1963 there were 2 million families in poverty despite the fact that the head worked all year as shown in Table 7.

Almost all the male heads who had worked full time all year in 1963 were also currently employed in March 1964 in poor and nonpoor families alike. Among the women year-round full-time workers, only 80 per cent of those at the head of families who were poor in terms of their 1963 income were still employed in the spring of the following year, compared with 96 per cent of those not poor. Among 1.8 million male heads of families who were poor despite their year-round full-time employment, more than a fifth gave their current occupation as farmers, an equal number were operatives, and nearly a fifth were laborers. Only 3 per cent were professional or technical workers. By contrast, among the nonpoor, 1 in 8 of the male family heads working the year around at full-time jobs were currently employed as professional or technical workers and only 4 per cent each were farmers or laborers.

Notwithstanding the current stress on more jobs, it is clear that at least for poor families headed by a full-time year-round worker—more than a fourth of the total—it is not so much that more jobs are required but better ones, if it is presumed that the head of the family will continue to be the main source of support, and that there will continue to be as many large families. In less than a fifth of the poor families headed by a man working full time the year around was the wife in the paid labor force, and in only about two-fifths was there more than one earner. By contrast, in the corresponding group of nonpoor families, one-third of the wives were working or in the market for a job, and 55 per cent of the families in all had at least one earner in addition to the head.

Not even for the 5.2 million poor families with a head who worked less than a full year can jobs alone provide an answer. Among the poor, about two-thirds of the male heads who had worked part of the year or not at all in 1963 gave ill health or other reasons—including retirement—as the main reason, rather than an inability to find work. Of the female heads less than fully employed in 1963, about five-sixths gave household responsibilities as the reason; though fewer claimed ill health or disability, they nevertheless out-

numbered those who said they had been looking for work.
Among the unrelated individuals, only 1 in 6 of the men
and 1 in 14 of the women not working the year around gave
unemployment as the chief reason. At best it will be difficult to find jobs that a large number of the underemployed
heads of poor households can fill, as the figures in Table 8
indicate:

Table 8—Family Head's Work Experience and/or Reason for Not Working

Work Experience of Head in 1963	FAMILIES		UNRELATED INDIVIDUALS	
	Male Head	Female Head	Male	Female
Total	100	100	100	100
Worked all year	39	15	21	11
Full-time job	35	9	17	7
Part-time job	4	6	4	4
Worked part of the year	33	28	28	20
Looking for work	19	7	11	4
Ill, disabled	6	4	4	3
Keeping house	—	15	—	6
All other	8	2	13	7
Didn't work at all	28	58	51	69
Ill, disabled	12	10	20	14
Keeping house	—	41	—	43
Couldn't find work	1	2	4	2
All other	15	5	27	10

Percentage Distribution of Units with Income Below Economy Level

Occupation and Poverty

The chances of a family's being poor differ not only with
the amount of employment of the head but also with the kind
of work he does. This is a reflection of the different pay
rates and lifetime earnings patterns that workers at different trades can expect. It appears, however, that the association is compounded: not only do certain occupations pay
more poorly than others, but workers in those occupations
tend to have larger families. Thus an income unlikely to be

high to begin with must be stretched to provide for more children, rather than less.

Of families headed by a male year-round full-time worker and with income above the economy level, more than half had either no children under age eighteen in the household or only one. Only 4 per cent had more than four. By contrast, among the corresponding group of families with income less than the economy level, fewer than a third had no more than one child in the home and nearly a fourth had five or more.

The poverty rates for families with heads in different occupations take on new meaning when ranked by a measure of earnings potential. There is a cycle in family income as well as in family size, although the two patterns are not generally in perfect correspondence. On the assumption that for the average family it is mainly the earning capacity of the husband that sets the scale at which the family must live, the poverty rates for families of employed male heads by occupation have been arrayed according to the median earnings (in 1959) by men aged thirty-five to forty-four. This is the age range at which on the basis of cross-sectional data, earnings for the average worker in most occupations are at their peak.

Two things are abundantly clear. In general, the poverty rates for families of men in different occupations are inversely related to the median peak earnings—that is, the lower the average earnings at age thirty-five to forty-four, the greater the risk of poverty for the family. In some instances, as among families of some of the proprietors, work of the wife and other adults may count as unpaid family labor rather than add earnings to the family income. The size of the average family with children seems also to vary inversely with earnings capacity, in terms of the number of children ever born to the wives aged thirty-five to forty-four of men employed in these occupations. The figures in Table 9 illustrate the patterns separately for white and nonwhite families with male head:

Table 9—Separate Work Patterns of White and Nonwhite Family Heads

Occupation Group	Median Earnings of Male Workers Aged Thirty-five to Forty-four[1]	Incidence of Poverty Among Families with Employed Male Head[2]	PER CENT OF WIVES AGED THIRTY-FIVE TO FORTY-FOUR OF EMPLOYED WORKERS WITH SPECIFIED NUMBER OF CHILDREN EVER BORN[3]		
			0–2	3	4 or More
White males:					
Professional and technical workers	$8015	2	56	23	20
Managers, officials, proprietors (except farm)	7465	5	57	23	20
Sales workers	6325	3	60	22	19
Craftsmen and foremen	5795	4	54	21	25
Clerical and kindred workers	5505	2	61	20	19
Operatives	5075	9	52	20	27
Service workers	4610	8	57	20	23
Nonfarm laborers	4095	15	49	19	33
Farmers and farm managers	2945	26	42	22	36
Farm laborers	2020	43	35	17	48
Nonwhite males:					
Professional and technical workers	5485	12	65	16	19
Managers, officials, proprietors (except farm)	4655	21	57	16	27
Clerical and kindred workers	4630	13	61	14	25
Sales workers	4010	NA	57	16	27
Craftsmen and foremen	3885	21	52	13	35
Operatives	3495	27	51	12	37
Service workers	2970	25	57	13	30
Nonfarm laborers	2825	45	48	11	41
Farm laborers	975	70	34	9	57
Farmers and farm managers	945	78	27	9	65

SOURCE: *U.S. Census of Population, 1960: Occupation by Earnings and Education,* PC(2)-7B and *Women by Number of Children Ever Born,* PC(2)-3A; and Social Security Administration.
   1. In 1959.
   2. Currently employed family heads in March 1964, with 1963 family money income below the economy level in 1963.
   3. Wives of currently employed men at time of 1960 decennial census.

For many families a critical point in financial status may be the arrival of the fourth or fifth child. At all occupational levels (except among wives of professional and technical employees) the nonwhite family tends to be larger than the white, but on the average nonwhite families are at a lower economic level than white families in the same occupational class. A more accurate, or at least a narrower, occupational grouping would probably show less difference between the sizes of white and nonwhite families at equivalent economic levels.

Some of the differences in number of children are related to different patterns of age at first marriage. But even among women who married at the same age there remains evidence of a difference in life style among occupational groups, in terms of number of children ever born.

The discussion here centers on children ever born rather than the more common statistic of children present in the home. Use of the latter figure results in serious understatement of the total number of children in large families who may be subject to the risk of poverty before they reach adulthood. Differences in the two statistics are greater for the low-income occupations, such as nonfarm laborers with their large families, than for high-income occupations, such as professional and technical workers with their smaller families. It appears to be the families with less income to look forward to in the first place who have more children.[18]

The statistics by occupation may throw light on the intergeneration cycle of poverty. It is not necessary here to repeat the admonition that education for our youngsters is a long step up in the escape from poverty. It is of importance, however, that in these days, when children generally are receiving more education than those a generation ago, the degree of upward mobility is affected by social environment as indicated by the occupation as well as by the education of the father. According to a recent report, among children of men with the same educational attainment, those with fathers in white-collar jobs are much more likely than children of fathers in manual and service jobs or in farm jobs to acquire more years of school training than their parents.[19]

Implications

The causes of poverty are many and varied. Because some groups in the population are more vulnerable, however, a cross section of the poor will differ from one of the nonpoor, measure for measure. Mothers bringing up children without a father, the aged or disabled who cannot earn, and the Negro who may not be allowed to earn will, more often than the rest of us, know the dreary privation that denies them the good living that has become the hallmark of America.

But there are others thus set apart, without the handicap of discrimination or disability, who cannot even regard their plight as the logical consequence of being unemployed. There are millions of children in "normal" as well as broken homes who will lose out on their chance ever to strive as equals in this competitive society because they are denied now even the basic needs that money can buy. And finally there are the children yet to come, whose encounter with poverty can be predicted unless the situation is changed for those currently poor.

Neither the present circumstances nor the reasons for them are alike for all our impoverished millions, and the measures that can help reduce their number must likewise be many and varied. No single program, placing its major emphasis on the needs of one special group alone, will succeed. Any complex of programs that does not allow for the diversity of the many groups among the poor will to that degree leave the task undone. The poor have been counted many times. It remains now to count the ways by which to help them gain a new identity.

NOTES

1. Published originally in *Social Security Bulletin*, Jan. 6, 1965.

2. Estimates are based on a per-capita average for all four-person nonfarm families. Costs will average slightly more in small households and less in larger ones. A member of a two-person family, for example, would need 74 cents a day for food and $2 a day for other items.

3. See U.S. Department of Agriculture, *Family Food Plans and Food Costs*, Home Economics Research Report No. 20, Nov. 1962.

4. With recommended adjustments for family size, small families are allowed somewhat more and larger families somewhat less,

and for all families the actual amounts of food suggested will vary with the sex and age of the members. Even in a four-person family, the per-capita cost will vary slightly from the figure cited, depending upon whether it includes teenagers with high food requirements or a younger child or an aged member with food needs less than average. Recent revisions in suggested food quantities to allow for changes in the recommended dietary allowances result in almost no change in the costs of the plans on the average. Foods for men of all ages and girls aged nine to twelve cost slightly less than before, and foods for women under age fifty-five cost slightly more. (*See* U.S. Department of Agriculture, *Family Economics Review*, Oct. 1964.)

5. U.S. Department of Agriculture, Household Food Consumption Survey, 1955, *Dietary Evaluation of Food Used in Households in the United States*, Report No. 16, November 1961, and *Food Consumption and Dietary Levels of Households of Different Size, United States, by Region*, Report No. 17, Jan. 1963.

6. See U.S. Department of Agriculture, *Food Consumption and Dietary Levels of Households in the United States* (ARS 626), Aug. 1957.

7. Willard Wirtz, statement in *Hearings Before the Ways and Means Committee, House of Representatives, Eighty-eighth Congress, on Medical Care for the Aged*, Nov. 18–22, 1963, and Jan. 20–24, 1963.

8. See Mollie Orshansky, "Budget for an Elderly Couple," *Social Security Bulletin*, Dec. 1960.

9. See U.S. Department of Agriculture, Household Food Consumption Survey, 1955, *Food Production for Home Use by Households in the United States, by Region*, Report No. 12, Jan. 1958, and *Farm Family Spending in the United States*, Agriculture Information Bulletin No. 192, June 1958.

10. An earlier analysis related to 1961 income, along the same lines but restricted to families with children, was reported in the *Social Security Bulletin* for July 1963. For that earlier estimate, since family income data were available only by number of own children, not crossed with total number of persons, it was necessary to make arbitrary assumptions about the additional relatives. The present figures, based on a more refined income grid and incorporating 1960 census data not previously available on characteristics of families and persons, represent not only an updating but, it is hoped, a refinement.

11. The special tabulations for this purpose were prepared by the Bureau of the Census, with the major responsibility for them carried by Eva T. Auerbach, Joyce A. Ingram, Arno I. Winard, and Frederick J. Cavanaugh.

12. Helen H. Lamale and Margaret S. Stotz, "The Interim City Worker's Family Budget," *Monthly Labor Review*, Aug. 1960.

13. U.S. Department of Agriculture, *Food Consumption and Dietary Levels of Older Households in Rochester, New York*, by C. LeBovit and D. A. Baker, Home Economics Research Report No. 25, 1964.

14. Council of Economic Advisers, *Annual Report 1964*, Chapter 2.

15. Gerald Kahn and Ellen J. Perkins, "Families Receiving AFDC: What Do They Have to Live On?" *Welfare in Review*, Oct. 1964.

16. Mollie Orshansky, "Children of the Poor," *Social Security Bulletin*, July 1963.

17. Mollie Orshansky, "The Aged Negro and His Income," *Social Security Bulletin*, Feb. 1964.

18. See also Bureau of the Census, *Current Population Reports*, "Socioeconomic Characteristics of the Population: 1960," Series P-23, No. 12, July 31, 1964.

19. Bureau of the Census, *Current Population Reports*, "Educational Change in a Generation," Series P-20, No. 132, Sept. 22, 1964.

The Poverty
of Aging

HAROLD L. SHEPPARD

The subject of the aged and
poverty is considered first[1] because the status of a society's
aged may well be taken as a measure of the degree to which
that society has met the problem of poverty in general.
When the aged have "reached the end of the road" or the
"home stretch in the race of life" in one condition or another,
we have some indication of the institutions and actions
taken by the general community prior to that period which
affect the outcome of individual life careers.

To begin with, the problem of the aged is essentially
one associated with the emergence of a modern, industrial-
ized society. Such societies have far greater proportions of
their populations over the age of sixty-five than do traditionally underdeveloped ones. At the same time, despite a
greater proportion of older persons, these societies use a

smaller proportion of their older members in their active labor force. The reasons are obvious, having to do with the increased (and increasing) longevity due to the improved practice of medicine, public health, and sanitation, with improved living and working conditions, and the like, as well as with the reduction in manpower hours required to produce goods and services.

More people are living to be "old," absolutely and proportionately, as compared to our own past, and as compared to other existing societies. Moreover, people are living beyond the age where they are needed in the labor force. Even within the United States today, the relation between industrialism and the age-occupation distribution is clear, as shown by the fact that the proportion of the aged male segment of the labor force engaged in agriculture is about two-and-a-half times the proportion of males of all ages in agricultural occupations.

The problems of poverty among the aged stem also from the fact that an increasing number of the sixty-five plus population are becoming definitely "aged," and within this upper-age bracket among the old, say, seventy-five and over, women will predominate, especially husbandless women with low incomes. By 1980 one-fifth of all the sixty-five-plus population will be females aged seventy-five and over. Employment is clearly out of the question for the vast majority of such individuals, men included. Retirement becomes the vital variable in the poverty condition of the aged, and the longer the average person lives in retirement, the greater are his or her chances of becoming impoverished. The radical decline in labor-force participation among the aged, from a rate of 70 per cent for men in 1890 to less than one-third in 1960 (including even part-time workers), is not due merely to the rising numbers of the very old among the aged. Even in the sixty-five to sixty-nine group, employment as a source of income is declining. For example, the labor-force participation rate, including part-time work, dropped for the sixty-five- to sixty-nine-year-old males from 57 per cent in 1954 to about 45 per cent in 1960. We can expect this rate to continue to decline in years to come.

Employment as a source of income for the total aged population of sixty-five and older is a status enjoyed only by about one-fifth of that population. The median income of all two-person families with aged heads (including those employed) is about $2500: this means that more than one-half of such families are below the poverty line of $3000. The median income of all aged persons living alone is about $1000; this means that more than one-half of aged individuals living alone—most of them women—are below the poverty line of $1500.

It is striking to note that there is little in the way of public thinking—and even in the official documents of our government agencies—that adequately conveys what may be called the dynamic and longitudinal facets of the phenomena involved. For example, the typical statistical presentations will tell us that the aged in 1960 had improved in their economic status, say, over 1950. The imagery here is that of a boat—labeled A-G-E-D—floating in a canal, through a series of locks that raise or lower the boat from one point in space to another point in space. To mix the image a bit, space represents time.

But this primitive model has very little to do with reality. One of the things we should be looking at, for example, is the following: what happens to a group of people, say, aged fifty-five to sixty-five in 1950 by the time they live to the year 1960, when they become at least sixty-five, and, at most, seventy-five years of age? That is the basic question, in my opinion.

The question usually asked is: are the aged of 1960 any better off, or worse off, than the aged of 1950? The first query pertains to the life career pattern of given individuals insofar as they experience relative deprivation over time, that is, relative to their earlier income. The second question, and the answers to it, shed light on how well the society has fared in assuring the aged of one era a decent standard of living as compared with the aged of another era.

To quote from the 1961 *Report of the Senate Subcommittee on Problems of the Aged and Aging,*

> . . . one major flaw characterizes much of the ordinary discussion about the income status of our aged citizens. This is the failure to reckon with the dynamic nature of the problem. For example, when it is said . . . that the median money income of aged family heads as a percentage of the median income of all families dropped from 60 per cent in 1949 to 52 per cent in 1959, there seems to be a tacit assumption that the aged of 1959 are the same people as those aged in 1949, but they are not exactly the same. The 4.8 million men and 5.5 million women aged 65 to 74 in 1960 were not "aged" in 1950, for example.
>
> The crucial question is, what change takes place in the incomes of a given age group as it moves into retirement status? When we say that between 1949 and 1959 the income of the male "aged" increased 55 per cent, we are really not talking about the same intact population. In reality, the median income of men aged 55 to 64 in 1949 was $2,366, but by 1959 the same men (minus those who died, etc.) experienced not an increase in their median income but a decrease.
>
> More specifically, the best data available on this point are provided by the Bureau of the Census, in its January 1961 report on 1959 incomes. The median income of men born in March 1895 and earlier was $1710 in 1949; 10 years later, the median income of the *same* group had *decreased* 8 per cent, to $1576. These figures, moreover, are in current dollars and not constant ones: an analysis using constant 1959 dollars would reveal that this group of men suffered an approximate 33 per cent *decrease* in real income from 1949 to 1959, while during the same period of time the real median income for men aged 24 to 34 in 1949 *increased* by approximately 57 per cent; for men aged 34 to 44 in 1949, the increase was approximately 34 per cent.
>
> The same analysis can be applied to the changes in assets and savings. In all of these trends, it is important to recog-

nize another aspect that is too often neglected, namely, the
effect of rising expectations in the general population—expectations which do not automatically abate upon retirement.
This aspect further aggravates the problem of an adequate
income for future generations of retired Americans. An
increasing number of such persons will be more insistent on
an adequate level of living than past generations of retirees.
The younger Americans of today will carry into their own
retirement of tomorrow many expectations and aspirations
that cannot be met if their retired income status is no better
than that of the aged of the present time.[2]

Another point I want to make relates to the controversial
document issued by the Ad Hoc Committee on the Triple
Revolution, in which it is argued that modern technology
increasingly requires a smaller and smaller proportion of
the population to create and provide goods and services,
and that therefore we should abandon the social institutions
and mechanisms that require employment in an occupation as a condition for obtaining food, clothing, housing, and
other services—with money as the primary intermediary
between employment and these ends. One does not have to
accept this radical suggestion for the total population's
problems to see its relevance to the problems of the retired
aged.

The point should be obvious; namely, that if there is
any class of human beings to which the Triple Revolution
applies it is the group of aged Americans who are retired.
Indeed, we have already accepted the principle of income
and material support without the intermediary of employment—although many students of gerontology would
hasten to add that we only tolerate this principle mea-
gerly and that we apply it begrudgingly and in a miserly
fashion.

A third point is less controversial, perhaps, but more
concrete and immediate, with consequences for the problem
of future poverty among the aged of tomorrow, all of us
included. The University of Michigan study[3] (by Morgan,

Table 1—Median Income of Men, by Age, for the United States: 1959 and 1949

(in current dollars)

			INDEX (35 TO 44 YEARS = 100)	
Age	1959	1949	1959	1949
Total	$3996	$2346	75	79
14 to 24 years	1131	1112	21	39
14 to 19 years	411	410	8	14
20 to 24 years	2612	1726	49	58
25 to 34 years	4747	2754	89	93
35 to 44 years	5320	2951	100	100
45 to 54 years	4852	2751	91	93
55 to 64 years	4190	2366	79	80
65 years and over	1576	1016	30	34

SOURCE: Bureau of the Census.

Table 2—Median Income of Men in 1959 and 1949, by Period of Birth, for the United States

(in current dollars)

	MEDIAN INCOME IN:		Per Cent Change, 1949 to 1959
Period of Birth	1959	1949	
April 1925 to March 1935	$4747	$1112	327
April 1915 to March 1925	5320	2754	93
April 1905 to March 1915	4852	2951	64
April 1895 to March 1905	4190	2751	52
March 1895 and earlier	1576	1710	−8

SOURCE: Bureau of the Census.

Cohen, Brazer, and David) reveals that out of 1967 spending units headed by nonretired persons aged thirty or over:

136, or 6 per cent will have no pensions.
1098, or 55 per cent will have social security only.
710, or 39 per cent will have social security *and* private pensions.

Some signs of possible poverty to come may be gleaned from the following findings, also from the University of Michigan study. They suggest the lack of advance preparation for old-age security:

1. Spending units who have had less than $500 in the bank for the past five years are more likely than not to report they will get along during retirement.

2. Nine per cent of heads between 30 and 45 see hard times in old age. Sixteen per cent of heads older than 45 see hard times in old age.

3. Assurance of financing of medical care during retirement is low.

4. More than one third of middle-aged and over (45+) have less than $5,000 assets of any kind.

5. About one half of non-retired people said they are now doing nothing or cannot do anything to add to retirement income. (This includes many who nevertheless are covered by social security.)

The authors go on to comment that

. . . aside from the automatic and largely compulsory retirement systems, and the accumulation of equity in a home, most people are making little other provision for retirement. The vast increase in retirement systems, particularly the Federal social security system, makes this less of a problem than it has been in the past. The question remains whether people, most of whom expect to retire by the time they are seventy years old, will find themselves dissatisfied with their economic situation when they retire.

The aged of today have had a lifetime in which to accumulate savings and other wealth, but their highest incomes in that working lifetime were not adequate to assure subsequent years of well-being. There is no assurance that the aged of 1975 or beyond will have had much improvement in the same conditions affecting the working lives of the aged of 1964.

Roughly 70 per cent of the nonretired (aged thirty or more) heads of spending units in the University of Michigan study indicate that they plan retirement after the age of sixty-five, or do not plan to retire at all. It will be interesting, in the decades ahead, to observe the actual behavior of today's working population, determining whether they retire

Table 3—Highest Income Head Ever Earned

	Aged	Nonwhite[1]	All Poor Families	All Families
		(percentages)		
$ 1– 949	13	19	14	4
950–1949	18	19	18	5
1950–2949	18	17	18	7
2950–4949	10	25	21	22
4950–7449	2	6	9	33
7450+	1	0	3	21
Not ascertained	38	14	17	8
Never worked	28	2	12	4
Mean highest income ever earned	$2230	$2490	$2949	
Mean budget requirement	$2401	$4144	$3676	
Number of families	137	128	755	2800

SOURCE: *Income and Welfare in the United States*, p. 200.
1. Excludes aged, disabled, single with children, those who worked less than 49 weeks in 1959 but usually employed.

Table 4—Hospitalization Insurance

	Aged	Nonwhite[1]	All Poor Families	All Families
		(percentages)		
Everyone in s.u.[2] covered	21	39	32	63
Someone covered	3	8	5	6
No one covered	74	51	62	30
Not ascertained	2	2	1	1

SOURCE: *Ibid.*, p. 204.
1. See previous table.
2. "Spending unit."

Table 5—Types of Poor Families, by Regions (1959)

Region	Aged	Nonwhite[1]	All Poor Families	All Families
		(percentages)		
Northeast	23	4	16	23
North Central	27	12	23	29
South	41	83	51	33
West	9	1	10	15

SOURCE: *Ibid.*
1. Excluding groups cited in above tables.

Table 6—Planned Retirement Age Within Earning Potential (Percentage Distribution of Nonretired Spending Unit Heads Thirty and Older)

Earning Potential of Spending Unit Heads

Planned Retirement Age	Nonw.	W. Farmers	WHITE NONFARMERS BY EDUCATION			All Non-retired S. U. Hds. 30 & Older
			0–11	12	Some College	
			(percentages)			
30 to 59	4	4	4	5	9	5
60 to 64	9	8	9	11	14	11
65 to 70	40	27	48	51	43	46
71 and over	1	0	1	1	2	1
Not ascertained	14	17	13	11	10	12
Do not plan to retire	32	44	25	21	22	25
Number of s. u. heads	270	155	748	399	382	1967

SOURCE: *Ibid.*

Table 7—Experience of Those Who Are Already Retired

Amount of Dissaving Since Retirement	WHETHER HEAD'S RETIREMENT WAS PLANNED		
	Planned	Not Planned	Total
Had savings at retirement; have used less than ¼	14	6	9
¼ to ½	4	8	7
½ to ¾	3	6	4
more than ¾	6	20	15
amount not ascertained	9	6	7
Have not dissaved; had no savings at retirement time, have none now	51	37	42
Have saved since retirement	13	17	16
Number	104	177	304

SOURCE: *Ibid.*

at the age they planned, and how any discrepancy between planned and actual retirement age affects their economic status. Table 7, which reveals the savings experience of people already retired, suggests to some extent what might be expected for those who plan, as compared to those who do not plan to retire.

According to the University of Michigan findings, 40 per cent of all families in the United States (with thirty-year or older heads and nonretired) are covered by private pensions. By contrast, 11 per cent of poor families (with thirty-year or older heads and nonretired) are so covered. *There is no guarantee that all of these will actually retire with a private pension.* We can only be certain regarding percentages now covered by Social Security and other government pensions: 93 per cent of all families, and 84 per cent of all poor families will have some form of Social Security benefit. This is apart from the question of the adequacy of such anticipated retirement incomes. But no one knows for sure how many of the persons now working for companies with private pension plans (40 per cent) will actually have a pension when they retire. Some estimates indicate that perhaps a maximum of one-half will be so fortunate—this, again, apart from the question of the adequacy of such retirement income.

The significance of these observations for those Americans now in their last working years, and for those working poor in general, can be seen in the following statements by the authors of the University of Michigan study:

> For persons fifty-five and older, the question of resources for the future is particularly critical. The incidence of both illness and unemployment increases for that age group, and the availability of a cushion of savings or insurance is important. . . .
>
> Neither the past earning experience nor the assets of the poor suggest that a large fraction were much better off in the recent past than they were in 1959. Their present level of savings and their rights to health insurance and pensions suggest that many will be worse off in the future. None of the poor can afford sickness or injury. Some will be unable to retire because they have no pension rights. This substantial long-term poverty suggests the need for an examination of the transmission of poverty from one generation to the next.[4]

For anyone to assert that today's retired aged should have saved while they were working—and presumably on a voluntary basis—is an indication of indifference or ignorance of economic facts. It is true that most people, for reasons of unawareness or lack of emotions concerning their future as retirees, make few if any private decisions that will improve such futures. But economic growth generally means that incomes and purchasing power improve in the process of growth, at least for those still contributing to the economy through employment. While so engaged when younger and employed, the aged of any given generation had to spend most of their wages and salaries merely to attain a decent standard of living. If they were able to save at all, it was generally very little, certainly in terms of future retired status needs. Furthermore, it has been argued that if the labor force were to engage in extensive private savings while employed in order to assure major improvements in its members' future retirement incomes, the withdrawal of current purchasing power would constitute an irretrievable economic shock to the Gross National Product; such excessive savings would result in widespread and persistent unemployment. If all this is correct, then, it might be further claimed that the employed nonretired population owes much of its present income and living levels to the currently nonemployed retired population, and that therefore the latter group should be rewarded (or supported) to an extent much greater than is currently sanctioned under present social policy.

The poverty of the aged, therefore, can be attributed partly to a social system which still insists on current employment as the basic requirement for human well-being, even though the technology does not have need for the labor of an increasing number of men and women in the upper age brackets. Moreover, there is every indication that the "entry age" into the status of retirement will continue to decline. The irony is that this decline is due partly to the pressures of younger workers trying to eliminate com-

petitors for jobs. This is one of the social consequences of
automation and cybernation, at least in certain industries
and certain occupations.

At the upper end of the "old age continuum," more and
more Americans will be able to live to the ages of seventy-
five, eighty, and even older. In this connection, while the
total aged population, that is, the sixty-five-plus group,
will increase between 1960 and 1975 by about 33 per
cent, the size of the population eighty-five and older will
increase, according to current estimates, by nearly
80 per cent! Medical science is adding years to life;
medical politics is helping to add poverty to these
years.

Unlike other disadvantaged groups in the recent past
and in the present, the aged have now very little power to
effectuate any significant change in the current pattern of
distributing wealth and income. There are some minor
exceptions, and these are usually in local situations, not on
the national level. Essentially, this lack of power is due to
the fact that the masses of the aged, unlike farmers, workers, or ethnic minority groups, do not coalesce as a self-
identifying group, Many of the *statistical* conditions for
political effectiveness—including population size, income
figures, and even percentages of total voting-age population
—are present and seem to be emerging more definitely.
But the *sociopsychological* conditions are not present. One
fact alone is worth repeating here:

> . . . in every presidential election since 1948 (except for
> 1956 when Eisenhower's qualities seemed to have affected all
> age groups) the older voters have shown a greater preference
> for the Republican candidates than have the young voters.
> In 1960 voters over 65 were the only age group that voted
> just as strongly Republican in 1960 as they had in
> 1956. . . .[5]

And the Republican Party, at the present time at least, is
the party least likely to support any basic departure from

contemporary public policy regarding the poverty status of the aged.

Given the fact that the only tool of bargaining power the retired aged would have is the vote—not their power to withhold their labor (which is nonexistent)—I doubt that any significant improvement in their poverty status will be achieved, short of a major revolution in the moral sentiments of the rest of the population.

Monthly Social Security benefits, which average about $80 for a male retiree, and about $125 for a retired couple, and which most retired Americans now receive in varying amounts, up to about $130 per month for a male retiree, are obviously much too low to provide any immunity from poverty for most retired Americans. Only a small percentage of Social Security beneficiaries receive private pensions. It is also estimated that, for some time to come, recipients of Old-Age Assistance will continue to number about 2 million.

The basic solution, consequently, for the poverty problem among the aged lies in major increases in public benefits, which, of course, would require larger contributions from those Americans now working and from their employers, either in the form of a higher percentage of the present taxable income, or by raising the ceiling on that taxable income, which is $4800. Private pensions will not, in the next several decades, offer the basic solution, and the Social Security system, which was created in order to provide a floor of old-age security, is, for most Americans, a floor under water. An additional form of improvement in the poverty status of older Americans would consist of a meaningful program of health care insurance financed through Social Security, but current proposals by the administration, even if passed, will probably be of such a restrictive nature that only a meager change will have been accomplished.

We cannot ignore the fact that nonemployment—retirement—is the crucial factor in the poverty status of the aged.

Taking just married couples with at least one member of sixty-five or older (a population group which is, on the average, better off than nonmarried aged males and females), about half of these couples have an earner. Of those with no earners, 60 per cent, involving about 3 million individuals, had 1959 incomes of less than $2000, well below the poverty line of $3000. We can expect nonearners to increase, both among couples and nonmarried individuals, as population and medical and industrial technology trends continue to exert their impact on the size and proportion of the aged groups not in the labor force. Present programs for assuring adequate retirement income and the outlook for any improvements offer very little assurance of significant progress for future generations of old Americans, especially if we consider the expectations and changing definitions of adequate standards of living within our own society.

There is a comfortable myth that many people entertain about the aged, to the effect that older persons do not need as much money as younger persons. This myth is presumably supported by citations of facts, namely, that older persons typically spend relatively less on clothing and household goods than younger families, relatively more on food and medical care. The facts do show that older persons spend less than younger persons, but from such facts a logical leap is made to the conclusion that the aged therefore *need* less income. The same sort of evasive logic has been used to sanction the low incomes of other segments of the poverty population: Negroes don't need as much money as whites since they require but enough money to buy low-cost food items such as chittlins and fatback and turnip greens; they are happy with hand-me-down clothes and two dresses and one pair of shoes.

The answer to this myth should be obvious, namely, that since older persons typically *receive* less income, they *spend* less, just like younger persons who have low incomes. In an analysis of consumer patterns of aged spending units, Sidney Goldstein has shown that:

The data for the higher income group (among the aged) suggest that those older units who continue to have high incomes continue to follow their earlier patterns of consumption. Only when their income level is markedly reduced, with the resulting need to spend relatively more for the more essential categories of consumer goods and services, are old family units forced to make sharp changes in the patterns of expenditures to which they are accustomed.[6]

I do not think that we can truly point with pride to our system of old-age insurance as having accomplished its original purpose of assuring adequate income to the aged. OASI payments amount to no more than 2 per cent of our GNP. If we add all other types of federal programs, the expenditures for the elderly might amount to 4 per cent, for a population segment that is about 9 per cent of the total population. It is evident that our incomes and the national economy can afford to sustain a decision to provide the retired aged with truly minimal incomes of, say, $3000 per couple, and $1500 per unmarried individual, because "the resulting increase in payments will incur no withdrawals of income, since the nature of the need for funds by the elderly insures that the increased . . . payments will be spent on consumption needs rather than take the form of savings by the elderly."[7]

Whether we will move, in a significant degree, to provide nonpoverty incomes to our aged depends, therefore, not on the ability of the economy, but rather on the willingness of the nation to share the benefits of an expanding economy with the aged. Historically, the ratio of nonproductive to productive persons has been declining (until very recently), although the aged make up an increasing part of the nonproductive population. The resultant increasing productivity allows us room for increasing supports for the aged (which, of course, raises the basic problem of full-employment policies), the proportion of national income now devoted to the aged being nowhere near the proportion that the aged represent in the total population.

Much of the data and reasoning in the foregoing argument point to a possible development usually not confronted—namely, that we may be witnessing certain trends and policies that will create a poverty class that did not always live in conditions of poverty. This possible development goes against the popularly accepted notion that poverty is bred by poverty, which, indeed, is the springboard for much in the following papers—those dealing with youth, especially Negro youth. But the extension of life in retirement, emerging as a result of increased longevity and also as a result of the gradual lowering of the retirement age, coupled with severely lagging adjustments in levels of retirement income to rising costs (apart from rising living standards), should be expected to provide the conditions for the emergence of such a population group in coming decades—one that lives for 10 to 20 years in poverty *after* having lived for 60 to 65 years in relatively comfortable circumstances.[8]

NOTES

1. The papers that follow will not exhaust themselves in debate over the true definition of poverty; they will concentrate rather on trends and programs that affect the status of the aged Negroes and youth, including some discussion of selected factors involved in the prevention and mitigation of poverty for these groups.

2. *Report of Senate Subcommittee on Problems of the Aged and Aging* (Washington, D.C.: Government Printing Office, 1961), pp. 71–72.

3. *Income and Welfare in the United States* (New York: McGraw-Hill Book Co., 1962).

4. *Ibid.*, p. 205.

5. Angus Campbell, "Social and Psychological Determinants of Voting Behavior," in *Politics of Age*, edited by Wilma Donahue and Clark Tibbitts (Ann Arbor: University of Michigan Press, 1962), p. 93.

6. "Consumer Patterns of Older Spending Units," *Journal of Gerontology*, July 1959, p. 332.

7. Herbert E. Striner, "The Capacity of the Economy to Support Older People," in *Aging and the Economy*, edited by Harold L. Orbach and Clark Tibbitts (Ann Arbor: University of Michigan Press, 1963), p. 27.

8. Existing data are not organized systematically and adequately to verify this proposition insofar as certain segments of today's retired aged are concerned. However, I do know of fragmentary evidence to this effect: for example, for seventeen public-assistance cases in the caseload of one social worker acquaintance, six of them are elderly women who were daughters of an equal number of wealthy families in the past. All of them are over the age of seventy-five.

The Young
Who Are Poor

HAROLD L. SHEPPARD

. . . . education appeared to be the
mechanism for upward mobility as well
as for the transmission of level of economic
status from generation to generation.
Education affects a man's earnings and his
progress during his lifetime, as well as
the education of his children. This is not just
a matter of skills and training. Foresight
and planning, which are essential to getting
ahead and assuring the education of one's
children, are affected by formal education as
well as by the attitudes and achievement
motivation of the head.

   Morgan, Cohen, Brazer, and David, *Income and Welfare in the
United States*, p. 444.

For our purposes it is not essential to settle the issue of whether growing up in dilapidated, overcrowded homes and crime and disease-ridden neighborhoods causes a child to (1) accept these environmental features as part of the normal order of things or (2) to become demoralized or (3) to rebel against these features of his environment.

What is essential is the fact that most poverty-family youth are deprived of the broad range of experiences open to children from higher-income families, and that their limited imagery of the world makes it more difficult for them to succeed in one of the crucial springboards from poverty—the school. Many poor parents cannot provide these experiences and broadened images because of their own limitations, not to mention ignorance as to the benefit of these necessary experiences and the value system centering in the institution of education.

Placement at high school into *one* of three or four curriculums marks the final casting of the die for the student's entire future life. If a youth is placed on a vocational education "track"—say, sometime between the ages of twelve and fourteen—he will have near-zero probabilities of qualifying for college, if indeed he has had developed in him any interest in college attendance at all.

Few, if any, youths and their parents make the vital decisions in this sphere. The educational system does this for them. The poverty-family parent or parents remain blissfully unaware of, or indifferent about, educational matters, or are awed by the bureaucratic setting of the school atmosphere, and too frequently abide by the school's decision.[1]

There is a culture system in the high school by which students segregate themselves according to common interests and common social status. For the small minority of individual youths who happen to be different from the others and who have advanced interests, but at the same time are swamped by a high-school environment of several hundred students with attitudes of indifference, hostility, and low aspirations concerning education and occupation, the pressures toward conformity and "leveling" are often too great to withstand. Examples of the experiences of children of Negro professionals in such situations could be cited here, and they explain much of the tendency for such parents to send their children to private prep schools.

Before long, one can expect drop-out rates as high as 50 per cent in such poverty-background schools, and here the Rubicon is crossed. We all know of the high percentages of such persons with normal and above-average IQ's, frequently as many as 50 per cent. If we add to this another 15 per cent of drop-outs with IQ's between 85 and 90, on the definite possibility that these can be improved with special techniques, we have a wastage of 65 per cent who might otherwise be drawn out of the vicious circle of poverty.

During the present decade, estimates are that 7.5 million of the 26 million new young entrants into the labor market will be drop-outs from high school—29 per cent of all these young entrants. Apart from the lower income that must be expected by virtue of not having finished secondary school, these drop-outs (or push-outs, properly speaking) can also expect unemployment rates significantly above those of high-school graduates, and rates for the latter are high enough to begin with.[2] In addition, the percentage of full-time workers among drop-outs is generally lower than among high-school graduates.

Upper-class experience provides students with a need for personal achievement that is expressed in their constant search for success, teaching them from infancy to face each new situation aggressively and to overcome it to the best of their ability. When they take a test, whether the subject is arithmetic or general intelligence, they normally try to do their best on it, for their ego is on trial—they must make good, and they generally do.

> On the other hand [the lowest-class] adolescent has been subjected to a family and class culture in which failure, worry, and frustration are common. He has not been trained at home to do his best in school. His parents have not ingrained in him the idea that he must make good grades if he is to be a success in life. Moreover, the class system as it functions in the school does not help him to overcome the poor training he has received at home and in the neighborhood.[3]

Despite the limitations and qualifications that experts —even the ones who construct them—place on IQ tests, the school people who use them too frequently violate these warnings. Such school authorities generally make decisions about the lives of children as if the tests truly measured "innate" intelligence. They judge, categorize, and treat youth according to the scores on the tests—with the notion that they are acting with due regard to some built-in, unchanging and unchangeable intellectual capacity of children. Here is a major juncture where structural impediments are inserted into the process of matching labor supply with occupational demands, thus adding one more assurance of poverty's vicious circle.

It is not too widely known, especially among parents in poverty families, that even with superficial techniques, IQ's can be significantly raised.[4] As a result of a few hours of familiarization in items similar to those in IQ tests, one professor increased average IQ scores of students by eleven points. This increase is significant when we consider that the average difference between IQ's of children from professional and managerial families and those of children from unskilled-labor families is between fifteen and twenty-five points. Other experiences include the raising of freshmen students' average IQ's from 110 to 120 in less than one year, a difference which can affect a child's chances of being admitted into a college. In the spring of 1964, groups of Negro youths in Washington, rejected by the selective service system for having failed "mental tests," were tutored intensively, with the result that their average scores were raised substantially. In large part, this type of induced change amounts to a cultural diffusion of reading ability, vocabulary accretion, and (to the right people) the seemingly simple task of merely knowing how to take tests. But even in the case of children labeled as mentally retarded, special psychotherapeutic techniques and special education techniques have been applied to raise IQ's, over a three-year period, by about forty points.

Before we can make significant progress in this field, we must first demolish the strong intellectual and emotional adherence to the deeply entrenched doctrine about congenitally low intelligence, especially among individuals in poverty categories, and more pointedly among Negroes. And after that, we have the equally difficult task of discovering the most effective techniques for change, and then—perhaps most difficult of all—getting the institutions and personnel involved to accept and use these techniques.

Charles Silberman, an economist and editor of *Fortune* magazine, has recently made similar suggestions in his *Crisis in Black and White*.[5] If we are going to make a dent in the long-run problem of poverty, which essentially calls for preventive techniques, we must begin as early as possible in the life career of potential candidates for tomorrow's adult poor class, notably in the educational experiences of slum children. Third-grade students in Harlem are one year behind in academic performance; by the time they reach the sixth grade they fall behind by two years. And, reaching further back, children from poverty families enter school without many of the intellectual and personality traits—all of which can be acquired—that the educational establishment takes for granted.

I refer to many subtle facets which have escaped the notice of people who take certain attributes for granted, or who tend to interpret the "deviation" of poverty children as being due to ingrained racial or biological differences, or at best to unchangeable cultural differences. In this connection, the same thing is true of administrators of training programs, who frequently believe it is not their responsibility to deal with such groups, and who would be much happier if only those individuals *easy* to deal with were referred to their programs.

As Silberman points out, slum youngsters, to a greater extent than typical middle-class children, lack the sense of auditory discrimination—the ability to distinguish seemingly minor but crucial differences in sounds—an ability that is vital to successful reading achievement. It is possible that living in two rooms with six or more people forces the child to learn how *not* to listen. He thereby fails to acquire an ability to distinguish between relevant and irrelevant noises. In the classroom, which is usually filled with more children in slum schools than in other neighborhood schools, he often hears only one package of fuzzy sound, especially if outside traffic is also added to the auditory environment.

Perhaps more important, the poverty-family child does not have the fortune of having adults correct his pronunciation. Often it is a matter of having no adults whatsoever during most of his waking hours. And when we come to the southern rural migrant to northern urban areas, his problems are aggravated further by the "fact that the phonic system of the language he speaks is quite different from the system of the language which the teacher speaks and which the reading primers use." Coming from a nonverbal household, the child seldom hears several lengthy sentences spoken consecutively. On the other hand, the teacher is likely to talk on and on for several sentences. For the poverty-family child, this might as well be another language. And it *is* another language.

On a more subtle level, the absence of, or limitations in, a verbal environment can mean a limited perception and image of the world. Objects in the environment—even including the self as an object—come to have an existence in behavior and thinking to the extent that the individual in large part learns names for them.

Along with the language handicap, poverty children become poorly motivated, essentially because they rarely experience any reward or punishment in the family for success or failure in school. If there is absolutely no mechanism for prompting children to gain and sustain academic interest and achievement, the school system as it is structured cannot succeed too well. In contrast to such middle-class phenomena as preschool books and reading encouragement by a parent, the poverty child usually does not even have books and pencils in his home environment.

Because of these preschool deprivations and because of our growing knowledge of the importance of early intellectual stimulation and some techniques of "artificial insemination" in the field of learning and personality development,

Silberman urges "nothing less than a radical reorganization of American elementary education. . . . To reverse the effects of a starved environment, the schools must begin admitting children at the age of three or four, instead of at five or six. The nursery school holds the key to the future—but a very different kind of nursery school from the one most Americans are familiar with."[6] The battle can be won or lost between the ages of three to six, he claims. By the age of six, the probabilities are increased that poverty children will have become even more immune to the best educational systems. This argument points up the need, again, for a universal system of child day-care centers for poverty families. Plato's ideal society, it will be recalled, included the separation of the children from the parents. If progress entails a break with tradition, and this is what we are talking about, then such a system is not a fringe benefit; it is a *sine qua non*. Unfortunately, day-care centers are typically a matter for welfare departments and not for boards of education, and thus their chances of support are damaged. On the other hand, boards of education tend to consider them as welfare, and not education, items.

To demonstrate the value of such programs, Silberman points to the accomplishments of Dr. Martin Deutsch, of New York Medical College's Institute of Developmental Studies. Using ten New York City schools, and five day-care centers, "Deutsch's ultimate objective is to develop a standardized curriculum and a set of teaching techniques that could be adapted around the country. It is designed to teach poverty children 'the verbal and perceptual skills they need in order to learn to read, and also to bolster their sense of self'."[7]

> There is a great deal of emphasis on teaching labeling—getting across the notion, first, that every object has a name, and, second, the more sophisticated concept that objects may have a number of different labels, each referring to different attributes. . . . Auditory discrimination is taught through a tape recorder, in which background noise is used to mask a relevant sound; the level of the noise is gradually

stepped up, to enhance the child's discrimination. To help
develop a sense of self, the rooms contain a great many
mirrors; many children have never seen themselves in
one . . . 85 per cent of the youngsters have never seen a
picture of themselves. . . .[8]

Even the parents have to become involved in this type of en-
deavor, a collective effort at converting themselves into Pyg-
malions. The parents are given instructions in helping their
children, including talking at home with the children, especially about school, as one way of letting the child know
that his parents—usually the mother—want him or her to
succeed in school. "This has enormous impact on the children's verbal ability, for they begin talking about school
when they get home, instead of remaining mute; and it has
profound effect on increasing motivation."[9]

We are talking here about nothing less than a mass ac-
culturation program, just as took place through different
techniques and in a much less planned manner, in the years
of mass immigration of Europeans into America, from the
late nineteenth century to World War I; just as the Israeli
government is now doing with its nursery schools for non-
European Jews, many of them born into families with medi-
eval cultures. For example, the Israeli Ministry of Education
is convinced that 80 to 85 per cent of the Oriental youngsters can be brought up to the reading levels of European
Jewish children, thus increasing the size of the nation's
population that will be able to go through high school, graduate from a university, and enter into responsible jobs in
government and industry.

One simple sentence by Silberman suddenly throws us
back onto some other hard facts: "One reason the Israelis
have been so successful is that they have far greater administrative flexibility than we do in America; the director
of research operates out of the office of the Minister of Education, so his research results can be immediately translated into administrative policy."[10] And from the top down,
the vast majority of educational personnel work is based
on the assumption that differences in IQ scores are not con-

clusive proof of inherent, biologically determined differences in intelligence and in learning ability. This is hardly the situation in the United States, where such administrative flexibility—and authority—is woefully absent, and where the myth of inherited intelligence still tragically operates in our public policy and procedures.

Of course, such a new approach can open its advocates to charges of segregation, an accusation which makes the most sincere school administrator neurotic and perhaps subject to dismissal, with the right kind of hysterical minority-group pressure. Kenneth Clark (a psychologist and a Negro himself and who wrote the sociopsychological brief in the 1954 Supreme Court desegregation case)—as one of the leaders of the Harlem Youth Project—clearly has the goal of integration in mind, but he earnestly feels that a system of compensatory education is required as a means to that goal: at least 50 per cent of Harlem's junior high school students need a program of massive remedial education. The alternative at the present time is to conduct a wholesale program of school integration in an education system incapable of adjusting to the needs of 50 to 80 per cent of its Negro *and* white poverty-family students. As Silberman writes, ". . . genuine integration will not be possible until the schools in Negro neighborhoods, and the schools in the white slum areas as well, are brought up to the level of the very best in the city—until the schools do their job so well that children's educational performance will no longer reflect their income, or their social status, or their ethnic group, or their color."[11]

Existing programs of training both the out-of-school youth and unemployed adults in the poverty population, outside of the general public education system for grammar and high school, include the Welfare Administration's training efforts to "aid" so-called able-bodied relief recipients as well as training programs financed through the Manpower Development and Training Act (MDTA) and the Area Redevelopment Administration (ARA) for the more "fortunate" unemployed. For the most part, the latter consist essentially of short-term courses, running from four to six months, but which can run as long as a year.

In addition to work-relief (MDTA and ARA, to which we will return below), there is, of course, the old, established vocational-education program which is ostensibly a preventive program and which is properly to be considered as part of the general public education system. Its manifest purpose is to prepare high school age youth for adult occupations so that they will not be confronted with unemployment problems in the future. Its actual function is another matter.

Vocational education, in the cities at any rate, has become the "back ward" of the schools, the dumping ground for children whom the school system is ill-equipped to help. In the 1950's, it was taken for granted that vocational-school graduates would have to start on unskilled jobs in the big cities. This is not the manifest intent of such programs. In New York City, the average IQ in vocational schools was less than 85. Employers, not only in that city but elsewhere too, were ignoring such graduates and hiring those from the general high schools, since such students are easier to train on the job than those who possess only a trained incapacity to learn.

In reaction to this problem, a new dilemma was created: in many cities, children with poor educational backgrounds, as measured crudely but pragmatically by IQ scores, were being screened out even from vocational schools. Some of the vocational schools began to introduce academic subjects, such as mathematics and science for the best students, perhaps with the vague hope that such children might want to enter, or could afford to enter, engineering schools.

The dilemma, of course, is that the schools were still stuck with youths rejected even for vocational-education high schools! The inability of the school systems to cope adequately with this problem underlies in turn much of the drop-out problem. These are the youths who need long-term MDTA-type training, and of an intensive compensatory nature to boot.

But even for those in vocational schools, only a small proportion are enrolled in courses leading to employment in occupations where job opportunities are expanding. Home economics and agriculture courses are nice, but it should be kept in mind that only 10 per cent of rural youths can expect to find employment in farm occupations. Yet two-thirds of all enrollees in federally supported vocational-education programs live in rural areas, and slightly less than one-third of those aged twenty to twenty-four live in rural areas. These are the future migrants to urban areas, who come to the city ill-equipped to escape from situations associated with the perpetuation of poverty.

It is much too premature to discuss the impact of the 1963 Vocational Education Act, but it does make possible—it does not guarantee—a radical departure from our 50 year old system of vocational education. It could provide meaningful preparation for vast numbers of youth—those in high school and those now unemployed or underemployed—for the realities of the changing labor market. Within a few years, $225 million per year will be authorized, in contrast to $55 million per year for traditional vocational education. The new legislation also specifically earmarks funds for the construction of facilities, vocational education research—a field which has suffered for decades—and for specific programs aimed at poverty family youths. There are even provisions for the construction and perhaps maintenance of five residential schools in large urban areas—possibly to become the first federal public schools in the Nation, outside of Howard University, the military academies, and military base schools.

Work Relief

The Welfare Administration's program is about two years old and it has had little effect on reducing the numbers of people on relief rolls. For one thing, few states have chosen to participate in the program. This experience is but one more piece of evidence against joint federal-state pro-

grams, in which the federal government makes available
funds and technical assistance, but leaves optional the
choice of each of the fifty states to take advantage of the
funds and assistance. Sometimes this failure is due to internal state agency differences as to which one should administer the federally financed program, sometimes to the
political party differences between the governor and the
administration in Washington, and sometimes—perhaps
most frequently—to the unenlightened nature of state legislatures.

Much of the spirit of the work-relief program is a punitive attitude based on the notion that people should not be
allowed to live if they don't work for a living. It is not carried out sufficiently in the spirit that, if so-called "able-
bodied" men and women are offered an opportunity to
experience improved education and job training by performing in socially necessary public works, they may then be on
the road to independence and ultimate employment in regular occupations compensated through normal payroll
sources at decent wage levels.

MDTA Programs and ARA Programs

Through December of 1963, nearly 3000 projects were
approved for training nearly 120,000 people. This was for
a 17-month period. Under ARA training programs, which
are administered by the same federal, state, and local agencies running MDTA, for a 25-month period ending December 1963, 574 projects were approved for training about
27,000 unemployed people.

Together, the two programs provided training opportunities for only 147,000 unemployed workers. This is a
relatively small figure, when compared to the annual average unemployed population size of about 4 million. In percentages, about 3½ per cent of the unemployed were offered
opportunities for training under MDTA and ARA. But it
should be added that about 70 per cent of the trainees do
find employment.

In assessing the importance of current training programs for one of the most critical population segments, our youth, it should be kept in mind that the biggest program with the most potential, MDTA, was not originally created for the purpose of attacking the youth unemployment problem. It was designed rather for those unemployed heads of families with at least three years experience in the labor market. Only 5 per cent of the appropriations for training allowances were allowed to be spent for youths aged nineteen to twenty-two, and even in those cases, such individuals were restricted to a maximum of $20 per week.

The 1963 amendments to MDTA which liberalized these age restrictions and lowered the age to seventeen may make a difference. Considering the fact that even under the original conditions, more projects were being requested than could be financed, it is doubtful whether the increased demand that apparently will be made possible by the new liberalized conditions can be met under existing authorized ceilings and by actual appropriations. For example, toward the end of fiscal 1964, with still three more months to go, a few million dollars worth of projects were not funded because the $100 million appropriated for fiscal 1964 was exhausted before the end of the fiscal year.

It might be argued that the number of projects and trainees can be expected to decline or level off in the near future, on the assumption that a pent-up demand for qualified workers will have been met, that is, that there are only so many job openings available to begin with, and that these will be filled as soon as the trainees complete their courses. In answer to this position, however, it should first be stated that such a view is too mechanistic and ignores the dynamic nature of the economy and the job market, including the phenomenon of attrition, and hence the need for replacements. Second, from what is now known about the actual human and administrative processes of implementing and stimulating training programs, I am convinced that we have only begun to tap the potentials of the "market" for such programs. It is doubtful, for example, that only 209 projects under MDTA between August 1962 and December 1963, and only one project under ARA between November 1961 and December 1963, all in California, constitute the full mileage that can be truly gained out of that state.

The essential point here is that a fully effective utilization of training programs will not be realized until local communities are organized and stimulated to apply for training programs. This in part calls for the difficult feat of coordinating on a practical basis public employment services, employers, vocational-education systems, labor unions, and civic officials. In general, if any one of these links is unwilling, disinterested, or inept, applications for training projects will not be forthcoming. And quite frequently, these community and state elements will not be brought together for such a purpose unless an aggressive, enthusiastic missionary from a federal agency works with the local community, and often over a sustained period of time. Given the limited number of such employees, only so many groups and commmunities can be reached in any given period of time.

Third, we should expect an increase in enrollments as a result of the 1963 amendments to MDTA, which include permitting trainees to work part time 20 hours per week without having their subsistence allowances reduced; raising the subsistence allowance $10 above the average unemployment-compensation amount in a given state; making it possible for more younger unemployed to participate than previously; extending the period during which the federal government finances 100 per cent of the costs (until mid-1965); liberalizing qualifications for admission to training; and formally allowing basic education as part of the program, and extending the maximum length of training for workers starting in such courses to 72 weeks, which would allow for "graduation" into a regular occupational-training course during this 17-month period.

More accurately, these new provisions set the *conditions*

for increased enrollments (and fewer drop-outs) in the MDTA training programs. Their mere authorization does not create increases. For example, as of this writing, more than four months have passed since the passage of the 1963 amendments described above, and nothing has been done to implement them. In a community in which I have been directly involved recently, South Bend, Indiana, the ex-Studebaker workers knew about the 20-hours outside-work provision, but when they asked the state employment service personnel about it, the latter pleaded ignorance, or, at best, lack of authority to permit the trainees to take advantage of the provision. Here is a case where the workers learned through their private organization, the auto workers' union, about national legislation before the local bureaucrats did. Here is a case in which no new appropriations were needed, but in which bureaucratic paralysis, from the Washington level on down, prevented much needed action.

In addition, when it comes to attacking the poverty group's training needs, the full exploitation of training-program potentials calls for an exhaustive, complicated process of stimulation and coordination, not just among the organizations cited above, but also among the workers themselves, who must be informed, encouraged, counseled, and motivated through techniques not yet adequately appreciated. The mass-media approach has proven highly limited in achieving this end.

NOTES

1. Patricia C. Sexton, *Education and Income* (New York: The Viking Press, 1961), p. 192.
2. U.S. Department of Labor, Bureau of Labor Statistics, *Special Labor Report* No. 21.
3. August C. Hollingshead, *Elmtown's Youth* (New York: John Wiley & Sons, Inc., 1949), p. 176.
4. See, for example, Patricia C. Sexton, *Education and Income* (New York: The Viking Press, 1961), pp. 48 ff., or any number of selected texts in social psychology, beginning with Otto Klineberg's, to name one.

5. New York: Random House, Inc., 1964.
6. "Give Slum Children a Chance: A Radical Proposal," *Harper's Magazine*, May 1964.
7. *Ibid.*
8. *Ibid.*
9. *Ibid.*
10. *Ibid.*
11. *Ibid.*

Poverty
and the Negro

HAROLD L. SHEPPARD

In the longer run, the remedies for poverty
should be concentrated upon those children
presently being reared in poverty. One of the
interesting things about poverty is that
relatively few people who are not born in it
wind up in it. Once out, people tend to stay out.
But, at the same time, the mere existence
of opportunities for betterment does not suffice
to bring all members of a group out of the
condition of poverty. There is a self-reinforcing
characteristic to poverty which renders
many steps against it ineffectual. The poverty
complex contributes to its own causes of
ignorance and disease and stunted aspiration.
      Robert Lampman, "One Fifth of a Nation . . . ," *Challenge,*
April 1964.

There is a self-reinforcing char-
acteristic to poverty which renders many steps against
it ineffectual." So says Professor Robert Lampman. Undoubtedly he is right. One of these characteristics derives
from the negative correlation between the number of chil-

dren in a family and median family income. The many
social conditions and consequences surrounding this statistical phenomenon are the subject of an article by Mollie
Orshansky, in the July 1963 issue of the *Social Security
Bulletin,* entitled "Children of the Poor." Families with one
or two children under eighteen have a median income of
about $6000, for 1961, and for families with six or more
children the median income is about $4750. A difference of
$1250 median income between families may not seem vital
until one seeks to construct the difference between standards of living, and of life chances, for a child having five or
more brothers and sisters in a family with less than $5000
income, and those for a child with one or no sibling in a
family with $6000 income. In the former group, there are
about 7 million such children. If we include families with
four or more children (families whose median income is
about $5300), then we come up with a figure of 17 million
children. In other words, perhaps one-half of these children,
or about 8.5 million, live in families with incomes of less
than $5300. The data are not organized to be more precise
than this. They do show however, that in families with four
or more children, and with less than $5000 income for 1961,
there were more than 8.3 million children under eighteen.

Despite all the emotions and strong theological values
involved, the problem of poverty and the attack on it should
include, in my opinion, some sober consideration of the role
of birth control. It could be argued, in this connection, that
a sharp increase in the use of birth-control techniques is
not a phenomenon in and of itself, but rather a single item
in the total syndrome of a break in the value and culture
patterns associated with generation-to-generation poverty.
But in any deliberate program of inducing change from
such patterns, concrete steps—such as education about
birth control—can often carry with them other dynamics
and by-products leading to the more general break in traditional patterns.

Equally important as a relevant factor in the perpetuation of poverty is that low-income status is disproportionately concentrated among those families with no father in the home. These children in nonwhite families are overrepresented in the poor population—compounded by the lack of year-round employment by the head of the family. Many of the problems of Negro advance out of the poverty class are an outcome of a vital sociohistorical condition, namely, the nature of many Negro underclass families and, especially, the dominance of the mother or other adult female in such families. This unique role has contributed to the problem of child-rearing and personality development, notably with regard to the Negro male. This is not the place to elaborate on the implications of relationships between the Negro male child and his dominant mother, but one interesting aspect has been noted by Pauli Murray of Yale University Law School, in a paper before the National Council of Negro Women in November 1963:

> The civil rights revolt, like many social upheavals, has released powerful pent-up emotions, cross currents, rivalries and hostilities. In emerging from an essentially middle class movement and taking on a mass character, it has become a vehicle to power and prestige . . . there is much jockeying for position as ambitious men push and elbow their way to leadership roles. Part of this upsurge reflects the Negro male's normal desire to achieve a sense of personal worth and recognition of his manhood by a society which has so long denied it. One aspect is the wresting of the initiative of the civil rights movement from white liberals. Another is the *backlash of a new male aggressiveness against Negro women*.[1]

This male aggressiveness against Negro women has some of its roots, according to some researchers, in the childhood role of Negro males in their families. The crucial point is that nonwhite children are much less likely to have a "normal" parental home. For one thing, the role of the mother, even in husband-wife families, is not strictly identical to that in white husband-white families. Second, one-third of all nonwhite youth live in a family with only one parent, more often than not, the mother—as contrasted with only one-tenth of all white children.

A Negro woman, if she is a mother in a family without a father, furthermore, is more likely than a white woman in a similar role to have been separated or deserted rather than divorced or widowed.

> The divorced or widowed mother is more likely to have formal financial support arrangements for herself and the children than the mother in a family that breaks up for other reasons. In the 1960 Census, three fifths of the white mothers with children under age 18 and no father in the home were divorced or widowed; only 2 per cent said they had never been married. By contrast, one third of the non-white mothers without a husband claimed that they were divorced or widowed, and 1 in 8 said they were never married to the father of their children.[2]

The data concerning Negro women suggest that the Negro woman "has a harder time finding a mate, remains single more often, bears more children, is in the labor market longer, has less education, earns less, is widowed earlier, and carried a heavier economic burden as a family head than her white sister."[3] In addition, she also carries a greater child-rearing burden in the sociopsychological sense, which has a bearing on the learning and achievement motivations of her children.

The typical occupations in which such women work are not covered by minimum wage laws or by unemployment insurance—domestic service in private households, small retail stores, laundries, and other service establishments. Much of such employment is only intermittent, and thus, even if they are in "covered" employment, this means that there is less chance of eligibility for average or above-average Social Security benefits—incidentally another source of the impoverished aged in the future, discussed in the chapter on the aged poor.

Mothers who seek employment under these conditions do

not have available adequate child day-care facilities. Re-training programs can be of limited use only, when such facilities are not provided while the mother is being trained. And the children themselves, along with those from families headed by male unskilled laborers, contribute dispropor-tionately to those first-year high-school cases with low apti-tudes and high drop-out rates. For the nonwhite side of the poverty problem, these facts are of pressing concern when we consider that nearly two-fifths of all nonwhite males are under the age of fifteen (as contrasted with less than one-third in the case of white males).

About 30 per cent of all youths entering the labor force in the next several years will not have a high school diploma.[4] The vast majority of these young people are born and reared in low-income families with few of the characteristics con-ducive to any sharp break with the culture of poverty. About 10 per cent will not even have a grade-school training. And no doubt they will continue the vicious circle—perhaps in a geometric fashion—by having large numbers of children who will inherit—and themselves bequeath—the legacy of poverty.

*   *   *

"All men want to work" is an almost universal assump-tion in the minds of those who direct and manage our indus-trial and other work situations, and the major preoccupation of the foreman or supervisor is to maintain personnel mo-rale and motivation at a level appropriate to organizational efficiency. The world of work, of commercialism and indus-trialism, functions through the maintenance and existence of sufficient numbers of people motivated by values of work and of striving as the normal, the "right thing to do." But this attitude toward work is not an eternal constant, nor is it universal among all human beings. It has historical origins and varies from one region to another. Indeed, even within one region such as the United States, there are variations among population strata. The world of work for most Ameri-cans as children begins in the form of make-believe role-playing games involving a number of occupations with which they are at least superficially familiar. They are constantly being asked by adults, "What are you going to be when you grow up?" And after a while they begin to look for a range of suitable answers to such questions. By the time such children reach high school, they have usually narrowed down the range and are expected to have more sensible answers, in the direction of meaningful, adult roles. Work is expected of them. Work is good. And work is available.

When the Negro child assimilates these values—in varying degrees—and at the same time recognizes the hypocrisy and obstacles involved in his being able to achieve the goals, this "dissonant situation creates tension within the individual that causes him to seek some solution to the conflict that will reduce the motivating tension or anxiety."[5]

Lower socioeconomic children "receive a work orientation" but they are also confronted daily with chronic unemployment and underemployment in the family and in the social group in which they live. Among Negro youth especially, the phenomenon is even more salient since the opportunity structure for Negroes is more restricted than for others—even during times of general full employment.

One basic pattern of response by lower-class Negro males to this "dissonance between the stated societal work values and his perception of a closed opportunity structure and chronic unemployment" involves a general playing down of work as a way of achieving income and a searching for other means. Another response involves even a general devaluation of the objects that income can purchase and thus of income itself. As Schwartz and Henderson say, ". . . a new community, in both the ecological and social-psychological sense, comes into existence in which new values are communicated and shared, and to which adolescent males are resocialized."

The Negro mother, who is frequently the dominant figure in the family, contributes to the stress on work as part of her children's aspirations. The matriarchal tradition plays a significant role in the Negro's internalization of the achievement motive and work ethic.

> The white culture demands that the lower class Negro conform to middle-class white values while the structure of opportunities for participation remains largely closed to him. Certainly, many of the conditions that must inevitably bring the despair to the Negro youth that Baldwin communicates so brilliantly are beginning to decay—by executive order. The process is slow; the Negro middle-class and leadership is impatient. One hundred years is too long to wait to be given what is rightfully the Negroes' in the first place. Whether the lower class is equally impatient is unknown.
>
> The emergence of an impatient stratum, however, is evidence of great change in the direction of accelerated assimilation of the general cultural values, including the sanctioned means of realizing those values, that is, through work and occupations that are characteristic of the dominant population. Added to this is the development of these patterns among *male* Negroes who are now demanding access to the channels for realizing these means and goals.[6]

But the core of the Negro poverty problem lies in the prospect that even if today "the lower class Negro were to be completely free and integrated into the dominant culture, having free access to opportunities of all forms, it might be no better for him. The adaptations over generations have in many cases become 'functionally autonomous.' They are, for many, now a preferred way of life; an appropriate life style that includes 'bunking in,' welfare chiseling, borrowing from working women, or women on relief, etc."[7]

The following are some of the Schwartz and Henderson findings and interpretations about Negro males 13–19 years of age in Detroit (1962):

1. Fifty per cent perceived their fathers as being the boss in their families. Without any previous similar inquiries, we cannot say for sure that this is higher than in the past, but it certainly is lower than among whites.

2. The boys expressed greater respect for dominant fathers than for dominant mothers.

3. The father-dominated home is more stable, even when the father is not working and has been unemployed for long periods.

4. There is greater alienation among boys in mother-dominant homes, including feelings of powerlessness and isolation.

5. Luck—"hit a number" or "find some money"—was perceived by most of the boys as their only means of escaping from poverty. And playing the numbers is not the same to them as gambling.

[Following an interview, a fifteen-year-old boy asked the interviewer: "How much do you make a week?" Upon hearing the answer, the boy frowned and replied, "My brother ain't got no college education—he ain't even got a high school education, but he makes more than you do." His brother "picked up" numbers.]

6. Little willingness to accept hard work and striving as desirable activity were found to exist. "The children of the unemployed don't perceive the pay-off. The implications for a 'culture of unemployment' [or of poverty] are clear."[8]

Many of the findings and conclusions of Schwartz and Henderson are reminiscent of the "Portrait of the Underdog," by Genevieve Knupfer, written nearly twenty years ago.[9] One finds here the portrait of the person with economic and educational limitations that produce a "lack of interest in and a lack of self-confidence in dealing with certain important areas of our culture," along with a greater acceptance of a belief in the inability of the individual to change his circumstances, and in the inadvisability of planning for the future. The low level of aspiration of the poverty-class youth—the severe restrictions that many of them put on what they allow themselves to wish for—may serve the function of making their lives more tolerable ("hope for nothing and never be disappointed"); but, as Knupfer states, this "can be just as unrealistic as excessive ambition."[10] To repeat, such an adaptation can acquire functional autonomy. This observation is significantly relevant to the question of success or failure of recent programs and proposals designed to attack the poverty problem.

While one pattern of response may be the rejection of work as a desirable activity, another response—involving acceptance of work—consists of the type of behavior described more than thirty years ago in a study of underprivileged German youth, wherein such "frightened" youth tended to choose blind-alley jobs because of anxieties about unemployment—"to crowd into overfilled, unproductive lines of work where they could produce nothing."[11] "Laziness," "lack of motivation," and so on are frequently the labels used by the undiscerning to explain many instances in which underprivileged individuals fail to "take advantage" of opportunities that hold promise of changing their life chances.

A special project in Norfolk, Virginia, was begun for the purpose of dealing with the training of "hard-core" unemployed Negroes, many of them in their twenties. It goes without saying that such individuals are finding it harder and harder to get the crucial first job, which in and of itself is an important psychological event in the lives of new labor-market entrants or severely long-term unemployed adults. The vicious circle of poverty can be entered at this point. Often it is only an intellectual exercise to search for *the* fundamental cause of poverty, a luxury that only idle researchers and academicians can afford. The greater challenge is to discover those points in the vicious circle which can be affected in order to deflect the otherwise circular movement. To repeat, the finding of the first job can be one of these points, and the number of points may be infinite.

The problem is serious, even in times of relatively low adult unemployment. During 1955–1957, when adult unemployment (for those twenty-five and older) was below 4 per cent, unemployment in the fourteen-to-twenty-four-age group was over 10 per cent. In recent years, it has been as high as 13 to 15 per cent. Data on duration of unemployment suggest that length of unemployment among youth is lower than for older workers, but the data do not cover those youth who give up and cease the search for work altogether. We do know, however, that the percentage of young males (sixteen to twenty-four) not working or seeking work, even among high school graduates not in college, was only about 3 per cent, in contrast to nearly 14 per cent among male drop-outs in 1960. In 1961, as of October, the rate jumped to nearly 14 per cent, even among high school graduates of June of that year, while the rate for drop-outs was slightly more than 16 per cent.[12]

Perhaps more relevant are some incomplete data (1952–1957) from the Department of Labor that indicate that (1) two-thirds of all youths who never look for jobs were drop-outs; (2) in contrast, less than two-fifths of those who do look for jobs were drop-outs; (3) long-term unemployment for drop-outs was twice as great as it was for graduates; (4) for nonwhite drop-outs in particular, first-job experience in unskilled manual labor jobs and in farm labor jobs—the typical markets for drop-outs—is more of a trap than a first step on a ladder to occupational and income progress.[13]

Although the information about Norfolk's male Negroes' unemployment experience is not available, we can be sure that corresponding rates are much higher than these. The effort expended merely to inform the Norfolk Negro community was a strenuous undertaking. I will not dwell here on the preliminary work involved in obtaining approval and coordination for the project. A complicated "selling" job had to be done, including special techniques of communication with the nonliterate Negroes, who at first did not accept the possibility that publicly announced training programs were meant for them as well as for other unemployed workers in the community. They had to be convinced that the intentions of the directors of the project were sincere and genuine. While we can understand how generations of exploitation and hypocrisy by the dominant group can breed an almost instinctual suspicion, we should also appreciate the possibility that such suspicions and feelings of defeatism can acquire a "functional autonomy" that operates to prevent decisions and behavior capable of taking advantage of new situations leading to a break in the poverty cycle.

The potential candidates for the special training program had to be convinced that if they volunteered they would not be insulted and humiliated during the course of the project, particularly when situations revealing their inadequacies were bound to develop. Furthermore, they had to be led to choose a long period of self-sacrifice—twelve months—since the subsistence allowances were much too low for many of these men, with families averaging four children each. Few, if any, of these individuals would ever have been chosen under the regular type of MDTA training programs, which require passing scores on the General Aptitude Test Battery.

If we think that some principle of gravitation and magnetic attraction takes effect as a result of an increase in aggregate demand and that this mystical process somehow or other miraculously sops up the unemployed underclass of Negroes in our urban industrial centers, we are in for some bitter disappointments. Aggregate demand in this context provides the bricks for the cathedral of full employment, but the mortar comes from another source which includes the human factors of social organization, communication, and motivation, as well as cultural transformations, to name but a few of the specific processes involved. The hardcore unemployable Negroes are characterized by more than the simple attribute of lack of skills, or obsolete skills. Subsidiary research in Norfolk on those men who could have applied for training but did not points up what I mean.

These men are not easy to locate. For example, many of them can be reached only by finding the address of their mail-drops which they may visit occasionally to see if any letters have been sent to them. In their experience, if word reaches them that someone has been asking for them—a stranger, white or Negro—it can only mean a bill collector or a law enforcement officer. "They drift and, with luck, float through life and the complications of women and peer-groups, alienated from the larger society, which is based on money values to which they cannot by any 'legitimate' route aspire." Nor do they even have the skills necessary for persistent success in illegitimate pursuits.

The overt purpose of the basic project was to (1) convey job-skills in a number of occupations, the curricula for which were designed with the assistance of employers, and taught by carefully qualified college instructors with practical work histories of their own; (2) teach literacy—not only in the ordinary sense of simple reading and writing, but also talking and listening skills, especially in the vocabulary of their specific occupations for which they were being taught —as well as the numbers systems associated with each of those crafts; (3) to prepare them for the future by conveying knowledge about the world of work—a knowledge which most of us, the fortunate ones, take for granted, much as we take language and vocabulary for granted without realizing their indispensable role in personality and intellectual development. This educational experience included occupational information, techniques of getting and keeping a job, and budgeting for the family. The project also included individual casework, such as diagnoses of potential drop-outs from the course, and intervening with social and health agencies, landlords, even the police and courts, all for the purpose of helping the trainee stay in the project, get a job, keep it, and advance in it.

As an indication of the immense and comprehensive nature of the challenge to break the vicious circle of poverty, and of what is in store for the nation if and when we do launch a war on poverty, it should also be pointed out that recognition was made of the need to restructure the social basis of these trainees' lives. This included the creation of a student council, a student newspaper, a credit union, and spontaneous "outings and excursions." Because of the importance of the trainee's home and family life in making for success or failure of the total project, his wife was brought into the project as a member of a separate group with its own side projects, such as getting their children into summer camps.

Here is a statement from unpublished notes about this project:

> When the project began, the idea of MDTA training in the 3 R's for the unskilled and uneducated was novel. Now it is less so, since the notion begins to be commonplace that a man who cannot read or do simple number-calculations has little chance today of learning a job that he can get and hold. It is now conceded that literacy training must and can precede or pace vocational training. . . . The stress on orientation to the world of work—the shape and interactions in the job-market, the psychology of the foreman and the manager, how loan sharks and credit unions operate, what a contract is in all the manifold senses of that term—also was once unique and also now begins to be accepted, at least in principle, in the sense of pre-training indoctrination sessions, client-centered griping and groping meetings in the search for identity as a worker, and for support in the course of a personal revolution in expectations, attitudes and behavior.

What about the real test of such an intensive attack on the vicious circle, that is, the pay-off in terms of "postgraduation" success or failure in finding and keeping jobs? For one thing, it was discovered that employer-by-employer solicitation discovered jobs that "were there all along—but the Negro community didn't know it." Mechanics were needed in a bus company, but Negroes had never applied before. Even department stores were looking for sales clerks and were more than willing to hire Negroes. The local telephone company hired its first Negro lineman from the electronics class. Two men obtained jobs on the assembly line in a motor manufacturing plant at $3.50 an hour. Maintenance men found jobs in the same plant at about $2.50 an hour—one of them a Baptist preacher for a congregation so poor it could not support him. A shipyard with about 2000 employees selected several of the trainees explicitly because the employer was confident about the skills they acquired in the courses, including sheet-metal work and machine mechanics.

If dignity is an objective phenomenon and not something concocted by social workers and moralists, this total re-formation (I hesitate to use the term "training," although the word in French for training is *formation*), should provide some test. Quoting again from the unpublished notes:

> When they came in, they were supposed to be "hard-core"— and they didn't care. They were untouched by all the publicity—simply didn't believe it. We told them it was an experiment attracting national attention—they didn't believe it. The Secretary of Labor came and made a speech to them; they didn't believe it. New York reporters came to watch them, visit them in their homes; they didn't believe it. So they weren't bothered. Then, after nine or ten months, suddenly they changed. Pictures were taken of them and printed in the local papers with captions saying they were "hard-core" and they were indignant, and said they wouldn't let themselves be photographed if they knew they were going to be identified that way.

When, later in the year, they were asked not to enter the main building of the college during a crowded regular college registration period, they interpreted this as meaning the course administrators thought they weren't good enough to mingle with university students, whereupon they held a protest meeting, an act which could not have taken place in the first weeks of the project, "when they just didn't care." Thanks to the training program, they also knew how to organize and conduct such a meeting, too. They had the confidence to talk, instead of brooding or quitting—a reaction that takes place every day in the lives of the Negro underclass. ". . . it is the lack of such experience and confidence that in part keeps men of this socioeconomic class down and dependent . . ."

There were failures too, partly related to the fact that government installations in the area were being eliminated, to some extent. Other private jobs were lost, due to production cuts. Underlying all of the attempts to break the circle by finding worthwhile employment for these once "culturally deprived" Negro unemployables is the persistence of the rigid reliance in the world of employers on credentials and documents as the magic indicator of an applicant's worth, including the police blotter. As the Norfolk project sociologist, John Blue, has pointed out to me.

> The hard-core man comes out of a pool-hall culture, where there is a high incidence of arrest. Their marital and family problems, their troubles with automobiles, are much more likely to result in police action than in the case of middle-class families. And the genuine hard-core man is likely to have a major police record.

Those agencies and individuals who have jumped into the training program with all feet and hands and heart have discovered the network of institutional arrangements and the obstacles and weaknesses in our society that function to bolster the self-generating forces which in turn perpetuate behavior and attitudes conducive to poverty. The phenomena they observe are dramatic illustrations of Robert Merton's discussion of the self-fulfilling prophecy.

There is the infamous ruling that forbids relief payments to families with an able-bodied unemployed male. This encourages both genuine and spurious desertions. For families without an employable male, the budget in Virginia, for example, is calculated on that state's own formula for minimum-subsistence needs—and then 80 per cent of that sum is paid. For a family with four persons, for example, about $140 per month is presumably provided.

In the Norfolk project, the final hundred men who began training had an average of nearly four children each.

Each trainee was entitled to $27 per week in training or subsistence allowances, and each week he had to sign a formidable document swearing that he did not earn any money from any other source. This meant that debts piled up, especially rent payments. Surplus food was denied them, and the entire project was put in jeopardy until an anonymous benefactor gave $29,000 for supplementary subsistence payments. Without this, the prospects for drop-outs from the training project were dangerously high. It is comfortably easy for sociologists and psychologists to write about the concept of "deferred gratification" and its relative absence among working-class individuals, in contrast to the restrained, virtuous middle-class people who acquire through a long childhood the psychic ability to refrain from indulging themselves today in order to be successful tomorrow. But stretching out $27 a week for six or more family dependents, and using restricted credit sources, including those of friends, can only be done for a limited period of time— especially as temporary summer jobs open up, tempting the money-starved trainee to "live for today and forget about tomorrow." It is questionable whether the act of dropping out of a training program for a temporary job paying more than twice the training allowance can be considered irrational. Anxieties alone can serve as a deterrent to effective learning.

That any "action" program in the War on Poverty can merely consist of a single-goal preoccupation, such as teaching a man how to read a tool gauge, is disproven by this project as well as others like it. Such an experience also raises the question as to whether the country will have the organizational and cultural "know-how," and personnel to meet a comprehensive blueprint for an effective attack on poverty. Money is not the problem. There is no question about the fact that the current program proposals, and many of those already in existence, aim at changing individuals, and not merely to promote improved social conditions (such as better housing, surplus food, more and better school plants, and the like), or alternatively to provide "opportunities" by accelerating economic growth through fiscal and monetary measures. Any program that aims at the treatment of individuals on a mass scale is faced with an infinitely more formidable set of challenges than a program based on setting loose those market mechanisms that require, by contrast, few, if any, conscious acts of human volition, persistence, and creative acts. Years, not months, of sustained programs of this nature will be required to move large numbers of impoverished Negroes and youths—of all races—into those behavior patterns and socioeconomic situations that will increase their life chances for evading the poverty circle. The alternative in our type of society is not pleasant. As Max Lerner has written in his *America as a Civilization:*

> In more static societies the underlying population has learned to accept its lot as a kind of fatality; in societies with a permanent proletariat, there is a proletarian consciousness which may offer some nourishment, so that poverty has a kind of psychic balance sheet. But in a rich consumers' civilization, with abundance so pervasively present, those who are caught in scarcity feel themselves not only the despised and rejected but come to despite themselves. They are the outsiders to whom the culture gives only denials, who lose their sense of confidence, and who in many cases do not even have the consolations of a traditional, deeply felt religion.[14]

The Norfolk project experience also points up the necessity of coping with many Negro impoverished "changes," not merely as individuals in some isolated, clinical sense, but as individuals who at the same time have other roles in groups (such as their families) that must be reckoned with, too, in seeking to change the individuals. The project directors also had to organize the wives into a group, as stated earlier. They had to reckon with the fact that in many cases, the wife was better educated than the husband, and often was better able to obtain a higher status job than her husband.

The wives frequently felt shut out by the new experience of their husbands. They were even jealous of their husbands and suspicious, since the men attended classes on a college campus sprinkled with attractive young female college students—students who dressed better and who, unlike themselves, patronized beauty parlors. Here was another source of potential collapse to the entire project: in one way or another, these wives were capable of getting their husbands to quit.

The project staff thereupon moved quickly to bring the wives onto the campus and to convince them that they played an important and vital role in determining the future of their husbands' lives, and thus the happiness of their families. Once on the campus, they discovered that many of the college coeds were not so rich and beautiful as they feared. The total involvement of the wives in the project led to opportunities to introduce them to the notion of birth control. It further led to activities enhancing the welfare of the children—as well as a special project of their own in which the wives charged themselves 5 to 10 cents a meeting to create a fund of $35 to pay for summer camp for an underprivileged child. Under ordinary circumstances, such an act on the part of disadvantaged relief-level families might have been considered a frivolous misuse of public funds, at least by rigid public-welfare standards, rules, and regulations.

In this connection, one might ask the question, why is it that the routine, established agencies had failed to identify such families and individuals in the first place—inadequate drunkards and narcotics addicts, families with "retarded" children included, and not just so-called ordinary hard-core family problems—and then to persuade them that help was available and possible? We certainly know that once the total social-service resources of a community are concentrated on a concrete goal, the results can be dramatically effective. The goal in this case was the deceptively simple one of keeping the husbands and fathers of a hundred families engaged and committed to twelve months of occupational training.

Underlying the basic problem of producing success in programs of all sorts concerned with changing individuals, whether you call them training programs, vocational education, nursery classes, or even Americanization classes, is the uneven nature of programs run by state and local officials who actually run federal-financed programs on the day-to-day, grass-roots level, and thus affect actual policy. They "are too preoccupied with past practices [and local internal problems] to readily respond to new national needs"[15] not to mention even local needs.

Public-assistance bureaucrats in local and state welfare departments often view the work-relief program as a throwback to punitive policies, and not as a possibility of helping welfare recipients to become more self-sufficient; hence, they do little to introduce or apply techniques to make the program succeed. Or they view it as an inconvenient challenge that disrupts the administrative routines of welfare investigation, and assistance handouts. In many vocational-education programs, it is difficult for the local and state administrators to shift from the comfortable days of providing courses in soldering, magazine-rack building, agricultural techniques, and homemaking. Many of them resent federal interest in the problems of occupational training, and feel no sense of urgency about national problems. Local employment-service officials, whose salaries are financed by the federal government, but who are hired and controlled by the states (at salaries set by the state), are preoccupied with filling employers' vacancy orders without too much active initiating of requests from employers, and with even less systematic effort into encouraging "job development" programs. Often this is due to staff shortages. The new training programs of MDTA and ARA also call for—if they are to become successes—a "reaching out" to find the truly hard-core unemployed, and together with local school authorities, to motivate them to enter training, and then to stay in the courses. These programs call for energetic action to find placements for the trainees in jobs for which they have been trained. In addition, many areas lack adequate personnel of sufficient quality to successfully train the hard-core unemployed. In some of the programs, such as in welfare areas, local and state matching funds are required, and it is frequently impossible to get legislatures to appropriate such funds to the degree necessary to meet the need.

Yet the greatest obstacle is the failure at nearly all levels to appreciate the unique nature of the problems and of the variables that must be faced head-on in the realm of psychology and sociology—along with the techniques of individual and group change seeking to break poverty's vicious circle. Until greater recognition of these problems, variables, and techniques is achieved, and built into the designs at the outset, the best-financed programs will face too many delays and disappointments. It is the joint responsibility of program administrators and of social scientists to hasten the day of such recognition.

NOTES

1. "The Negro Woman in the Quest for Equality." Italics not in the original.

2. Mollie Orshansky, "Children of the Poor," *Social Security Bulletin*, July 1963. Before we make too many strictly moralistic and cultural explanations of the behavior of Negro women, a demographic note should be added, namely, that in 1960 there were 422,000 more nonwhite females in the child-bearing ages fifteen to forty-four than there were nonwhite males in the same age bracket. Only part of this excess can be explained in terms of possible greater nonreporting of nonwhite males. Much of the explanation lies in the impact of greater "environmental insults"—for example, higher death rates—for nonwhite males, that result in their lower survival and longevity rates.

3. Pauli Murray, *op. cit.*, p. 11.

4. *The Challenge of Jobless Youth*, Report of the President's Committee on Youth Employment, April 1963, p. 3.

5. Michael Schwartz and George Henderson, "The Culture of Unemployment: Some Notes on Negro Children," in A. B. Shostak and W. Gomberg, *Blue Collar World* (Englewood Cliffs: Prentice-Hall, Inc., 1964), p. 459 ff.

138 HAROLD L. SHEPPARD

6. *Ibid.*
7. *Ibid.*
8. *Ibid.*
9. *The Public Opinion Quarterly,* Spring 1947, pp. 103–114, and reprinted in Reinhard Bendix and S. M. Lipset, *Class, Status, and Power: A Reader in Social Stratification* (New York: The Free Press, 1953).
10. *Ibid.*
11. Quoted by Knupfer from M. Lazarsfeld-Jahoda and H. Zeisel, *Die Arbeitslosen von Marienthal* (Leipzig: Psychologische Monographien, 1933).
12. U.S. Department of Labor, *Profile of Youth—1963,* Report of the U.S. Senate Subcommittee on Employment and Manpower, Part I, 1964).
13. *Ibid.*
14. New York: Simon & Schuster, Inc., 1957, p. 339.
15. From a *Wall Street Journal,* April 29, 1964, article on training programs by Jonathan Spivak.

The Employed Poor:
A Case Study

CHARLES V. WILLIE AND WALTER E. RIDDICK[1]

The mythology of poverty created by the affluent has been one among several deterrents to a solution of the problem. In spite of the fact that about 20 per cent of the households in the United States received less than $3000 a year while less than 6 per cent of the labor force was unemployed,[2] the myth persists that poor people are those who will not work. Another myth is that anyone who works hard enough can get ahead.

This is an exploratory study of a population in Washington, D.C., to determine the association, if any, between these myths and reality. It analyzes (1) characteristics of the employed poor, (2) differences, if any, between their characteristics and other households that have pulled themselves out of poverty by their own "bootstraps," and (3) consequences of upward mobility for families that rely upon their own ingenuity.

This study is of *the employed poor*. They consist of 190 households whose employed heads averaged less than $3000 in 1963. The households studied are located in the District of Columbia in the Cardozo High School area. An inner-city section in northwest Washington, it consists of four square miles, 18 census tracts, and 104,278 persons, according to the 1960 census. The area is relatively heterogeneous, consisting of poor and affluent households, and white and nonwhite persons. But it is predominantly a low-income and Negro area: 70 per cent of its population live in census tracts classified as below average in socioeconomic status[3] and 72 per cent are nonwhite. This school district has been selected as the Target Area for launching several demonstration programs designed to prevent juvenile delinquency.

Before these programs were designed, information about the area's population was obtained in a field survey conducted during the summer of 1963. Approximately 1000 households were randomly selected in six census tracts representative of the various status levels in the area. Interviews of one-hour duration were conducted by residents of the area who were employed and trained to administer a schedule of questions, some of which dealt with economic problems.

To get an indication of how the employed poor might climb out of poverty using their own resources, the household heads with limited earning capacity were divided into two groups: total annual income for the household was below the poverty level of $3000 in one group and above in the other. Approximately 70 per cent (or 133) of these low-earning workers were in families with an annual median income of $2369 while 30 per cent (or 57) were in households with an annual median of $4625 and were classified as "marginal." Marginal families have climbed beyond the poverty level in spite of the limited earnings of the head because of other sources of income and therefore are a good example of "bootstrap" upward mobility. The population of

190 households represents about one-fifth of the sample of 1000 households in the Cardozo Area.

The heads of marginal families, like the heads of poor families, average $50 a week or less, but their annual family income is above the poverty level of $3000. This report is a comparative analysis between poor and marginal households to determine differentiating factors other than annual family income.

Demographic characteristics such as age, race, and marital status are presented for the two populations studied. Similarities and differences in employment, earning capacity, and educational characteristics of members in poor and marginal households are discussed. The extent of contact or involvement with community services and associations is also noted. As an exploratory study consisting of small numbers of cases, the findings are presented not as definitive answers but as tentative conclusions warranting further research.

Findings

One hundred and thirty-three of the 1000 households in this study are below the poverty level, even though the head is employed; 93 per cent of the heads in these poor families are full-time employees and the remaining number are part-time workers. This clearly is contrary to the myth that people are poor because they will not work.

Poor and marginal households consist of white and Negro persons. The proportion of employed Negroes who head poor households is 92 per cent, as compared with 77 per cent heading marginal households. While Negro households are predominant in each group, because Negroes are the predominant race in the Cardozo area, both categories of poor and marginal households are multiracial.

Poor and marginal families are similar as to their large number of female household heads, approximately 43 per cent for both groups combined. Slightly less than half of the poor households and slightly more than half of the marginal households consist of two parents. About 11 per cent of the poor households consist of unmarried men, as compared with only 2 per cent of the marginals. Other than these minor differences, poor and marginal households are similar in marital status of their heads.

The employed heads of poor families tend to be young; one-fourth are under thirty years of age, compared with one-eighth of the heads in marginal households. Both household groups contain children from infancy to age nineteen. However, poor households have 38 per cent of their child population under five years of age, compared with 24 per cent of the child population among the marginals. Another contrast is in the proportion of teenagers fifteen to nineteen years—27 per cent in the marginals and only 11 per cent in the poor households. Thus, employed heads of poor households tend to be younger and their families tend to consist of a higher proportion of small preschool children than found among the marginals.

Marginal households are slightly larger, averaging one person more per household than poor families. In addition, the marginals have more large households of five or six or more persons. About three out of every ten of the marginal households may be classified as large, compared with approximately two out of every ten of the poor households. This is because a higher proportion of marginal households consist of primary family members as well as relatives and nonkinsmen; 46 per cent of the marginal as compared with 27 per cent of the poor households include persons other than parents and children. Of the characteristics analyzed thus far, household composition is a major differentiator of poor and marginal families.

These two groups are similar in that the heads are employed in the same types of job. A large majority of poor and marginal heads are blue-collar workers. About half in each group are service workers. There are few laborers (only 7 to 9 per cent) and few skilled workers (less than 7 per cent in either group). A modest difference that should be noted, however, is the higher proportion of clerical workers among the marginals—19 per cent compared with only 7 per cent among the poor. Excepting these minor variations, most of the household heads in this study work in the service industry.

While large proportions of both poor and marginal household heads work for businesses engaged in retail and wholesale trade and in private households, a modest difference between the two groups is the higher proportion of marginals employed by the federal government. This is the source of employment for 20 per cent of the marginal as compared with 7 per cent of the poor household heads. These proportions are similar to those for marginal and poor heads engaged in clerical work and apparently involve the same persons, since most governmental work is of a white-collar nature.

A most striking difference is that the wife in the marginal household is much more likely to be employed than the wife in the poor household. Three out of every four wives in marginal families are employed, and better than half are employed full time. The converse is true of the other group. Three out of every four wives in poor families are not gainfully employed. This difference between the two groups is more striking than that observed for households consisting of primary and extended family members. Possibly the presence of adults other than parents in the household is related to whether or not a mother with young children works. Also, there may be motivational factors associated with the higher proportion of working wives among marginals.

Most of the wives in marginal families are engaged in service work. Of the few wives in poor families who are gainfully employed, most are service workers too. However, the median weekly income for marginals of $51 is about $11 higher than the median for working wives in poor families. This may be because seven out of every ten employed marginal wives render a service other than that of private household work, as compared with five out of every ten employed wives in poor families. Interestingly, the median weekly income of working wives in marginal families is one dollar higher than the median weekly earnings of their employed husbands. The few working wives in poor families tend to earn less than their menfolk.

The number of multiple wage earners in marginal families is increased not only by working wives but by the employment of relatives and other household members. For example, three or more members are gainfully employed in about 20 per cent of the marginal households, compared with 3 per cent of the poor households. This means that most poor households have only one gainfully employed person of limited earning capacity. The marginal household head, also with limited earning capacity, has his low wages supplemented by the incomes of one, two, three, four, and in one instance five, additional wage earners living at the same residence. The prevailing pattern, however, is two wage earners in the marginal and one wage earner in the poor household.

The median weekly earnings of heads of poor and marginal households are about the same—$49 and $50, respectively—and so are their educational achievements. Thirty-six per cent of the poor and 37 per cent of the marginal heads have only an elementary-school education or less. College graduates are under 2 per cent in both groups. Of heads who have graduated from high school, the 42 per cent in marginal households is slightly larger than the 31 per cent in poor households, but this difference is probably of little consequence in a sample of this size.

A marked difference between poor and marginal households, however, is in the formal schooling of spouses in two-parent families: 46 per cent of the wives in marginal households are high school graduates, compared with 27 per cent among the poor.

Wives in two-parent marginal households also tend to be high-school graduates more frequently than husbands.

This may account for the fact that they also tend to earn as much or more than their husbands. In poor families, the median earnings of the few working wives is nearly $10 a week less than that of their spouses, and they also tend to have less education than their husbands.

Another persistent myth is that the poor are new arrivals who have come to take advantage of city charity. Our study reveals that the poor as well as the marginal households are headed by relatively *long-term residents;* 50 per cent of the poor and 62 per cent of the marginal households have employed heads who have lived in Washington, D.C. more than 20 years. Nevertheless, these households have few contacts with community services and associations. Of the 133 households with employed heads and an annual family income below the poverty level, only nine (6.7 per cent) had been in contact with the Public Welfare Department during the year preceding this study. More than half had not received any help from a public agency in the past 12 months.

In general, the poor and marginal families headed by low-income workers are cut off from the mainstream of the community. The members in 90 per cent or more of the poor and marginal families in this study had not actively participated in any union, political, fraternal, religious, parents', or citizens' group in the community during the year prior to the 1963 summer survey. These data suggest that the poor are strangers in our midst whom we do not know and thus have been appropriately labeled "our invisible poor."⁴

The similarities and differences between poor and marginal families, headed by husbands of limited earning capacity, are probably best illustrated by two case studies of Cardozo households reconstructed from data recorded in the interview schedules. The names of these families are fictitious but their problems and possibilities are real. A vignette of a poor family is followed by a sketch of a marginal household.

*   *   *

At age twenty-six, John Parker has a wife, three children, and a crushing lack of funds. On the surface, the Parkers seem to be better off than many of their neighbors, for John presently earns $70 a week. However, with only a ninth-grade education, unskilled construction work is all that he can find. Due to the weather and the plentiful supply of laborers, he is often idle for several weeks at a time. Consequently, the Parkers' annual income is less than $3000. After paying monthly rental of $76 and buying food, there is little money left for other needs such as medical care and recreation.

The Parkers have been married three years; Mrs. Parker is only nineteen. She left school in the tenth grade. Three daughters were born in rapid succession. Mrs. Parker confided that she would like to limit the number of children but that she knows nothing about family planning. She is, therefore, in a state of despair.

For a family of five, the Parkers need at least a three-bedroom dwelling unit. They live in a dilapidated one-bedroom apartment totally inadequate for a five-person household. The Parkers want a larger and better-kept place but have little hope of finding one and not enough funds to pay for it. They are dissatisfied with the neighborhood as well as the dwelling unit.

The Parkers have thought little about their children's futures except that they do not want them to grow up in the present neighborhood, which Mrs. Parker describes as run down and full of crime. Although they view present circumstances as temporary, they have no idea of how or when these may change. The Parkers have little contact with the community. They belong to no social or civic organizations and attend church infrequently. Although impoverished, they do not receive social-welfare services, not even medical clinic services. They know very few people in their neighborhood and have no desire to meet any.

The John Parker family is typical in many respects of today's poor families. Both Mr. and Mrs. Parker are school drop-outs and consequently untrained for continuous employment in a technology-dominated society. They married at a very young age and assumed child-rearing responsibilities early. Yet the Parkers have not accepted their present condition as permanent.

Mr. and Mrs. Clay are parents in a family with marginal resources: the family income is better than $4000 a year. This family has improvised and, by its own bootstraps, climbed above the poverty level.

Nine persons are crowded into a five-room apartment in the Clay household. Beside the parents and their five children, Mrs. Clay's mother and a lodger live with the family. Without the financial contributions of the latter two persons, the Clays would be in poverty, for Mr. Clay brings home only $48 a week, hardly enough to provide basic needs. Mrs. Clay does not work; her youngest child is only three. The mother-in-law, who has a fourth-grade education, is a private household worker. Her weekly income of $30 relieves some of the strain on the family's limited resources, but not nearly enough. In order to "make ends meet" the Clays have taken in a roomer. His contribution to the finances of the family is small, but it and the mother-in-law's earnings have raised the family to a marginal-income level above the poverty line.

Mr. and Mrs. Clay were born in North Carolina, and both moved to Washington in 1949 seeking a better life. They had lived in Washington several years before they met. At the time Mr. and Mrs. Clay married, she had a daughter by a former husband living with her mother in North Carolina. Soon after the marriage, the mother-in-law and step-daughter moved to Washington. Mr. Clay, with a high-school diploma, expected to increase his income steadily. Today, far from his expectations, he is a mover for a storage company with earnings insufficient to support his family.

In spite of their marginal resources the Clays have remained fairly independent. Except for toys and food at Christmas from the Salvation Army, they have not turned to the many social-welfare and family services available in the community.

The neighborhood in which the Clays live is far from the best. It is characterized by poor housing conditions and high adult and youth crime rates. The Clays fully realize this, and would like to have a large house in the country with a yard. Their financial status makes this impossible.

In general, the Clays have little contact with their community. Mrs. Clay recently joined a mothers' club that meets monthly at a nearby church, but other than this, the Clays have no contact with social or civic organizations. They do occasionally attend a neighborhood Methodist Church.

The Clays are a very close family. Mr. and Mrs. Clay take great pride in their five children, and say they are doing their best to rear them into responsible adulthood. The Clays try to entertain their children in the home and keep them off the streets. Mrs. Clay teaches the girls to sew and reads to the boys. She is also the household's chief disciplinarian. The Clays consider their child-rearing practices successful, pointing out that none of their children has ever been in trouble with the police.

Their marginal economic status has not dampened the Clay's aspirations for their children's futures. They want the children to enter professions—the girls in nursing and the ministry, the boys in law and medicine. However, beyond the knowledge that more than a high-school education is required, the Clays have little idea of what is entailed in fulfilling these goals.

In summary, there is little to sustain the Clay family other than their sense of significance and optimism for the future. They are making ends meet because of the presence of multiple wage earners in the household, including a relative and a lodger. The sacrifice of privacy, therefore, has been the major cost for movement out of poverty.

Summary and Conclusions

This analysis indicates that some families are poor even though the head of household is employed, that families with heads of limited education may climb out of poverty through the contributions of multiple wage earners, and that the second wage earner is usually the wife, but that family income may be further supplemented by the contributions of relatives and lodgers in the household.

The analysis also shows that employed wives in families in which the husband is an unskilled worker tend to have more formal schooling than the husband and earn as much or more than the head of the family. Working wives are usually employed in unskilled service jobs. The data suggest that whether or not a wife works depends not only upon her level of education but upon the presence or absence of young preschool children in the household. A kinsman in the household, especially a grandmother or other adult who can care for young children, provides an additional opportunity for the mother to work. The number of cases in this analysis are insufficient for determining the relative contribution of each of these three factors to a mother's opportunity to work.

The analysis also indicates that poor families are not necessarily newcomers to the city. A majority of the heads of households had lived in Washington more than two decades. Notwithstanding the longevity of their residence, few families were in contact with community health and welfare services, even though annual family incomes were marginal or below the poverty level. The number of families with members participating in neighborhood associations is miniscule.

Of the 190 families in this sample whose heads are employed in low-paying unskilled jobs, 30 per cent of the households pulled themselves out of poverty by their own bootstraps, with mulitple wage earners and contributions of lodgers or extended family members in the household. Utilization of this method of climbing out of poverty will probably diminish in the future as the kinds of jobs which the second wage earner holds—primarily unskilled service and private household work—decrease. Unless the skills of the household heads or their spouses are upgraded among this 30 per cent, they too will slip into the category of the employed poor as the unskilled jobs that provide supplementary income disappear.

A household of multiple wage earners and persons who make contributions in rental or child-care service means one way of climbing out of poverty. This method could have disorganizing side effects. A household consisting of persons in addition to primary family members sacrifices some of its privacy. Though consequences of this sacrifice have not been studied adequately, accumulated evidence demonstrates that enduring cohesion is more difficult to achieve among persons who are drawn together on a contractual basis. Moreover, the intimate fulfillments of family life are sometimes jeopardized when nonfamily members or nonprimary family members share living quarters with a family.

These findings point toward the need for further research on working wives of husbands with limited earning capacity. We need to know the kind of person the wife is and the impact of her work upon the husband, the children, and the social mobility of the family. These findings might displace many of the myths that currently indicate the consequences of work for wives and mothers.

In the meantime, the Cardozo study has already shattered the myth that poor people won't work, and that the poor are the newcomers to our cities. It also indicates that opportunities for bootstrap upward mobility are diminishing for the poor as the kinds of jobs that other members of the household once obtained to supplement the low earnings of the household head are fast vanishing.

NOTES

1. The authors acknowledge with appreciation the assistance rendered by Austin Gerald Harris, statistical clerk, Washington Action for Youth research staff.
2. Department of Commerce, *Statistical Abstract of the United States* (Eighty-fourth edition; Washington: Government Printing Office, 1963), pp. 219, 340.

3. Charles V. Willie and Anita Gershenovitz, "Juvenile Delinquency in Racially Mixed Areas," *American Sociological Review,* **29** (Oct. 1964), pp. 740–744.

4. Dwight Macdonald, "Our Invisible Poor," *The New Yorker,* Jan. 19, 1963.

Appalachia:
Realities of Deprivation[1]

WILLIAM J. PAGE JR., AND EARL E. HUYCK

President Lyndon B. Johnson, in transmitting to Congress his bill on Appalachia on April 28, 1964, called for "an active beginning to end an old problem in Appalachia." National attention and concern have been focused on this highland region by the President's Appalachian Regional Commission established by the late President John F. Kennedy on April 9, 1963. The commission consisted of a representative designated by each of the governors of the Appalachian states and a representative of each of the heads of major federal departments and agencies. The commission was charged with the preparation of a comprehensive action program for the economic development of the Appalachian region.

The facts of Appalachian conditions are not new. In 1902 and again in 1935 the federal government published extensive reports of this region. In 1961 an analysis of the region was published by the Conference of Appalachian Governors. In 1962, a fully documented study of southern Appalachia was published under private sponsorship. Over this 62-year span, the conditions described in each report are discouragingly similar; their recurrence in these studies is the chronicle of a region bypassed.

The Natural Endowment of Appalachia

Appalachia is a region apart—geographically and statistically. It is a mountain land boldly upthrust between the prosperous eastern seaboard and the industrial Middle West —a highland region which sweeps diagonally across ten states from northern Pennsylvania to northern Alabama. It contains 165,000 square miles—an area slightly larger than California—and includes all of West Virginia, and parts of Pennsylvania, Maryland, Ohio, Virginia, Kentucky, Tennessee, Alabama, North Carolina, and Georgia. This mountain land that delayed the westward march of settlers early in the nineteenth century has become a bypassed region in the twentieth century.

Appalachia's rich natural endowment has benefited too few of its 15.3 million people. The average Appalachian, whether he lives in a metropolis, in town, on the farm, or in a mountain cabin, has not matched his counterpart in the rest of the United States as a participant in the nation's economic growth. The most serious problems are low income, high unemployment, lack of urbanization, low educational achievement, and a low level of living.

The President's Appalachian Regional Commission has emphasized that the major objective of a regional development process is clear: Appalachia must attain an employment base which can sustain its people at a level of dignity and prosperity comparable to the relatively affluent nation of which it is part. The conversion and processing of its raw materials should be done locally to the fullest extent possible. New industries, dependent not on the resources of the

Table 1—Population of Appalachia, by State, and Balance of United States, by Type of Residence, 1950 and 1960

Appalachian Portion of—	Total Population	Per Cent of Total Population			
				RURAL	
		Urban	Total	Non-farm	Farm
Alabama:					
1960	2,077,496	54.9	45.1	33.6	11.5
1950	1,954,649	45.1	54.9	25.4	29.5
Georgia:					
1960	675,024	27.8	72.2	60.1	12.1
1950	619,766	23.3	76.7	36.9	39.8
Kentucky:					
1960	886,113	17.9	82.1	59.2	22.9
1950	1,041,242	15.0	85.0	39.9	45.1
Maryland:					
1960	195,808	45.3	54.7	48.3	6.4
1950	189,701	44.4	55.6	43.8	11.8
North Carolina:					
1960	776,828	23.0	77.0	58.3	18.7
1950	762,229	21.2	78.8	37.4	41.4
Ohio:					
1960	743,860	34.9	65.1	52.6	12.5
1950	676,715	32.6	67.4	39.0	28.4
Pennsylvania:					
1960	5,932,025	63.0	37.0	33.2	3.8
1950	5,784,652	62.6	37.3	29.1	8.2
Tennessee:					
1960	1,607,689	42.6	57.4	40.9	16.5
1950	1,529,762	37.7	62.3	30.5	31.8
Virginia:					
1960	572,950	23.0	77.0	58.8	18.2
1950	599,028	18.7	81.2	46.5	34.7
West Virginia:					
1960	1,860,421	38.2	61.8	55.3	6.5
1950	2,005,552	34.6	65.4	44.9	20.5
TOTAL APPALACHIA:					
1960	15,328,214	47.5	52.5	42.8	9.7
1950	15,163,296	43.9	56.1	33.6	22.4
BALANCE OF UNITED STATES:					
1960	163,997,457	72.0	28.0	20.8	7.3
1950[1]	136,162,502	66.2	33.8	19.3	14.4

1. Includes Alaska and Hawaii in 1950, but rural farm and nonfarm data were not available separately for those areas. Rural data for those areas are treated as part of nonfarm data.

region, but on the strategic location and potential market
which Appalachia represents, must be located in the region.
Recreational resources must be developed with coordinated
intensity if their employment potential is to be realized.
Agricultural diversification should be accelerated; mining
and timber employment and income, expanded.

Population Change

Americans have traditionally been apt students of the
geography of opportunity; their migrations have clearly
marked the regions of growth and decline. Population trends
in Appalachia offer the most convincing statistics to prove
the deficit of opportunities which pervades the entire region.

The Appalachian *birth rate*, for decades higher than the
nation's, dropped nearly to that of the rest of the nation in
the decade 1950–1960. Yet the population of the region
itself grew by only 1.1 per cent in those years, compared
to a growth of 20.4 per cent in the balance of the United
States (Table 1). During that decade, 2 million *more people
left the region than moved in* (Table 2). By contrast, California, a state of approximately the same size and population as Appalachia, gained 2½ million more people than
it lost.

In relation to the total population, the *rural farm population* declined strikingly from 22.4 per cent in 1950 to 9.7
per cent in 1960, nearly the level for the balance of the
United States. In the interim the *rural nonfarm population*
increased more rapidly in Appalachia than elsewhere, but
by 1960 only 47.5 per cent of Appalachia's residents lived in
urban areas—elsewhere in the nation, 72 per cent lived in
urban areas.

The *most productive age group (eighteen to sixty-four)*
in the rest of the United States expanded by 8.6 per cent in
the period 1950–1960 but in Appalachia declined by 5.1
per cent (Table 3). The decline in the eighteen to sixty-four
age group is more pronounced in nonmetropolitan areas

(6.4 per cent) than in metropolitan areas (3.1 per cent). During the period 1955–1960, some 45 per cent of the out-migrants from Appalachia were in the age group twenty to thirty-four. Thousands who are educationally and vocationally most able to contribute to the development of their communities are leaving for better opportunities and living conditions elsewhere.

Table 2—Net Migration From Appalachia by State, 1950–1960

| | NET MIGRATION, 1950–1960 | |
State	Total State	Appalachian Portion of State
Alabama	−368,442	− 191,827
Georgia	−213,569	−53,656
Kentucky	−389,730	−367,333
Maryland	+319,978	−14,751
North Carolina	−327,987	−106,722
Ohio	+408,576	−18,068
Pennsylvania	−475,286	−529,112
Tennessee	−272,605	−172,426
Virginia	+14,722	−113,079
West Virginia	−446,711	−446,711
Total	−1,751,054	−2,013,635

Low Income and High Unemployment

In Appalachia, almost 1 in 3 families lives on an annual income of $3000 or less (Table 4). Elsewhere in the United States, that figure drops to one family in every five. Per-capita income for the balance of the United States, $1900, is 35 per cent greater than the Appalachian figure of $1400. The per-capita income for the Appalachian portion is substantially below that of the remainder of the state—and 45 per cent below in Kentucky (Table 5). Only 8.7 per cent of Appalachian families—but 15.6 per cent of other U.S. families— have incomes over $10,000 a year.

In 1960 there were 380,000 *unemployed workers in Appalachia—7.1 per cent of the labor force*—compared to 4.9 per cent elsewhere. But the deficiency of job opportunity is far greater, for these figures do not take into account the

Table 3—Per Cent Change in Total Population and by Select Age Groups, Appalachia and Balance of United States, 1950–1960

State or Region	Total	Under 18 Years	18–64 Years	65 Years and Over
Appalachian portion of:				
Alabama	6.3	9.4	0.9	36.4
Metropolitan	16.9	29.1	7.0	47.2
Nonmetropolitan	−1.4	−3.0	−4.0	29.4
Georgia	8.9	8.5	6.4	32.2
Metropolitan	25.9	30.7	20.2	41.6
Nonmetropolitan	6.7	5.7	4.5	31.0
Kentucky	−14.9	−15.7	−18.9	25.5
Metropolitan	4.4	9.4	−1.8	33.1
Nonmetropolitan	−15.9	−16.8	−19.9	25.0
Maryland[1]	3.2	9.2	−2.9	23.1
North Carolina	1.9	−1.9	0.5	36.1
Metropolitan	4.6	10.0	−3.5	47.6
Nonmetropolitan	1.4	−3.8	1.4	33.6
Ohio	9.9	20.7	3.1	12.3
Metropolitan	1.8	10.3	−5.4	14.7
Nonmetropolitan	12.0	23.3	5.3	11.8
Pennsylvania	2.5	15.4	−6.9	24.7
Metropolitan	4.1	19.8	−5.6	30.1
Nonmetropolitan	−0.2	9.2	−7.4	17.4
Tennessee	5.1	4.8	2.0	33.3
Metropolitan	11.1	19.6	3.4	42.3
Nonmetropolitan	1.8	−2.2	1.2	28.9
Virginia[1]	−4.4	−7.9	−5.1	25.1
West Virginia	−7.2	−5.1	−12.6	24.5
Metropolitan	3.4	11.1	−4.1	32.3
Nonmetropolitan	−11.3	−10.5	−16.1	21.7
APPALACHIA	1.1	5.8	−5.1	26.7
Metropolitan	6.6	19.9	−3.1	33.2
Nonmetropolitan	−2.4	−1.5	−6.4	22.7
BALANCE OF UNITED STATES	20.4	40.9	8.6	32.3

1. There are no metropolitan counties in the Appalachian portions of Maryland and Virginia.

many men and women who, in despair of ever finding jobs, have given up the search and withdrawn from the labor force. In Appalachia that group is extremely large. If the average proportion of Appalachians employed or seeking work equaled the national average, there would be an additional 700,000 persons in the labor force, a figure which far exceeds the number of unemployed.

Table 4—Distribution of Family Income, 1960, Appalachia and the Balance of United States

State or Region	All Families	PER CENT FAMILIES WITH INCOME: Less Than $3000	$10,000 and Over
Appalachian portion of:			
Alabama	513,921	36.7	8.3
Georgia	170,598	37.3	5.1
Kentucky	209,007	57.3	3.6
Maryland	51,143	24.2	9.2
North Carolina	194,729	40.2	5.3
Ohio	187,264	29.5	7.5
Pennsylvania	1,530,250	19.5	11.4
Tennessee	405,606	39.0	7.2
Virginia	137,518	42.5	5.0
West Virginia	462,078	32.6	8.4
TOTAL APPALACHIA	3,862,114	30.7	8.7
Metropolitan	1,591,432	20.8	12.3
Nonmetropolitan	2,270,682	37.5	6.2
BALANCE OF UNITED STATES	41,266,279	20.5	15.6
Metropolitan	27,028,958	14.8	19.2
Nonmetropolitan	14,237,321	31.3	8.9

The deficiency of job opportunities in the Appalachian region in recent years is the result of *severe declines in employment in mining and agriculture.* Only 1 in 15 persons is now employed in agriculture in Appalachia. Between 1950 and 1960 these two sectors together released 641,000 workers, or more than half of their 1950 work force. During this period the increase in manufacturing, construction, and service employment (567,000) was insufficient to prevent a net decrease of 1.5 per cent in total employment (Table 6). By contrast there was a 15 per cent increase in employment in the rest of the United States.

The job deficit in Appalachia would be even greater but for the heavy out-migration which occurred in this period. The population of Appalachia hardly increased—a bare 1.1 per cent—between 1950 and 1960 because the natural increase was offset by an almost equivalent volume of *out-migration.*

From the facts on income and joblessness, we can infer

that the "real" Appalachian standards of living are below national norms. The evidence mounts as we look at some direct indicators. For example, *retail sales* in Appalachia in 1962 were equal to 6.4 per cent of national totals, a figure well below Appalachia's 8.5 per cent share of U.S. population. Had Appalachians purchased retail goods at a rate proportionate to their population, an additional $4 billion in goods would have been sold in the area. Capital accumulation is likewise low. *Per-capita savings* in 1960 amounted to $514 in Appalachia in contrast to $920 elsewhere.

Table 5—Per Capita Income, Appalachia and Balance of United States, 1960

(in dollars)

State	Appalachian Portion	Rest of State	Total State
Alabama	1254	1231	1246
Georgia	1194	1393	1359
Kentucky	841	1519	1321
Maryland	1589	2031	2002
North Carolina	1169	1269	1251
Ohio	1396	2003	1956
Pennsylvania	1680	2047	1854
Tennessee	1257	1369	1318
Virginia	1008	1698	1598
West Virginia	1378	1378	1378
TOTAL APPALACHIA			1405
BALANCE OF UNITED STATES			1901

Unhealthy People in an Unhealthy Environment

Few social phenomena are clearer than the circularity of poor health and low income. Severe personal health problems in Appalachia include nutritional deficiencies, dental diseases, chronic diseases, infant deaths and communicable disease problems, especially enteric and diarrheal. Health services are not readily available because of shortages and maldistribution of health manpower and lack of funds for purchase of services. The Appalachian area has 94 *physicians* per 100,000 population, compared with a national

average of 141 per 100,000. Low per-capita income and tax
base predictably underlie low per-capita expenditures for
health services. Expenditures for public health in Appalachia are less than half the level needed to improve public
health to the level of the rest of the United States. The
particulars of the "health gap" make a distressing catalogue.

High infant mortality has long been associated with
inadequate prenatal, delivery, and postnatal care. In 1960,
when the infant mortality rate (deaths per 1000 children
under one year of age) for the nation as a whole was 26.9,
there were eight Appalachian counties in which rates were
at least twice the national average—and one county had
nearly three times (76.9) the national infant mortality rate.
In the Appalachian counties of one state, midwives attend
13 per cent of births, and 18 percent of the infants are
delivered out-of-hospital, compared to 3 per cent and 6 per
cent respectively for the state as a whole.

*A child runs a course of health obstacles more difficult
in Appalachia than elsewhere* in the United States. Malnu-
trition, parisitic infestation, mental retardation, heart disease, and neurological defects are common diagnoses. The
cumulative effects of these conditions and lack of treatment
produce high rates of chronic ailments in older age groups.
One of the outcomes is a *shorter and less productive work-
life* reflected in excessive loss of workdays because of acute
and chronic illness. The average Appalachian worker ex-

Table 6—Employment in Major Industry Groups for the Appalachian Region, 1950 and 1960

Industry	EMPLOYMENT 1950	EMPLOYMENT 1960	Per Cent Change	PER CENT EMPLOYMENT IN EACH GROUP 1950	1960
Agriculture	706,250	335,742	−52.5	14.1	6.8
Mining	462,341	191,255	−58.6	9.2	3.9
Construction	270,692	286,060	+5.7	5.4	5.8
Manufacturing	1,394,302	1,592,135	+14.2	27.8	32.2
Services	2,179,430	2,534,138	+16.3	43.5	51.3
ALL INDUSTRIES	5,013,015	4,939,330	−1.5	100.0	100.0

periences two more days of work loss from these causes than a comparable worker elsewhere. The Public Health Service estimates that, translated to wages, the excess of lost work costs Appalachian workers $140 million annually.

Tuberculosis is widespread in most of Appalachia. One area reports prevalence (number of cases per 100,000 population) almost 70 per cent higher than the national figure. The same area reports incidence (new cases per 100,000 population) 30 per cent higher than the national rate and tuberculosis mortality 6 per cent greater than that of the rest of the country. *Typhoid fever*, once a scourge of the nation and a fairly reliable index of poor environmental sanitation, still is prevalent in Appalachia. One small area accounts for nearly a third of all typhoid carriers in one Appalachian state.

Dental disease is another critical health problem, especially among children. One state reports a rate of diseased teeth one-third higher than among non-Appalachian children, with the usual corollary—one-fourth as much dental care received by Appalachian children. Fluoridated water is unavailable to 82 per cent of the population. Other reports document the expected outcome: 60 per cent of aged persons without teeth and only one-half to two-thirds of these persons with dentures.

Environmental health deficiencies increase the incidence of disease and contribute to economic disadvantages. A state survey of Appalachian community water supplies provides these dismal figures: only 62 of 109 communities (77 per cent of the population) have *public water supplies*. Only 17 systems are rated "good," 28 are "doubtful," and 17 are "bad." Raw sewage—1.5 million gallons per day in one state —is discharged into streams and rivers. *Unsewered communities* number 160 at present (Table 7). Only 4 of thirty-three larger communities, containing 12 per cent of the population, in a selected Appalachian area have adequate sewage-treatment plants.

Mining operations of past years have contributed heavily

Table 7—Needs for Sewage Treatment Works in Appalachia

| | SEWERED COMMUNITIES | | UNSEWERED COMMUNITIES[1] | |
| | | | | Cost of Treat- |
State	Number	Cost (000's)	Number	ment Works (000's)
Alabama	30	$9131	21	$4145
Georgia	4	3544	0	0
Kentucky	24	6228	3	517
Maryland	4	1971	8	1867
North Carolina	40	21,397	2	329
Ohio	10	2966	4	1251
Pennsylvania	236	87,584	74	15,808
Tennessee	12	9879	7[2]	153[2]
Virginia	28	5832	0	0
West Virginia	98	33,175	41	10,188
TOTAL	486	$181,708	160	$34,258

SOURCE: U.S. Department of Health, Education, and Welfare; Public Health Service.
1. Cost of collecting sewers unknown.
2. No cost information available on six projects.

to water and air pollution. Mile after mile of stream show the havoc wrought by acid drainage from mines, which makes the water unfit for most purposes. Hundreds of unsightly coal refuse piles exist, some of them burning year after year.

Hospitals and other community health facilities are inadequate to cope with existing problems. Appalachia has only 96 public health centers for its 340 counties; 44 additional centers are needed. The need of 12,500 hospital beds represents a shortage of 20 per cent, but the need of additional nursing-home beds is even greater—30 per cent. Even cursory study of tax potentials indicates that these needs cannot be met from local revenues. Having built necessary hospital facilities, Appalachia would still have to cope with the fact that eight of the ten states have less of their populations than the national average (76 per cent) protected with *hospitalization insurance.*

Educational Deficits

Economic growth depends to a large degree on educational excellence. While assistance can be provided in Appalachia from outside the region, the primary drive for recovery must originate inside its own boundaries. Yet the educational resources to mount that drive are inadequate. The region has not produced a sufficient corps of educated persons in the past; it lacks the tax base to provide an adequate education effort in the future.

For every hundred persons over twenty-five years of age elsewhere in the United States, eight have *failed to finish five years of school* (Table 8). In Appalachia, that figure rises to more than eleven. Although the level of educational attainment in the Appalachian portion of three states is above the national average, in the remainder of these states the percentage of persons failing to finish five years of school ranges from 11 per cent to 22 per cent. It is estimated that 1½ million of Appalachia's inhabitants are functionally illiterate.

Thirty-two out of every hundred Appalachians over

Table 8—Educational Levels of Persons Twenty-five Years Old and Over for Appalachia, by States and Balance of United States, Metropolitan and Nonmetropolitan, 1960

State or Region	Persons 25 Years Old and Over	PER CENT COMPLETED		
		Less Than 5 Years Schooling	4 Years of High School or More	4 Years of College or More
Appalachian portion of—				
Alabama	1,083,026	15.0	30.1	5.8
Georgia	351,144	17.7	22.8	3.7
Kentucky	434,175	22.1	17.4	3.0
Maryland	111,969	7.7	31.9	4.4
North Carolina	414,301	16.3	28.8	5.0
Ohio	407,444	7.1	33.3	4.0
Pennsylvania	3,443,354	7.2	38.4	5.7
Tennessee	857,720	15.9	28.5	5.5
Virginia	293,481	19.2	23.6	4.0
West Virginia	999,731	11.0	30.6	5.2
TOTAL APPALACHIA	8,396,345	11.6	32.3	5.2
Metropolitan	3,660,966	9.1	38.2	6.5
Nonmetropolitan	4,735,379	13.4	28.0	4.3
BALANCE OF UNITED STATES	91,041,739	8.0	41.8	7.9
Metropolitan	60,251,979	6.9	44.6	9.0
Nonmetropolitan	30,789,760	10.3	36.5	5.8

twenty-five have finished *high school,* contrasted to almost forty-two persons of similar age elsewhere. No section of Appalachia reaches the national norm for the rest of the United States and one state dips to 58 per cent below that norm.

Appalachia also suffers from a *shortage of college graduates.* In the rest of the United States, eight of every hundred persons over twenty-five years of age have completed at least four years of college. In Appalachia that figure drops to five. Again, none of the ten states reaches the figure for the rest of the United States, and in the most deficient state, only three of every hundred persons twenty-five and over have completed college.

If the 8.4 million Appalachians over twenty-five years old were educated to the same degree as their counterparts in the rest of the United States, there would be almost 800,000 more high school graduates in Appalachia and the region would have 227,000 more college graduates. Many of the region's college graduates are included in the heavy outmigration of young adults in the twenty to forty-four age group.

The prospects for improvement in Appalachian education are dimmed by the *region's inadequate tax base.* The balance of the nation's per-capita income is 35 per cent greater than Appalachia's; this inevitably cripples a state's income and sales tax collections, common sources of school revenue. Furthermore, Appalachian property has an assessed per-capita value ($1271 in 1961) that is 38 per cent less than the non-Appalachian property value ($2050). Levies on property constitute the major educational tax base both in the region and the nation.

Federal investment in Appalachia has not been proportionate to either its population or its needs. In fiscal year 1963 Appalachia's 8.5 per cent of the nation's population received 4.9 per cent of the federal dollar, exclusive of trust fund and interest expenditures. This relatively low level of federal spending, combined with the inadequate economic base of the region, explains part of the region's past distress and indicates the need for a larger federal investment in the immediate future.

Welfare Problems

In fiscal year 1964 all levels of government expended $476 million in Appalachia for *public assistance*—federal government, $260 million; states, $109 million; and local governments, $7 million (Table 9). In Appalachia 5.9 per cent of the total population receive public-assistance payments as compared to 4.1 per cent elsewhere. Appalachia's 8.5 per cent of the U.S. population accounted for 11.9 per cent of the nations public-assistance recipients in June 1963. Even with the current level of expenditures, monthly payments per recipient for each category of public assistance are low in Appalachia in comparison with the rest of the nation (Table 10). For example, Appalachia's medical assistance to the aged in June 1963 accounted for 12 per cent of persons in the United States receiving such aid, but only 6 per cent of payments. Public-assistance programs still do not reach all who are needy. Many of the Appalachian states have not implemented welfare activities authorized in the relevant federal statutory amendments of 1961 and 1962.

Sources of income in one Appalachian county—neither at the top nor at the bottom in economic rank—suggest

Table 9—Public Assistance Expenditures in Appalachia

| | FISCAL YEAR (in millions) | | |
Source	1962	1963	1964
All	$326.5	$345.1	$376.2
Federal	222.3	239.0	259.9
State	98.7	98.9	109.2
Local	5.5	7.2	7.1

SOURCE: U.S. Department of Health, Education, and Welfare; Welfare Administration. These minimum estimates were made by applying the percentage of the total state population residing in the Appalachian portion of the state in 1960 to the federal grants to the states for assistance. As such they do not reflect variations in the patterns of receipt of assistance within each state; generally there is a higher proportion of the population receiving assistance in the Appalachian portion of the state.

Table 10—Recipients and Payments from Public Assistance Programs Supported by the Federal Government in Appalachia and Balance of United States, June 1963

	Appalachia	Balance of United States	Appalachia as Per Cent of the Total United States
Total public-assistance payments:			
June 1963[1]	$33,634,400	$347,987,200	8.81
Per-capita[2]	$2.19	$2.12	
Total public-assistance recipients:			
June 1963[1]	907,710	6,697,504	11.94
Per cent of total population receiving aid[2]	5.92	4.08	
Public-assistance programs, June 1963,[1] by type:			
Aid to families with dependent children:			
Payments	$13,436,300	$108,341,700	11.03
Families receiving aid	131,540	831,146	13.66
Per cent of total families receiving aid[2]	3.40	2.01	
Children receiving aid	392,418	2,559,967	13.29
Per cent of total persons under 18 years of age receiving aid[2]	7.01	4.36	
Old age assistance:			
Payments	$12,752,300	$156,398,700	7.54
Persons receiving aid	203,371	1,995,545	9.25
Per cent of total aged, age 65 and over receiving aid[2]	14.21	13.50	
Medical assistance to the aged:			
Payments[3]	$1,495,100	$25,117,900	5.62
Persons receiving aid[3]	16,246	120,090	11.92
Per cent of total persons age 65 and over receiving aid[2]	1.14	0.81	
Aid to the permanently and totally disabled:			
Payments	$2,924,500	$31,608,600	8.47
Persons receiving aid	52,061	409,477	11.28
Per cent of total population receiving aid[2]	0.34	0.25	
Aid to the blind:			
Payments	$1,283,200	$6,715,300	16.04
Persons receiving aid	18,933	79,452	19.24
Per cent of total population receiving aid[2]	0.12	0.05	
General assistance:			
Payments[4]	$1,743,000	$19,805,000	8.09
Families receiving aid[4]	32,371	742,629	4.18
Per cent of total families receiving aid[2]	0.84	1.80	

SOURCE: Published and unpublished reports of the Department of Health, Education, and Welfare and the U.S. Bureau of the Census.
  1. Kentucky data included in Appalachian figures are for December 1962.
  2. Based on 1960 U.S. census data (8.5% of the U.S. population, 8.6% of the total

trends and provide a basis for understanding the extensive involvement of welfare programs in the economy of the region. The county's unemployment rate was 6.8 per cent in 1957 and 19 per cent in 1959. In 1961, unemployment affected 24.2 per cent of the county's total labor force of about 20,000 workers. *Vocational disability*—at the same time a cause and an effect of persistent poverty—was found among 11 per cent of the county's population in the sixteen to sixty-four age group.

An average of 14,500 people, 23.6 per cent of the total population, received monthly welfare payments. Money allocated to that county for welfare programs increased from $181,000 in 1940 to more than $2 million in 1960. Not included in the allocations for direct payments was surplus food, valued at $1 million annually, distributed to an average of 16,800 persons. Income maintenance through Social Security payments ($426,000) and unemployment compensation ($1 million) added substantially to total welfare costs.

Inadequate Housing

Another index of poverty is the condition of housing. In Appalachia, 26.6 per cent of the homes need major repairs and 7.5 per cent are in such a dilapidated condition that they endanger the health and safety of the families (Table 11). The comparable percentages for the rest of the United States are 18.1 and 4.7, respectively. The situation is more aggravated in rural areas. Here almost one out of four homes has basic deficiencies that require correction to provide adequate housing; one out of ten is dilapidated. More than half of the farm homes lack adequate plumbing. In the

U.S. families, 8.1% of the total persons under 18 years of age and 8.8% of total persons age 65 and over resided in Appalachia in 1960).

3. There were 29 states with MAA programs in June 1963, including Alabama, Kentucky, Maryland, Pennsylvania, Tennessee, and West Virginia in Appalachia.

4. Appalachian data presented here are underrepresentative of the total Appalachian participation, due to the exclusion of data from Kentucky. Kentucky data were not available in a form which would allow the derivation of separate data for the Appalachian part of the state. This also explains the low percentage of the total families receiving general assistance.

rural sections of one state almost half of the homes need either major repairs or replacement, and more than three-fourths of the farm homes lack plumbing totally or have inadequate plumbing.

The value of Appalachian housing is far below that in the rest of the United States. The percentage of owner-occupied housing worth less than $5000 in Appalachia is double the U.S. average, while regional housing worth more than $15,000 is about half the national average. In each of these categories, the balance of the Appalachian states more closely resembles the national figure.

Table 11—Condition of Housing in the Appalachian Region, and the Balance of United States—1960

(number in thousands)

| | Condition of Housing | | | | | | |
| | SOUND | | DETERIORATING | | DILAPIDATED | | |
Area	Num-ber	Per Cent	Num-ber	Per Cent	Num-ber	Per Cent	Total
APPALACHIAN REGION[1]	3418	73.4	888	19.1	350	7.5	4655
Urban	1898	80.8	339	14.4	112	4.8	2348
Rural	1520	65.9	549	23.8	238	10.3	2307
Nonfarm	1302	66.6	449	22.9	205	10.5	1956
Farm	218	62.1	100	28.6	33	9.4	351
BALANCE OF UNITED STATES	43,933	81.9	7188	13.4	2542	4.7	53,663
Urban	32,901	85.7	4228	11.0	1279	3.3	38,409
Rural	11,031	72.3	2960	19.4	1263	8.3	15,254
Nonfarm	8763	72.8	2242	18.7	1034	8.6	12,039
Farm	2268	70.6	718	22.3	229	7.1	3215

1. Excludes Appalachian Ohio.

What Needs to Be Done: Program Recommendations

The program recommendations of the President's Appalachian Regional Commission fall into three groupings. The first two involve investment—in social overhead (transportation network, community facilities, and so on) and in human and economic resource development, which are closely interdependent. For example, investment in educational facilities alone, unaccompanied by other measures which would create employment opportunities, might actually hamper the region's economic progress by generating an increased out-migration of the more capable. Similarly, a single-minded development of the natural resources of Appalachia would be as ineffective now as it was in the past in sustaining regional income, unless it were coupled with programs designed to develop other job opportunities in industries which would process these resources. To achieve balanced programing in a total effort over a period of time, the third set of recommendations provides for an Appalachian Regional Commission to allow existing and proposed public and private agencies and interests at state, national, and local levels to focus on the realistically defined problems of this region.

The commission has identified *four priority areas of investment* for the immediate future:

[1] The provision of *access* both to and within the region.

[2] Programs to use the region's great *natural resources* —coal, timber, and arable land—more fully.

[3] *Construction of facilities* both to control and exploit the abundant rainfall of Appalachia.

[4] Programs in which immediate improvements in *human resources* can be attained.

The proposed programs of access and physical-resource development are validated only by the enlargement of hope and genuine opportunity they offer to this region's most valuable resource—its people. But programs must also be initiated which are focused more directly upon the people themselves.

The unmet needs of the people in Appalachia are primary—food, clothing, medical care, housing, basic education, skills, jobs, hope, dignity—and they are interrelated. The school-lunch program encourages attendance and assists scholarship. Adequate housing protects health. A decent job is necessary to the preservation of dignity.

With the exception of the health feature, the program recommended by the commission to meet the human needs of the Appalachian people is concentrated within existing activities of the federal, state, and local governments expanding and accelerating already authorized programs where known deficits exist in those funds available for Appalachia.

Human Resources

TRAINING AND EDUCATION

An unfilled job is more than a man unemployed. The potential employee and his family remain at the survival level; the direct and multiplied product of the employee are lost. Present opportunities are unfulfilled because qualified applicants are scarce. The combination of too few vocational-school buildings and a hostile terrain, for example, has seriously restricted the area effectively served by existing schools.

The Manpower Development and Training Act, the Vocational Education Act, and the Cooperative Research Act should be supplemented in order to provide for in-service training of teachers, development of instructional materials, and demonstration and research projects.

An immediate effort should also be made to reduce the high incidence of illiteracy in Appalachia. Training programs for specific skills are inapplicable where the prospective trainee can neither read nor write. New amendments to existing training legislation permit heavy emphasis on the problems of illiteracy, but special funding is essential to meet the region's greater needs.

Unless education, training, and retraining are intensified, tomorrow's opportunities will be lost. Action here will require greatly increased expenditures in the whole field of training. The efforts of state and local government to increase their own spending will be to some extent frustrated by the inadequacy of the region's tax base.

EMPLOYMENT SERVICES

Appalachia's relatively dispersed rural, nonfarm population requires special attention. The size of present staffs has prevented their doing much more than servicing claims for unemployment compensation. Emphasis has necessarily been on past problems rather than future opportunities. Counseling, guidance, registration, and placement, both for jobs and for training, will be possible only if the employment services within the region can be expanded significantly.

VOCATIONAL REHABILITATION

Vocational-rehabilitation opportunities for the mentally and physically disabled must be extended and improved through the provision of comprehensive vocational rehabilitation services, with special emphasis on physical restoration and other remedial services, as well as on prevocational and vocational training. The importance of this program in a region characterized by high-risk employment and poor health is obvious. Mining, particularly, has left its scars upon the men of the region. For all of these men, the rehabilitation services offer a new opportunity to live a satisfying and productive life; this opportunity should be extended to greater numbers.

WELFARE SERVICES

Emphasis upon programs designed to broaden the future for many must not obscure the fact that for others, less fortunate, welfare assistance will be necessary. Community welfare resources need to be strengthened. The welfare services which form a part of the underpinning of satisfactory economic and social life, such as homemaker services, day-care services for children, foster care, and other child-welfare services, and programs and centers for older persons, should be expanded within Appalachia. In addition, it should be recognized that financial support will continue to be necessary for many aged, disabled, and mothers with children.

The emphasis should be on constructive programs. More states should extend the aid to dependent children program to families where parents are unemployed, and should couple this program with a community work and training program. Under such a program, welfare recipients not only perform important community tasks which would otherwise go undone but they also receive training and education which can become a bridge to more gainful employment. Special funds for demonstration programs and technical assistance should be appropriated.

HEALTH

The region's shortcomings in training and in skills are matched by health and nutritional deficits. These needs warrant the initiation of several demonstration community health centers—including the construction and operation of fixed and mobile medical facilities, the hiring and training of personnel, the treatment of water and sewage (Table 7), and pest control—in areas selected both with reference to need and to promise.

The *regional health center* would provide space for many activities in maternal and child health, mental health, chronic and communicable diseases. There would be diagnostic services as well as rapid screening for health defects. The center would include under one roof all personnel, records, laboratories, and conference and training facilities. Office space would be made available to encourage physicians and dentists to practice in the distressed area. Space for research personnel would be provided. Environmental health services would be programed and coordinated from the health centers.

NUTRITION

The nutritional problems of the region persist despite the dedicated efforts of state and federal officials who administer the federal school-lunch and commodity-distribution programs. Increased funds will be needed to permit the extension of the school-lunch program to those schools not now participating. The commodity-distribution program cannot, however, be corrected by simply adding additional funds. The very nature of the program restricts the variety of the foods distributed; as a result many suffer from a lack of certain essential nutrients. The food-stamp program— which has operated in selected pilot counties in Appalachia —has demonstrated its merit in overcoming these deficiencies.

Housing

Health is also threatened, in many instances, by inadequate housing. The need of the elderly and the disabled for housing may be met through an expansion of the Farmers Home Administration's program of small grants to rural homeowners with severely restricted earning potential. But many in the region could afford to improve or replace their inadequate housing if adequate credit resources were locally available. The need for additional credit resources is dramatically demonstrated by the oversubscription of the Farmers Home Administration's loan program for rural homeowners. Lack of funds forces a continual turning away of applicants, with the result that substandard housing persists, suppliers' opportunities are diminished, and employment opportunities never come into existence.

These elements are but a partial catalogue of the human needs of Appalachia. The needs are apparent; they can be measured both by slide rule and by human eye. But the poverty they represent is not one of the spirit. The traditional rugged independence of the Appalachian people, although eroded in some areas, is still the base upon which any recovery program must be founded.

If their elemental needs can be met, these people will take whatever additional action is necessary to achieve full participation in the nation's expanding economic thrust. No single program can be devised to answer these fundamental requirements. Instead, a variety of programs must be brought into a coordinated attack. The "mix" will vary with the situation and must necessarily remain flexible.

Proposed Regional Organization

In seeking a developmental organization tailored to the nature and dimensions of the Appalachian problem, the Commission recognizes two extremes of size which that organization must serve: the bigness of the total region and the smallness of the local jurisdiction. The approach and the structure must be regional to encompass the diversity of problems which are found in so large a region. It must also be able to assist the states' efforts to aid the multitude of local development units which alone can carry out the arduous, day-by-day work of development.

The new developmental organization must also perform the vital function of *coordinating the many programs now conducted* in the region by federal, state, and local agencies. There have been countless past examples of successful cooperation in meeting a specific problem, but in many instances, governmental units cannot spare the funds or the personnel essential to a well-planned, interagency or intergovernmental cooperative effort.

The new organization would offer a continuing instrument for such cooperation in the future, serving as a *clearinghouse* for all such public units and private development activities within the region. The clearinghouse could provide an area or community with specific solutions already proven successful elsewhere. Wasteful duplication of research could be avoided, and desperately needed state and local funds could be more effectively spent. The new organization would assume the following responsibilities:

1. Inventory and analyze the region's resources, sponsoring research necessary for policy, program, and plan development.

2. Suggest formulas for adapting federal allocation procedures to meet the particular needs of Appalachia; to review federal, state, local, and private programs and, where appropriate, recommend modifications which will increase their effectiveness.

3. Encourage and assist the formation of multicounty development districts designed to aid the small, technically inadequate local jurisdiction.

To fulfill these responsibilities, *the Commission has proposed the creation of an Appalachian Regional Commission* composed of the governor (or his appointee) of each participating state and a federal representative appointed by the President. A state representative and the President's representative would serve as co-chairmen; an executive director would direct the business of the Commission.

The Commission should create citizens' councils to advise it on general or specific regional problems, and it should work with appropriate local organizations or jurisdictions in carrying out regional projects. Existing organizations, such as the various area development groups, municipal authorities, and municipalities themselves, would be appropriate local organizations or "development districts," where they are approved by the state. Where appropriate local organizations do not exist, the commission may assist in the establishment of development districts and may provide technical assistance to them, as well as to state and local agencies and to private parties.

The Commission believes that solutions to the problems of Appalachia can be found—indeed, must be found, since time has shown that its passage alone does not solve, but only deepens, problems. It is no less evident, from experience, that the unique tangle of problems in Appalachia calls for a uniquely tailored program, and that neither the states alone nor the federal government alone are adequate to this challenge which involves them both so closely.

Recognizing that it is essential to begin, the Commission has recommended that the federal, state, and local governments act in concert, within a framework which permits their cooperation and encourages private initiative. This, it feels, is the only possibly successful approach.

NOTES

1. This article was published originally in *Health, Education, and Welfare Indicators*, June 1964.

Poverty
and the Law

ZONA FAIRBANKS HOSTETLER

*Laws grind the poor, and the rich men
rule the law.*
—Oliver Goldsmith

One outgrowth of the recent national concern with poverty has been an awareness—indeed, a revelation to many—that law affects the lives and affairs of the poor with far more immediacy than had been previously suspected.[1] It has been a common assumption, of lawyers and nonlawyers alike, that since the poor do not have valuable assets or business affairs, they do not have legal problems—except, perhaps, for those occasions when they are tried for criminal activities.[2] The fact of the matter is that practically all aspects of everyday life for the poor are fraught with legal problems. For the poor man, rental of an apartment, purchase of a car, application for unemployment compensation, welfare aid, medical care, or Social Security, may all present major legal crises. Not only does the poor man have legal problems, but he often has them in multiples, though he may not have recognized all of them as such. Worse, many of the poor have legal problems without respite.[3] Moreover, law affects the poor adversely, and in a discriminatory manner, because for all practical purposes they are excluded from the legal process by which law is used, tested, challenged, and shaped to redress grievances and obtain justice. While the comments that follow are more impressionistic than exhaustive, it is the purpose of this paper to suggest that disenfranchisement and alienation from the legal process are an integral part of the pattern of life of the poor.[4]

Buyer Beware

Purchases of merchandise are an important part of the lives of the poor. Although we have not generally thought of the poor as a major buying group, David Caplovitz, in his book *The Poor Pay More,* has revealed that not only do the poor buy,[5] but their lack of shopping sophistication and vulnerability to "easy credit" schemes subjects them to exploitation and legal entanglements. The following case example is typical.[6]

> Mrs. Williams is a mother of seven children and supports them on a monthly income of $218 received from public welfare. Nevertheless, a furniture firm sold her several items of furniture over a period of time including a stereo set for $514. For each purchase she entered into a separate installment contract with the firm. She was never given copies of the contracts. Subsequently, after months of payments, it was discovered that the contracts had interlocking clauses and the fine print allowed the firm to repossess all of the items purchased as soon as there was a single delinquent payment on any item. The trial court held that Mrs. Williams had signed a contract which was binding and not against "public policy."[7]

One of the interesting things about consumer practices of the poor is that, notwithstanding the fact that many of

them are bad credit risks, credit purchasing is nonetheless
easily available to all—even to those who are unemployed
and whose entire income consists of welfare payments.
Merchants extending such credit use high mark-ups to cover
their risk. In Caplovitz's study, 40 per cent paid more than
$300 for their television sets, and 13 per cent paid more
than $500.[8] In some instances the goods are openly sold at
high prices. In most cases, the inflated price is hidden in
installment payments, finance charges, service fees for late
payments, insurance, and legal costs. In many states the
seller is under no obligation to make clear to the buyer what
the total cost of the purchase will be. In addition, credit
charges are not regulated in all states, and most state courts
have held that general usury statutes do not apply to credit
sales.[9]

Failure to meet installment payments frequently results in immediate repossession. In some jurisdictions, repossession of items without the return of equity is illegal
—yet most of the poor have no idea of the law or how to
enforce it. In many cases the items sold and subsequently
repossessed are of such inferior quality that little is realized
upon resale to another buyer. To the astonishment of most
poor persons, they find that though they no longer have
the merchandise, they are still legally liable for the difference between what the merchant receives upon reselling
the repossessed goods and the original contract price, plus
interest, court fees, and other charges. Here is a second case
example:

> Mr. X who supports his family on an annual income of
> $3800 went to a used car dealer to look at old cars. He had
> been drawn there by a newspaper advertisement of a "re-
> possessed Chevrolet for $600 with $1 down." When he
> arrived he was told that the Chevrolet had been sold. The
> salesman then talked him into buying a Cadillac assuring
> him that it was in tip-top condition, that he, the salesman,
> had been driving it to and from work, and that everything
> was in perfect working order. He further assured Mr. X that

he would take care of any needed repairs discovered within sixty days. Mr. X bought the car, turning in his old car, paying $300 down (which he had to borrow) and signing an installment contract and negotiable note for $1600. Two days later, the car was unable to pass the state required inspection and $140 was needed to repair the brakes, steering and lights. Two weeks later, the transmission died. Mr. X complained to the car dealer who said he would take care of repairing the car. The car was never repaired. A few weeks later, a finance company repossessed the car for lack of payments, sold it for $300 and then brought suit against Mr. X for $1554. In the meantime the car dealer had gone out of business.[10]

Mr. X's automobile was sold for a mere $300 despite the fact that it had been sold to him only two months previously for $1900. This could be evidence that the car was originally sold to Mr. X at an exorbitant mark-up. It could also be evidence of a not uncommon practice whereby two or three merchants or finance companies band together and buy each other's repossessed goods at low prices. In most states, the sale of the repossessed car would have to be the best that could be reasonably obtained, preferably at a well advertised public auction, but even if the buyer knew this, proving that the sale had been a fraudulent one would be difficult, particularly without investigative and legal help.

A frequent practice of "easy credit" merchants is to sell promptly the installment contract and negotiable note to a finance company. In many jurisdictions, the finance company, unless it can be proved that it is in partnership with the seller, is not liable for the misrepresentations or the promises of the seller and is entitled to the full sum set forth in the agreement, plus interest and costs. The buyer's only recourse in such a case is to bring a suit for fraud against the seller, but the buyer usually does not know what his legal remedy might be, does not have a lawyer, and cannot prove his case.

I bought a set of pots and pans from a door-to-door salesman. *They were very poor quality and I wanted to give them*

*back but they wouldn't take them. I stopped paying and told
them to change them or take them back. . . . They started
bothering me at every job I had.* Then they wrote to my
current job and my boss is taking $6 *weekly from my pay
and sending it to pay this.*[11]

Harassing, nasty and humiliating telephone calls at
home, at work, at all hours of the day and night, day after
day without letup, to both the buyer and his relatives,
friends, and employer are a common collection tactic of
exploiting merchants and their collection agents. Calls on
the job are very effective because many employers feel that
they cannot afford the extra clerical costs of making complicated payroll deductions and forwarding garnishment
payments, nor do they want to be bothered themselves with
harassing calls. Thus they do not hesitate to fire workers
who are having debt difficulties. Sometimes, as happened
in the case noted above, the employer may enter into an
agreement with the creditor without regard to the validity
of the debtor's claim that he does not owe anything.

Even where the buyer is unemployed, the merchant can
find effective ways of coercing him into paying. Thus, in
New York, where it is against the Welfare Department's
rules for a welfare recipient to buy on credit, a favorite tactic of unscrupulous creditors is to threaten disclosure of
such purchases to the welfare authorities.

Tenant Traps

Exploitation also occurs in the housing area. That the
poor pay proportionately higher rents than the middle class
for what they get in return is now well known. That the
premises rented are more often than not in disrepair, rat-
infested, without adequate heating or plumbing, and in
violation of housing codes, is also well known. Less well
known is the extent to which landlords have been able to
use the legal process to perpetuate slum conditions. A case
example:

Mrs. X rented a small frame tenement row house in the city for herself and her five children. The banister was loose when she moved in, but the landlord promised to repair it. He never did. Subsequently it broke beneath the weight of a two year old child causing him to fall and break a leg. Mrs. X had the banister fixed and sent the bill to the landlord. He refused to pay citing the fine print in the lease that the tenant was liable for all repairs including those caused by structural defect.

A lease clause making the tenant responsible for repairs caused by structural defects is common in slum areas. In the foregoing case, the landlord used a store-bought lease form but inserted an unconscionable condition.[12] The middle-class tenant rarely faces this trap, because few landlords expect that they can take such advantage of their "better clients." Even where the slum landlord has the technical responsibility for making repairs, he frequently ignores his obligation. The demands for housing in urban areas, particularly in the crowded slum ghettos, are so great that landlords are under no pressure to make repairs, even when the premises are in gross violation of a city's housing code. They know that there is always someone else willing to move in.

In many cities when serious violations of the housing code are disclosed, the family can be evicted for living in unsuitable conditions. If the family is not evicted, the landlord can usually claim successfully that he is unable to repair the premises while they are occupied.

It is very difficult to enforce housing codes against slum landlords. Quite often, the most that is done is to give the landlord a warning or to assess a small nondeterrent fine against him. In many instances, when the landlord is forced to make repairs, he then taxes their cost to the tenant under the lease provision making the tenant responsible for all repairs. If the tenant doesn't pay the assessed costs, he is subject to eviction under the lease. Finally, tenants are discouraged from lodging complaints about needed repairs with the authorities by the threat of retaliatory eviction or rent increase.

In some cases, particularly retaliatory eviction cases, a slum landlord evicts a tenant without any notice and without giving the tenant any chance to appear in court. One way to accomplish this is simply to tell the tenant who does not know any better that he is "evicted" as of that moment. In New York City, it is such a frequent practice for the landlord or his hired process server to throw away the notice of eviction proceedings that the practice has become known in legal circles as "sewer service."[13] In other cases the slum landlord acts pursuant to another unconscionable provision inserted in the lease whereby the tenant waives any right to notice of an eviction hearing.

Even when a landlord acts wholly lawfully, the regular eviction procedures often work to the disadvantage of the slum tenant. In most states, landlord-tenant cases are heard in a summary proceeding. Summary proceedings are intended to provide an early and informal hearing where both parties can present their sides of the case to the judge. In fact, what happens is that the landlords are represented by lawyers but the tenants are not. The result is that only one side of the case is articulated. Another feature of summary proceedings is that personal notice is not required. In New York, for example, the landlord is required only to mail the tenant a copy of the notice and to nail a copy to the door. Nancy LeBlanc, of Mobilization for Youth's Legal Service Division, describes the use of this eviction procedure as follows:

> Unfortunately, it is my conclusion based on several hundred cases, that the process server almost never "nails," he only mails. Since in summary proceedings, the tenant has only five days in which to answer from the date of service, the fact that he receives his notice only by mail means he usually has three days to answer, not five. . . . Further, the five day rule is strictly enforced, so that a tenant must

either obtain the consent of the landlord or an order from court to file a late answer.

Since personal service is not required, another serious problem often arises—that of nonservice. . . . and the first time [the tenant] learns an action is pending against him is when he receives the notice from the City Marshal that he is to be evicted in 24 hours. At this point, the tenant must have immediate legal help if he wants to defend against the action. If he wants to pay the rent, and the landlord is willing to take it, he will usually be charged a heavy fee for the Marshal's costs—generally 3 or 4 times as much as the landlord would be permitted to collect if the tenant went to court and the court set costs.[14]

Finally, the use of eviction procedures as a collection device for nonpayment of rent also has harsh effects on poor tenants. Many slum landlords don't bother trying to collect overdue rent. They simply bring an eviction proceeding within one to three days after the rent is delinquent. This means that for a poor person, any sickness, unemployment, cessation of a welfare check, or other emergency, reaches crisis proportions when the rent payment comes due.

The Elusive Remedy

More important than the fact that the poor are continually beset with legal problems different in kind, magnitude, and frequency from those encountered by the general population is that the mechanisms for adjusting legal problems do not operate the same way for a poor man as they do for one with means.

The poor man usually has no idea that he has a legal remedy nor where he can go to seek help.[15] Caplovitz reports in his study that when asked where they would go for help if cheated by a merchant, some 64 per cent did not know. They could not name any community agency such as the Small Claims Court, the Legal Aid Society, or the Better Business Bureau. Only 3 per cent said they would turn to a lawyer, and only 9 per cent of those with problems actually did seek professional help.[16] Even in those instances when the poor man suspects that he has a legal remedy, other obstacles stand in his way. The following, for example, is a very realistic obstacle faced by many:

> My wife and I bought some furniture and for the first few months we paid our money to the store. Then the store sold out, so we had to start paying the second store. (The second store noted what they had already paid in their payment book, but it did not appear in the store's own records.) *The store told us they were going to take us to court if we didn't pay $150 more. But I'd rather pay the extra money than go to court and lose any days of work, because I just got my job and I don't want to risk it.*[17]

Without the assistance of counsel, there are serious psychological obstacles to overcome. For example, a landlord-tenant proceeding appears to the slum tenant to be stacked against him. He first receives a form piece of paper telling him to appear at the courthouse on a certain day. Assuming that he understands the import of the paper and overcomes the problems of getting to the courthouse, when he arrives, the scene is one of baffling confusion to him. No one is there to help those inexperienced in the ways of the courthouse. The tenant may eventually find his way to the clerk's office where the usual early-hour bedlam reigns. Lawyers are bustling about, calling upon harassed clerks for files and docket sheets, signing papers, and filing documents. It is a bewildering sight to the nonlawyer, even if he is fairly educated—to the poor man it is incomprehensible. If the latter manages to work his way to the clerk's desk, a busy clerk may finally take notice of him and ask him what he wants. The inarticulate, confused tenant doesn't know what he wants. He starts telling about how he received a piece of paper, shuffling through his pockets for it. The clerks are not social workers and they have little patience or sympathy with the numbers of tenants who appear each day, and their attitudes unmistakably reflect this. At the outset the encounter with the legal process is bewildering and unfriendly at best.

The tenant may finally locate the courtroom in which his case will be heard.[18] There his suspicion that the law is for the "rich man" may be symbolically reinforced by the physical setup of the room. Typically, there is an area of several yards around the judge's bench which is marked off by a waist-high partition. Inside the partition sit the landlords, or their agents, and their lawyers. (Rarely does a tenant have a lawyer.) The landlords, their agents and lawyers, are well-dressed in suits and ties, and there is an atmosphere of conviviality and acquaintanceship among them as they chat amiably with each other. When the judge arrives, he too is often included in the group by an exchange of friendly comments and looks of mutual understanding. Moreover, those within the partition speak a common language replete with references to technical legal terms which are wholly foreign to the tenants.

On the outside of the inner circle stretch the rows of tenants, miserably dressed and obviously poor. There is little talk as each sits quietly, some clutching in their hands a wad of dirty dollar bills. Then the ritual begins. The clerk starts by reading aloud the names of delinquent tenants. The majority of tenants do not show up, so that the names are read in rather rapid succession, with the landlord or his lawyer coming in on cue after each name with the word *default*, followed by the judge on cue, *judgment*. The monotony of the recital has some resemblance to a bingo game with an occasional response from the tenants' row, whereupon the game is halted momentarily to the sometimes obvious inconvenience of those in the inner circle. The tenant very self-consciously makes his way to the front of the room, where he haltingly (or sometimes with false bravado) starts explaining that he has had unexpected medical bills, or the house doesn't have any heat. In many courts he is interrupted rudely and asked if he's got "the money" with him. If he does, he pays, including interest and costs, and is curtly dismissed. If he does not, the landlord may agree to give him another five days or so in which to pay, upon failure of which judgment will automatically ensue and the marshal can be sent to evict without further hearing. If he cannot promise to pay or the landlord isn't willing to wait, he is told that within a few days the marshal will appear and move all of his belongings onto the street. The tenant may protest that his family has no place to go. A benevolent judge will direct him to a social-welfare agency, which, in the face of acute housing shortages, can often do little more than offer sympathy, and perhaps refer him for a night's emergency lodging when such emergency lodging is available.

Middle-Class Advantage

For the middle-class person the procedures for resolving disputes are different.[19] In the first place, when he feels that he has been the victim of a fraudulent deal or that the landlord is violating the housing code, he knows that remedies are available to him. As an educated citizen, he can often deal with it on his own. A call, or a threat to call, the Better Business Bureau, a lawyer, or the city authorities may be enough to take care of the matter. As a next step, the actual employment of an attorney can work miracles. Frequently a mere telephone call from a lawyer to the effect that he is representing John Doe will be sufficient. In any event, the man of means can employ counsel either to solve a complicated tangle of legal questions arising out of a dispute, or to create one.

Having an attorney is helpful in other ways. For example, if a case is continued at the request of the complaining party or of the court, the rules require that a brother member of the bar be notified, and indeed often his permission must be obtained. Cases may be continued or postponed at the request of a lawyer, but generally not for a defendant acting on his own. In some instances, a friendly clerk of the court will notify the lawyer at his office just before it is necessary for him to appear. In many legal proceedings it isn't necessary for the client to appear if his lawyer is there. In some instances, information about a man's case will be given by the court clerk over the phone to his lawyer, but not to the individual himself.

Even when a middle-class citizen has no legal defense to the action, but has simply failed to make payments on a lease or sales contract, the use of the legal process is different. Landlords and creditors seldom resort to court on the first day or two after nonpayment by a person of means, and thus the tenant or debtor has additional time to make up the debt. Moreover, the person of means can absorb a financial loss to a fraudulent seller more easily, and the delays, loss of work, and legal costs of taking a case to court as well.

Most important of all, the middle-class citizen with a valid defense and an attorney to represent him has a meaningful opportunity to present his side of the case. The poor man does not. In a landlord proceeding, for example, the action may be dismissed because notice was not served on the tenant, or the required amount of time for quitting the premises was not set forth accurately in the notice, or the landlord never actually demanded the rent prior to commencing the action. These are rather technical arguments, but any good lawyer would present them on behalf of a client. The poor man, who does not have a lawyer, does not have the benefit of these defenses. The fact that they exist for his benefit in theory does not help him if they are not presented. The same is true of substantive defenses such as failure to deliver the goods purchased, breach of warranty, or fraud in inducing the purchaser to buy. Without a lawyer to amass the proof and present the legal arguments, the poor man is deprived of an otherwise valid defense and perhaps of a valuable counterclaim as well.

Moreover, without a lawyer, certain legal defenses may never be tried. For example, in the recent New York City rent strikes, the tenants refused to pay rent to slum land-lords under an obscure section of the New York Real Prop-erty Law, permitting them to pay the rent to the court until the landlord corrected outstanding violations of the city's housing code. What is interesting is that though this law had long been on the books, prior to the recent offer of legal assistance to the residents of Harlem and the Lower East Side, the law was virtually unused—not only the landlords' attorneys but the judges were unaware of its existence and its provisions.[20]

In the absence of a lawyer, new legal theories may never be advanced, nor new legal principles established. Miss LeBlanc and her colleagues of the legal services unit of Mo-bilization for Youth are now presenting imaginative legal arguments on behalf of their tenant clients on New York's Lower East Side. One interesting question presently on ap-peal is this: when the tenant proves that he was never served (so that the entire dispossession proceeding, includ-ing the eviction, are void), can he reoccupy the apartment from which he was illegally evicted? As Miss LeBlanc notes, "Since tenants have for years been illegally evicted, it is a remarkable tribute to the general unavailability of legal counsel to poor people that this question has never been re-solved by the courts of New York State."[21]

Another handicap that stems from being without a lawyer is that cases are not appealed. And only when there is an appellate court decision is it considered binding on similar cases before lower court judges. Thus, in the land-lord-tenant area again, the decision of one judge is not bind-ing on another. As Miss LeBlanc notes:

> . . . without an appellate decision as precedent, each judge
> is king in his own courtroom, the law which is applied is
> extremely uneven, and the results obtained in any one case
> depends more upon which judge hears the case than the
> merits of the case, the preparation of witnesses, and the skill
> of the lawyer, if the tenant has one. This does not instill in
> tenants very much respect for the law—rather it suggests

. . . that there really is no such thing as a "rule of law."[22]

Inequality before the law occurs in almost every kind of legal proceeding. This can be illustrated by the differing results shared by all income groups in one kind of problem —marital discord. Divorce is a luxury available only to those who can afford attorneys' fees and court costs. In jurisdictions such as New York, where there are few legal grounds for divorce, the rich may get a divorce by visiting Mexico and Reno, but this alternative does not exist for the poor. Even in less strict jurisdictions, divorce is available only to those who can afford to hire a private lawyer and pay the costs.

Thus the woman in poverty who marries at sixteen and who two years later is deserted by her husband is doomed to a life of "official" but hardly satisfying marriage. Her only chance for a husband-wife relationship is an illicit one, with the consequent birth of illegitimate children and its attendant stigma and psychological damage. Even if a second man is willing to marry her and assume legal responsibility for the children, he cannot do so unless she obtains a divorce. But she cannot obtain a divorce without a lawyer, and it is almost impossible to obtain one.[23] Most legal-aid organizations inexplicably refuse to handle divorce actions. The few that will, often attach conditions that are not generally required of the population at large. For example, the legal-aid organization may insist that the parties must first make use of a marital reconciliation scheme of the agency. The scheme may be a good one, but the fact remains that the poor are required to do something that others are not. Some legal-aid organizations will represent a client in a divorce action only if the divorce will be "socially useful." This again is the use of a double standard, since the well-to-do can have a divorce when there are legal grounds for it, but the poor can have one only when there are both legal grounds, and the divorce is viewed as socially useful. There is the further dubious presumption that a legal-aid lawyer

has the ability to determine what is or is not "socially useful." The policy manual of one legal-aid organization indicates that in the example noted above divorce would be
deemed socially useful. But obviously such a policy penalizes the woman who simply wants to be freed of a deserting
husband in order to marry another and have lawful children. In effect the policy requires that she first enter into
an unlawful relationship and have illegitimate children before she will be given the benefit of legal assistance in securing a divorce to which she is legally entitled under the laws.

Government and the Accused

Not only in their disputes with each other and with
other private citizens are the poor at a disadvantage, but
this situation holds in their encounters with officialdom
too. Even the area which has been the most publicized bat-
tleground of the poor and the law—the criminal area—has
been fraught with inequality, notwithstanding the fact that
judgment against the poor here means not only loss of property but loss of liberty and even life as well.[24]

Public attention has, of late, focused on the inequities
of the criminal process vis-à-vis the poor.[25] Much has been
written about the recent Supreme Court decision (*Gideon
v. Wainwright*) that a state conviction could not stand because the government had not provided the defendant with
a lawyer as he had requested.[26] The only surprising thing
about the decision is that it was not made long ago, especially since the indispensability of counsel to a fair trial has
been known for some time.[27] In 1932 Justice Sutherland
wrote:

> The right to be heard would be, in many cases, of little
> avail if it did not comprehend the right to be heard by coun-
> sel. Even the intelligent and educated layman has small and
> sometimes no skill in the science of law. If charged with
> crime, he is incapable, generally, of determining for himself
> whether the indictment is good or bad. He is unfamiliar with

the rules of evidence. Left without the aid of counsel he may
be put on trial without a proper charge and be convicted
upon incompetent evidence or evidence irrelevant to the issue
or otherwise inadmissable. He lacks both the skill and the
knowledge adequately to perform his defense, even though
he may have a perfect one . . . he faces the danger of
conviction because he does not know how to establish his
innocence.[28]

Other questions regarding adequate representation of
indigent defendants were not covered by the Gideon decision, and, therefore, still remain for future resolution. Thus
the question of legal counsel for persons accused of misde-
meanors is still unsettled. Indigent persons are now tried,
sentenced, and convicted for substantial periods of time
without benefit of counsel. Clearly the truth of Justice Sutherland's statement as to the indispensability of counsel to a
fair trial is not contingent upon the length of time one's liberty is to be taken away. Even where a suspended sentence
is given, the convicted person still has a record for life which
not only damages his reputation and causes him and his
family personal anguish, but it may also be a basis for re-
voking his driver's license or his right to vote, suspending
his security clearance, denying him a job, or even preclud-
ing his admission to governmental job training programs.

The Gideon decision did not deal with the fact that indigent persons brought before juvenile courts are not everywhere entitled to free counsel, nor are persons whose paroles
are about to be denied or revoked, nor are jailed persons who
believe they have been convicted by unconstitutional procedures.[29] Of particular significance is the fact that a state is
not yet under any obligation to provide counsel to an arrested indigent at all stages prior to trial.[30] This means that
the poor man is at a decided disadvantage during the in-
terrogation proceedings and immediately thereafter. Upon
arrest, a man with money immediately obtains a lawyer
and is thereby protected from physical or mental coercion.
The poor man, however, must wait for whatever counsel

may be assigned him.[31] Arnold Trebach's study of convicted
prisoners in New Jersey penal institutions revealed that the
mean average length of time between arrest and first contact with assigned legal counsel for the indigent New Jersey
prisoner was 56.89 days and the median average was 35
days. In contrast, the mean average of those who could hire
a lawyer was 3.94 days and the median average less than
a day.[32]

Finally, simply appointing a lawyer to defend an indigent will not assure him a fair trial if the lawyer is not a
competent one who will give him something more than
cursory representation. Judge Lumbard has described the
practice of assigning counsel as follows:

> In many cities and in most of the counties in the United
> States, each judge assigns individual counsel in each case
> as needed. . . . When advised that an indigent needs coun-
> sel, the judge usually picks out some lawyer who happens to
> be in the courtroom. Many of the lawyers so assigned have
> been recently admitted to practice and have had little or no
> experience in criminal cases. The lawyer then spends a
> few minutes with his new-found client at the side of the
> courtroom or perhaps in an anteroom under the scrutiny of
> the bailiff or the Marshal. In most of such assignments, after
> a few minutes of conference, the defendant is advised to
> plead guilty, and he feels that he has no choice but to do so.
> Everyone who participates in these proceedings knows that
> this is a farce—the judge, the district attorney, the assigned
> lawyer, the bailiff, and, of course, the defendant himself.
> The point is that a defendant able to retain his own counsel
> gets far different treatment.[33]

Although the new Federal Criminal Justice Act and some
pending state bills provide compensation to assigned counsel, there is serious question in view of the fact that the fees
to be paid under such acts are very low—a maximum of
$500 in the federal act—whether any more qualified lawyers
than before will be induced to represent indigent defendants.
It has been suggested by some that the plans, if not care-

fully administered, will turn out to be legal aid for indigent lawyers.

There is also the question of whether there is equality before the law if the rich man can afford investigators, medical and psychiatric examinations, research assistants, and other aids to proving his case, and the poor man cannot. Under the new Criminal Justice Act, a maximum of $300 is to be allowed for such aids in federal courts. There is no general requirement of similar financial aid in state courts, where the majority of criminal cases are tried. Failure to uncover facts or present expert testimony at the trial level is particularly damaging to a man's case because under our adversary system, court decisions, including those of appeal courts, are made only on the basis of evidence which is in the record.[34] Poor persons are further disadvantaged in defending themselves at trial by court rules requiring the payment of fees to subpoena needed witnesses.[35]

In addition to the failure to provide poor defendants with competent counsel, and the means to uncover and present all of the evidence available in his behalf, the administration of criminal justice treats them unfairly in other ways. The practice of alternative sentences, for example, unjustly penalizes the poor no guiltier than others. As Supreme Court Justice Arthur Goldberg, has pointed out, the familiar "choice" of paying a fine of $100 or 30 days in jail is no choice at all to the man who cannot raise $100.[36]

The unfairness of jailing poor men for their failure to raise the bail money that men of means can do more easily is finally receiving nationwide attention.[37] A recent national study concludes that "all available studies confirm two dominant characteristics in the national bail pattern. In a system which grants pre-trial liberty for money, those who can afford a bondsman go free; those who cannot stay in jail."[38] Jail for the poor man has meant separation from family, loss of employment, stigma and expense to the city for imprisonment and relief to the family.[39] In addition, recent studies have statistically determined that defendants remaining in

jail are handicapped in preparing their defense, are much
more likely to be found guilty, and much less likely to be
granted probation.[40]

Some of the worst examples of unequal treatment by
the law occur in the area of law-enforcement practices. Arrests for vagrancy and alcoholism are typically arrests of
the poor. Indeed, the crime of vagrancy is typically defined
as "an idle person who loiters without visible means of support and fails to give a good account of himself."[41] It is the
poor who are subjected most to the clearly unconstitutional
police and judicial practice of "banishment"—that is, orders
to leave the state, county, town, or even section of town,
upon penalty of jail.[42] Arrests for what the police call "investigation" or "suspicion" are typically arrests of the poor.
Supreme Court Justice Arthur Goldberg in a lecture at New
York University Law School recently noted:

> When the police conduct a roundup of "suspects," they
> generally do so in poor neighborhoods, rarely in middle class
> communities. As a result, more poor than rich are arrested
> for crimes they did not commit. We do not know how many
> of these people lose or fail to obtain jobs because of an
> "arrest record" resulting from guiltless involvement in such
> episodes. Nor do we know how many poor people are even
> aware of their rights in such situations: for example, their
> right to consult an attorney, to sue for false arrest, or to have
> their arrest records expunged (in jurisdictions which have
> procedures permitting this). Moreover, psychologists and
> sociologists tell us that young people who are close to choos-
> ing a criminal identity may have this choice confirmed by
> their repeated treatment as a criminal type.[43]

There is class bias in the enforcement of homosexuality
and other sex laws. Thus, a man of means arrested for
homosexual and other deviant behavior will often be released without trial on the payment of a fine or promise to
seek psychiatric help.[44] Many practicing lawyers have been
able to get prosecutors to drop other less serious criminal
charges upon the promise to obtain medical or psychiatric

help for their clients. This is not to say that such clients, if in need of psychiatric or medical help, should not have this alternative, rather than being subjected to the criminal process; it is simply that under the present system, only those with means can have this option. The same is true of rich juveniles. As Professor Paulson of Columbia University has noted:

> Wealthy persons have delinquent children, of course, but they are quite often able to shield them from juvenile court, and therefore, from the possibility of probation supervision or commitment to a public institution. Restitution to the victim can be arranged. Private psychotherapy can be paid for, and, if necessary, a private institutional placement can be arranged.[45]

A National Social Welfare Assembly memorandum tells of a "growing tendency . . . to apply intentionally a different standard of law enforcement to persons because of their poverty especially if that poverty is reflected in dependence upon tax supported benefits such as public assistance." Examples given included the practice in three New Jersey counties of subjecting mothers of illegitimate children to prosecution under otherwise rarely enforced adultery and fornication laws upon their application for public assistance; the case of a Connecticut woman recently arrived from a southern state subjected to deportation proceedings; and the practice in several states of threatening to institute neglect proceedings with consequent removal of children from their mother's custody as a means of discouraging applications for assistance from unwed mothers. Thus, in Florida, according to the report:

> A mother of illegitimate children applying for assistance is granted aid if otherwise eligible but told that her situation must be studied by a special "review team" in order to determine whether court referral on neglect charges is not necessary. While relatively few referrals are actually made and virtually no children have been removed by court order, the effect on a group of mothers whose loyalty to their children

is a dominant characteristic has been dramatic—i.e., 45
per cent voluntarily withdrew from the assistance rolls.[46]

Government Giveth—and Taketh Away

While lawyers and lawmakers have lately begun to appreciate that unequal justice is afforded the poor man who
is confronted by government's criminal processes, they have
as yet paid scant notice to the disparate treatment afforded
him when he comes into contact with other institutions of
modern-day government—which is often.

Charles Reich in a noteworthy *Yale Law Journal* article
has documented the phenomenal development of local,
state, and federal government as a major source of wealth,
or what he terms "the new property."[47] Claims on this property are not within the exclusive province of the poor, of
course, but for the poor man, government payments of
Social Security, welfare aid, and unemployment compensation are literally a matter of life or starvation. Accompanying these lifeblood services are a myriad of legal
technicalities, rules, regulations, and procedures which have
an immediate impact upon the poor. Such laws, of course,
do not administer themselves—laws depend upon men for
interpretation, application, and execution. To a very large
extent, then, law for the poor man consists of those decisions by government and quasi-governmental personnel
who regularly deal with the poor. As Edward Sparer, Director of Mobilization for Youth's Legal Service Division, has
observed:

> No longer is the primary contact of the poor man with
> the law in the ordinary courtroom (criminal or otherwise)
> but in the anteroom of a city, state or federal agency as he
> awaits a determination of vital significance to him and his
> family.[48]

Reich notes with some alarm the fact that distribution of
government largesse has been increasingly made by government on its own terms, without the safeguards of pro-

cedural due process, and held by recipients subject to conditions which express the "public interest." Nowhere is this tendency more evident than when the recipients are the poor. More than any other group they are denied any "right" to government wealth, and more than any other group they are subject to arbitrary official control. Indeed, in many instances, the condition precedent to receiving public assistance because of poverty is a waiver of basic constitutional rights deemed by most men essential to individual freedom and dignity.

One of the worst violations of constitutional rights is the practice which exists in many jurisdictions whereby local welfare department officials arrive unannounced in the middle of the night to search the homes of persons receiving public assistance in order to check on their eligibility.[49] Often there are no warrants. In some instances there are mass raids designed as general checks on eligibility.[50] To date, no court case has ruled on the legality of such practices[51] although considerable consternation was caused in public-welfare circles by Professor Reich's article, in which he concluded, after reviewing the relevant case law, that midnight welfare searches are a "flagrant violation of the fourth and fourteenth amendments."[52] As Reich notes, however, "persons on public assistance are in no position to enforce a constitutional right of privacy. They lack the means and knowledge to litigate constitutional questions."

Another example is the much publicized LaFountain case in upper New York state. There five men on public assistance who had been participating in a state work program for families on public assistance were assigned to cut brush in near-zero temperatures along a country road where the snow was several feet deep. They refused to do this but offered to do other work. They were sent home and subsequently convicted to from four to eight months in prison for "a wilful act designed to interfere with the proper administration of public assistance and care." Thanks to the intervention of the American Civil Liberties Union, the New

York Court of Appeals reversed the conviction.[53] In some localities there is a practice of discouraging needy persons from applying for, or remaining on, relief rolls, by publicizing the names of welfare recipients. Indeed, newspapers covering the controversial Newburgh plan discovered that relief recipients were being photographed without their consent when they came to receive their checks. And then, there was the notorious attempt by the Virginia legislature in 1962 to make sterilization of indigents having more than a given number of children a condition precedent to welfare assistance. After much publicity the bill was amended to permit voluntary sterilization.[54]

In 1961 New York State passed a Welfare Abuses Act denying public assistance to any person (or his children) who came to New York with the primary purpose of getting on New York's public-assistance rolls. Within ten months, 2730 applicants for public assistance were denied relief on the ground that they had come to the state seeking it. The burden of proof was on the applicant that such was not his purpose. Emergency aid was given only to about one out of every nine rejected. After two years, as the number of rejectees had continued to mount, Edward Sparer interviewed some of the families and found them literally on the brink of starvation. Every case in which he intervened was reversed as he exposed the fact that undertrained caseworkers were regularly making two invalid presumptions in construing the act: (1) that a person who comes to New York without an adequate plan of support and presumably knowing that he or she will need welfare help, therefore comes for the purpose of obtaining welfare help; and (2) that emergency aid under the law should be given only to those who agree to leave the state. Sparer estimates that of the 2730 cases denied in the first 10 months alone, fully 2700 would have been reversed on appeal had appeals been taken.[55]

The Welfare Abuses Act has received a great deal of publicity, as have Sparer's successful defenses thereunder.

Most cases in most cities and towns go unnoticed and unchallenged. Yet "low visibility decisions" involving serious legal questions and vitally affecting the lives of the poor occur daily. A study of a private family-service agency in the District of Columbia[56] revealed, for example, that city welfare caseworkers had decreased the amount of welfare assistance to a family on the ground that a typewriter given to one of the members, a teenage student, so that she could teach herself typing, constituted additional "income"; a similar decision of "additional income" was made with respect to a scholarship covering tuition for night school courses at a community college, as well as to a tuition *loan*. Similar decisions of "additional income" have been made with regard to insurance and court-awarded damages for injuries or loss of goods.

Official decisions which Mobilization for Youth lawyers found had been made with respect to their clients included (1) the suspension of a deserted mother and her children from a welfare program because of anonymous complaints that she occasionally slept with a man; (2) the eviction from a public housing project of a man, his wife, and five children because of the imprisonment of a sixth offspring; (3) the suspension from school of a child that left him out on the street and out of school or any alternative occupation for several months; (4) the unemployment insurance referee's determination that a man had "provoked" his own firing and was therefore ineligible for such insurance; (5) the welfare department's refusal of assistance to a New York resident and her baby, born in New York and living there for over a year, on the ground that it would be more "socially valid" for her to live in another part of the country where her stepmother had allegedly offered her shelter (though nothing else), even though she would not be eligible for welfare aid in the other state because of her New York state residence.[57]

In the District of Columbia, there is a rule requiring a year's legal residency in the District before one is eligible for public assistance. The family-service-agency study[58] revealed that the following decisions had been made with regard to that requirement: (1) welfare assistance was denied to a child because during the summer he had gone to visit his grandmother for two months, and had, therefore, in the view of the welfare-department caseworker lost his legal status as a resident and could not regain it until he had lived in the District for another full year; (2) an entire family of eight children lost their status as "residents" when the mother accepted live-in employment as a domestic two miles away across the border in Maryland, even though the children remained in the family home in the District where they had lived since birth; (3) a mother and two infant children were held ineligible for welfare aid upon the imprisonment of the father for violation of the parole rules of another state on the ground that the father's violation made him a fugitive from justice. Apparently his being a fugitive from justice was deemed to taint the wife and child sufficiently to disqualify them from public aid, even though they had lived in the District two years.

Questions of residency can present very complex and technical legal questions even for lawyers. Yet low-level government workers are required to apply their own untutored views of the law, unchallenged and unreviewed. It might be noted that many lawyers believe that there is some question regarding the validity of basing eligibility for public welfare on residency criteria, but as with midnight welfare searches, no one has yet brought a test case.

A ruling of ineligibility because of lack of a year's residency has very harsh effects. The family which has just moved has no residency anywhere, either in the state moved to or the state moved from. Moreover, in most communities there is *no* agency, public or private (not even Travelers' Aid, which receives community funds only to help those actually in transit) to provide aid to families of children literally starving, until they have remained in one place for a year. For migrant families who are continually on the move, the plight is even worse—often they are never residents of any state.

Residency requirements are but one of the criteria used by welfare administrators to weed out "ineligibles."[59] Elimination of ineligibles, which is a primary preoccupation of the dispensers of government services to the poor, by its very nature, involves legal determinations; yet they are almost never challenged. Needless to say, there are no statistics available regarding the amount of death, illness, and human suffering caused by erroneous legal determinations.

Many times "low visibility decisions" are in conflict with each other. Consider the following story:

> There is the 19 year old mother of a small baby totally without income, who is ineligible for public assistance because she is, under Welfare Department rules, employable. Since she is utterly unskilled, Hospitality House tried to enroll her in a Federally-sponsored restaurant service training course. She was rejected, since the Employment Service wants the course to be successful and consequently discourages people who will be difficult to place. The girl is receiving no training then, because the Employment Service considers her unemployable, and she is receiving no relief because the Welfare Department insists on classifying her employable.[60]

The fact that questionable laws and legal determinations of government go unchallenged is due in large part to the failure of government to provide procedural safeguards. Nowhere do they seem to be more noticeably lacking than in those agencies dealing with the poor. With such agencies, the following questions are almost always pertinent:

How is the poor person even to know the grounds and basis for an adverse ruling?[61] How is a woman to rebut a presumption that because a man is found in her apartment one night he is in fact adequately supporting her and her children?[62] How is the person affected to know what kind of a factual presentation will alter the case and how to put forth such a presentation in the most advantageous posture?[63] How is the poor person to know whether the ruling

is consistent with the intent of the statute or with constitutional requirements, or even with similar decisions by the
same agency?[64]

For many agency determinations affecting the poor there
is no right of review or right to counsel. In other cases,
while the right may exist in theory, the aggrieved applicant
is never meaningfully advised of the right; active measures
are not taken to provide him with counsel, and nowhere is
there any mechanism for assuring that his case will be
presented completely, accurately, and in the best possible
light for him. Moreover, recent attempts by others to act as
advocates have not met with warm response on the part of
welfare administrators.[65]

In fact, there has been an almost total absence of advocacy on behalf of the poor before public agencies, especially
those that exist primarily for their benefit. The problem is
more deeply rooted than the mere lack of numbers of available advocates. As Edward Sparer has observed, not only
the legal profession, but the professionals in social work and
agency administration, as well as the great majority of the
public, simply have not accepted the basic proposition that
legal advocacy is as essential to justice where the poor are
the beneficiaries as where those with means are concerned.
Sparer attributes three rationales to this posture:

> First, it is widely thought that there is generally *no right*
> to governmental intervention and assistance; second, gov-
> ernmental agencies dealing with the poor are created to *help*
> the poor and not exploit the poor; therefore, legal help is
> hardly needed to contend with such agencies; third, govern-
> mental agencies dealing with the poor often base their judg-
> ments on *expert social evaluations* of what's best for any
> given poor person or family; to interject the rigidity and
> contentiousness of lawyers advocating against the position of
> the agency is, in result, to militate against the best interests
> of the poor themselves.[66]

In contrast, the importance of advocacy in the administrative process has long been recognized by those persons of
means affected by it.[67] Many a lawyer earns his living by

the representation of business clients before various administrative agencies. Such a client does not lack for rarefied arguments, novel legal theories, thorough research, creative ideas, legal scholarship, briefs, statistics, and documents in his effort to obtain a television channel, a zoning variation, or an airplane route. The presentation of his case is regarded by society as a healthy, countervailing pressure against administrative inertia or error, even well-meaning error, and against competing pressures on the agency brought by other interested groups. Moreover, no stigma attaches to an assertion of right to a governmental handout when that handout consists of a subsidy to an airline or maritime fleet unable to make it on its own. A handout to humans unable to make it on their own, however, is regarded quite differently. As Elizabeth Wickenden has so well stated: "The recipients or would-be recipients of public aid are not only the victims of every failure in our social system —from racial discrimination and unemployment to family desertion . . . but on top of all that they must carry the full weight of our generalized disapproval."[68] Yet it is essential to fair administrative law that the poor man's grievances and interests be as completely and forcefully asserted, and as respectfully heard and resolved, as those of the rich man. Recent suggestions have been made as to institutional means by which this might be accomplished.

Some have advocated the extension of traditional legal-aid programs to embrace comprehensive neighborhood legal assistance.[69] Others have called for the establishment of a community agency or agent similar to the Scandinavian *ombudsman* or the English Citizen's Advice Bureaus. An *ombudsman* is an "agent of the people" who hears and adjusts citizen complaints against government civil servants. A powerful and prestigious person, the *ombudsman* is concerned with both the petty and large cases of official abuse. His office reviews both civil and criminal proceedings to ferret out evidence of prejudice, favoritism, undue delays, and inequities. Visits are made periodically to prisons and

other institutions where private interviews are held with
inmates upon request. Free legal aid is recommended to
complainants who want to bring actions against state officials.[70] The English Citizens Advice Bureaus offer a variety
of neighborhood aids, including detailed advice and assistance with regard to governmental programs, laws, and
regulations.[71] Such neighborhood assistants are needed in
this country—and they need not be lawyers necessarily—
to help the poor person overcome the inconvenience and
demoralization he experiences in working his way through
the bureaucratic maze.[72] The important point is that lawyers,
public agents or *ombudsmen,* and citizen advocates, if
effective, are more than just "services." They are essential
to the viability of the rule of law and to restoring to the
alienated poor a sense of equal participation in the legal
process. As Attorney General Katzenbach has noted:

> You and I, in our daily lives, act as our own advocates.
> The poor do not. They concede defeat. They fear to argue
> because they fear retaliation. The poor need advocates, not
> simply to present their side of the story but to give them
> hope, to demonstrate that the law is not an enemy, but a
> guardian, and that public officials are not their masters, but
> their servants.[73]

A Public-Relief Saga

The almost total dependence on the legal determination
of someone else to provide daily sustenance, or to prevent
its being taken away, is exacerbated by the tortuous process
through which the poor must go to obtain the determination.
Delays, waiting rooms, endless uncertainty, red tape, more
delays and more waiting are an inevitable part of the price
one pays for government assistance. Nor are these attributes
found only in governmental organizations.[74]

The full impact of the process cannot be appreciated
until one has followed all the steps in detail. The story of
a typical case handled by legal-aid lawyers in the District
of Columbia would read as follows:

Mrs. X is the wife of an uneducated laborer and the mother of six children. Sometimes the husband gives his wife money for rent, food, and clothing, and sometimes he does not. Sometimes he disappears for several weeks and the family is left destitute. His income varies according to whether he works, which sometimes he does and sometimes he does not. In good weather his fortune in finding a job is better, and he can make a subsistence income. Sometimes he pays the rent and other bills and sometimes he does not.

After a particularly long absence, when the children are hungry, perhaps kept home from school because of inadequate clothing or in need of medical care, the wife, who is down to her last dollar or two, may apply for public assistance. First, there is the difficulty of getting to the public-welfare office (there is only one central office and it is necessary to apply in person unless the applicant is incapacitated). Upon her arrival, there is the usual depressing waiting room, forms to fill out, and long delay before someone can see her. She will then be interviewed. After answering numerous questions about the most personal details of her life, she will then be informed that she is ineligible for assistance because she has a husband who is employable. She will then be told that her husband must come in for an interview. If he fails to come in, the department may continue to deny the family aid.[75] If the husband does come in, he will be asked to sign an agreement to pay the wife a certain part of his earnings each month. If he signs, this agreement may be used in the future as a basis for denying any assistance to his family even though he fails to live up to its terms.[76] If the authorities can be convinced that the husband is not contributing to the family's support, the wife will then be told that she must bring a court action for support against the husband before the welfare department will render assistance. (This advice is frequently given to women who for one reason or another have no legal ground or practical expectation of recovery against the husband.) The wife may or may not be advised about the legal-

aid organization. (In some communities, of course, there is
no legal-aid organization.) Rarely does the welfare worker
make any attempt to call the lawyer and discuss the case
to see if there is a legal basis for suing the husband and how
long it will take. In any event, no appointment is made for
her to see the lawyer because the legal-aid organization does
not see poor clients by appointment.

The wife may need surplus food, emergency aid, shoes,
medicine, eyeglasses, or special schooling for a retarded
child. If she is lucky she may be questioned at the time of
her interview at the public-welfare department about her
need for these things and directed to the proper source,
public or private. More often than not, having informed the
wife that she is currently ineligible for assistance, the caseworker considers his job done. In any case, none of the
things she might need for herself and the children is dis-
pensed at the same place; hence, it means many trips, baby
sitters, bus fares, waiting rooms, interviews, and more application forms.[77]

If the wife does get to the legal-aid society's office down
town, she again is confronted with an eligibility screening,
waiting room, and red tape. She is also, incidentally, asked
for one of her few remaining dollars as a fee (though it
will be waived if she says she can't afford it). If she survives
the eligibility screening, she will be interviewed by a lawyer
and advised that even if she has legal grounds for bringing
the suit, and some chance of winning, it will first cost her
$12 to pay the price of filing suit and serving the complaint
on the husband. It is likely that at this point, her husband
gone several weeks, she does not have 12 cents to spare,
much less $12. Moreover, when the husband returns home,
even if she is still inclined to bring suit against him (which
involves going to court and testifying before everyone), any
money she receives from him must go first to buy food,
clothes, medicine, and to pay the bills, particularly the rent
bill. Thus she is caught in a vicious circle. Though there is
a court provision that one who is a pauper may obtain the

permission of the court to have the court costs waived, this rule is often narrowly construed by both attorneys and courts to exclude all members of a family when any member has employment income, whether or not he shares it with the rest of the family, or when any salable asset such as a car is owned (regardless of the need for the asset).

If the wife does manage to find $12, or if the court costs are waived, then there is the problem of getting the lawyer to draft and file the complaint, and, depending upon how much he has to do, this may take several days or more. Following this, there is the problem of finding the husband in order to serve the complaint upon him. He may have no fixed place of employment and his wife may have no idea where he can be found. After a period of time has elapsed, say three to six weeks, during which period the wife and children have been without any resources whatever, they can start receiving emergency public assistance, if they have applied for it.[78] (Some communities do not have emergency aid.) The family will not be eligible for permanent public assistance unless there is an affidavit from an attorney or the United States marshal that they have been unable to locate and effect service upon the husband. Moreover, the wife and children will still not be eligible for either permanent or emergency public assistance unless they satisfy all of the welfare department's residency and means requirements. In some instances, eligibility will be denied on the ground that the mother is employable. Neither emergency nor permanent public assistance is payable retroactively to the date the family was first without resources. The first check never includes, for example, money for rent and other unpaid bills which have accrued during the six weeks or more that the application for help has rested on someone's desk.

If the marshal is able to locate the husband and serve the papers upon him, the husband then has twenty days in which to file his answer, after which period the wife's lawyer can then ask the court to place the case on the ready

calendar for trial. After another week or two, the case will
be heard by the court. At the trial date, the wife and her
lawyer must appear in court and prove her side of the story,
including proof of her husband's earnings in order to claim
a certain percentage for herself and the children. If she is
able to show that the husband is earning at the time, say
$200 per month, the court may award her and the children
$100.[79] If the amount awarded is less than the amount
deemed essential for necessities under the public-assistance
department's rules, the department will then pay the difference.[80]

More often than not, the court order against the husband
has little effect because the husband fails to make the payments, or he pays for a week or two and then defaults for
the next three weeks, or he pays a different sum each time
so that no certain sum can be counted on, or he loses his
job or quits work altogether, or he absconds from the jurisdiction (or hides out somewhere within the jurisdiction).
In any of these cases, the wife cannot receive an automatic
increase in her public-assistance check. She must first bring
another suit asking the court to find the husband in contempt of court and send him to jail. This means another trip
to see a legal-aid lawyer, more waiting, delay and red tape,
more filing of papers, another attempt by the marshal to
find the husband, another five days wait for him to file his
answer, and another week or two for the case to be heard in
court. When the case is finally heard by the court, the husband may then be sent to prison for thirty days, if the judge
is convinced that the husband has steady employment and
can afford to pay something toward his family's support.
At this point, the public-assistance department will increase
the wife's income to make up for the amount that she is not
receiving from her husband. (Of course, she hasn't been
receiving it all along, but only now it is official that she
isn't.) She receives an increase only from the date that the
husband is imprisoned, not from the date that he failed to
make the payments. Even then, the increase in the public-

welfare check does not come at once because of clerical technicalities. In fact, there may be a delay of two weeks not only in receiving the increase but in receiving any check at all because of the necessity of changing the pay-out records.[81]

Upon the husband's release from prison thirty days later, the public-assistance check is automatically decreased again on the theory that he is once more able to provide for his family, unless the welfare department can be convinced that he has not been able for a medical or other good reason to go back to work. If he does return to work, the public-assistance check is decreased, even if he still does not make any payments to his wife or makes them only sporadically. And again, the decrease in the welfare check means another two weeks' delay in the wife's receiving any check at all, since the pay-out records have to be changed again.

And, of course, throughout this saga, every time the public-assistance check is withheld, or delayed, the rent becomes overdue, eviction notices are served (including those from public housing authorities), heat and telephone and electricity are turned off, bills pile up, creditors harass the family, and the children are without the necessities of life. If the husband continues to fail to make his payments, the wife's only recourse is to go back to legal aid and bring another contempt charge against him, which will put him in jail for another thirty days. Thus, the woman welfare recipient is continually forced to go to court to keep the payments coming.

Law—the Poor Man's Enemy?

Added to the inconvenience, waiting, red tape, delay and uncertainty that the poor person must continually face in his encounters with the institutions of law is the fact that everywhere these people are treated as though they were devoid of feelings and sensibilities. At best they find a middle-class bias and unmistakably paternalistic attitude

that they are clients rather than citizens; at worst they meet
outright rudeness, prejudice, harassment, and abuse. The
total effect on a poor person of rigid administrative rules
and policies, aggravated by an all-pervasive attitude of welfare colonialism is to stultify any latent desires to participate meaningfully in the legal determinations that affect
his life.[82] An occasional poor person may struggle out of the
slum to a different way of life; an occasional Gideon, despite
his wretched past, driven by an inner sense of dignity and
entitlement, will battle for his legal rights. But most do not.

Thus of vastly more significance than the fact that the
poor have many legal problems is the fact that years of
inequality in resolving them, lack of advocates on their
behalf, and the official stripping from them of the last ves-
tiges of personal dignity, have succeeded in alienating the
poor from the legal process in which the rest of society
participates. This sense of alienation may manifest itself in
apathy and resignation in some, cynicism, disrespect, and
even rebelliousness in others. The poor speak of "the law"
in much the same tones as the Negro speaks of "the man."[83]
For them, the legal system is one written, applied, and
enforced by others, for others. As former Attorney General
Robert Kennedy stated, "For the poor man, the law is always
taking something away." Particularly expressive is Woodie
Guthrie's explanation of his popular folk ballad, "Pretty
Boy Floyd," that the outlaw was popular "primarily because
he was an enemy of the law and order that had done nothing
to prevent or remedy the chaos in the lives of the poor in
the area."[84]

> As through your lives you ramble,
> Yes, as through your lives you roam,
> You won't never see an outlaw drive
> a family from their home.

We have recently begun to appreciate that there is a "culture
of poverty"—a way of life passed down from generation to
generation.[85] We have not as yet fully grasped the extent to

which distinctively different attitudes toward the law and the legal process are a part of this culture, nor the implications that their continued perpetuation will have for the rule of law.

The Responsibility of Law

One may wonder why the interrelationship of law and poverty has been by and large a neglected area of concern, particularly by the legal profession whose *raison d'être* is the implementation of the concept of equal justice under law. In part, the legal profession has simply failed along with the rest of the educated populace to appreciate fully the existence, both quantitatively and qualitatively, of the heretofore "invisible" poor. Several individual, and highly respected, members of the profession have long called for measures aimed at lessening the inequities in the legal process, particularly in the criminal area.[86] Unfortunately, however, individual awareness, concern, and indignation cannot be said to have pervaded the profession as a whole. Law schools have done little in the past to sharpen their students' awareness of the practical application of legal rules to the poor. As Professor Charles Ares of New York University Law School notes, "even the course in bankruptcy law is called 'creditor's rights.' "[87] The law-school curriculum is oriented toward those legal problems of concern to the wealthiest clients. The courses in administrative procedure are typically concerned more with determinations regarding sales of securities than with aid to dependent children. In criminal law, problems of criminal theory are emphasized. "We study the burglary, not the burglar."[88] Indeed, criminal law is barely touched upon by many of the better known law schools—at Harvard Law School, only one two-hour semester course is required.

After law school, the prestige jobs are with those law firms representing the richest clients, and the best legal talent graduating from law schools has gravitated toward those firms. Criminal-defense work, legal aid, and similar occupations have been looked down upon as *déclassé*.[89] They also have generally offered far less remuneration than is obtainable in the firms representing wealthier clients.[90]

Many individuals in private practice with a sense of responsibility do offer a great deal of uncompensated counsel to persons unable to pay for it, but even though the hours thus spent seem inordinately excessive to individual lawyers, they cannot begin to resolve the great portion of the poor's legal difficulties. Many communities now have formed legal-aid organizations, but despite the dedication of those who staff them, lack of adequate financial support from the bar and the community has severely restricted the scope of their assistance.[91] Because some members of the bar are openly hostile to anyone receiving free legal aid if he can possibly be made to pay for it, legal-aid standards of indigency for eligibility have often been strict and rigidly enforced.[92] Except in a few of the largest metropolitan areas, legal-aid organizations are generally understaffed, underpaid, and heavily dependent on volunteer help. Thus they have been unable to accept many kinds of cases (typically those that involve a great deal of time), to make house calls, to open neighborhood branches, and generally have had to be content with devoting only the barest minimum of time and legal ingenuity to any one case.[93] In addition they have too frequently exhibited the same kind of impersonal, middle-class bias which has alienated the poor from the other service organizations.[94]

Nor has there been much public pressure to provide more adequate legal aid. Other professions have not done as much as they might to expose the inequities of law, to sensitize the lay community, and to prod the legal profession into action. As Blaustein and Porter noted in their 1954 survey of the legal profession: "To appreciate why the poor are denied justice and to see the need for organized legal aid service requires a knowledge and understanding of our legal institutions which few laymen possess."[95]

There are, however, some encouraging signs of change. The national concern for poverty has stimulated new professional appreciation for the existing inequities in the legal process. Several universities and law schools have proposed or instituted interdisciplinary research institutes for the study of the sociology of law with particular emphasis on the legal problems facing the poor.[96] Some have initiated clinical training programs.[97]

There is also some indication of growing public concern. The federal government has sponsored conferences on bail and the extension of legal services to the poor. A Federal Criminal Justice Act has been passed. One feature of the President's War on Poverty, administered by the Office of Economic Opportunity, is the creation of neighborhood legal-service centers to provide an easily accessible corps of well-paid, competent lawyers especially skilled in cases involving such matters as usurious interest rates, Social Security applications, welfare-review-board hearings, minimum-wage laws, housing codes, and other legal problems of importance to the poor. The hope of such programs is that they will offer not only legal assistance for those problems which reach the crisis stage of a court proceeding, but also advice and assistance in how to plan their affairs and avoid legal problems.[98] Finally, from the judicial branch have come two decisions of far-reaching significance suggesting that traditional views of the organized bar regarding professional ethics may no longer be allowed to stand in the way of new methods of providing group legal services to both the poor and those of modest means.[99]

These expressions of interest are only a beginning. Many believe, however, that there are signs of a social revolution in the making, leading to new legal institutions, the shape and form of which are not yet clearly discernible, but which have as their motivating force the meaningful inclusion of the poor in the legal process. It is also agreed that any such revolution will of necessity involve social stress. If government is to provide advocates to challenge government

decisions, if the poor are to be given an effective voice in
asserting their interests to the detriment of other interests,
if the poor are to challenge rather than mutely accept
another's determination of "what is best" for them, conflict
among existing social groups is inevitable. Thus, the New
York Welfare Department's unhappiness with Mobilization
for Youth's challenge to its administration can be expected
to be shared by numerous other welfare administrators as
welfare clients, buttressed by legal and citizen advocates,
exercise their right of question and challenge. It can also be
expected that the proposed community action and neighborhood legal programs which are aimed at eliminating poverty
and giving the poor themselves a voice and a part in that
elimination will meet with some community resistance.[100]
It can also be expected that the new programs will face
opposition from some members of the bar. While other professions have become aware of the lack of identification and
rapport between the poor and middle-class professionals
who in the past had been sent in to "serve" them and of the
need for indigenous leadership, gang leaders, and community organizers, the use of roving lawyers to practice preventive and educational law has offended the sensibilities
of traditionalistic minded members of the legal profession.
To those lawyers, aggressive community legal aid amounts
to such violations of the canons of ethics as "soliciting
business," "advertising," and "unprofessional conduct." In
Connecticut, the members of the bar have been more blunt
in their opposition to neighborhood legal programs, sensing
in them plans for soliciting business away from established
neighborhood lawyers.[101]

Finally, it cannot be overlooked, though full development
of this theme is not within the scope of this paper, that
the use of the legal process has its political dimension as
well. Law and lawyers are employed by a knowledgeable
citizenry to accomplish a wide variety of community and
sociopolitical goals—to obtain sewerage service or better
schools, to force the authorities to enforce a law or pick up

the garbage, to obtain or to defeat an urban-renewal plan. Similar use of the legal process by a poverty-stricken neighborhood, however, caused shock waves throughout Chicago's power structure.[102] Even the assertion of legal rights against private interest groups can have widespread neighborhood ramifications and political repercussions, as the recent rent strikes in New York have indicated.

To allow—indeed to foster—effective citizenship participation by the poor in the legal process at all levels where that process affects their vital interests on the same terms afforded other groups is one of today's great challenges to a society dedicated to the concept of equal justice under law.[103]

NOTES

1. This paper does not examine anew the question of who is poor and how many poor there are but rather adopts the consensus of others that a large percentage of the population—probably about a fifth—live at or near what is commonly regarded as a level of subsistence. (*See,* for example, *Report of the Council of Economic Advisors—1965;* M. Harrington, *The Other America,* New York, 1963; D. Macdonald, "Our Invisible Poor," *The New Yorker,* Jan. 19, 1963; *Conference on Economic Progress, Poverty & Deprivation in the United States,* 1962.) In addition, while it is recognized that there are many individual differences within as large a group as one-fifth of the nation, for purposes of this discussion, that group will be referred to simply as "the poor."

2. Attorney General Katzenbach, in a recent address at a federal conference regarding the need for extending legal services to the poor, noted this prevailing attitude with the comment: "Michael Harrington has aptly described the millions living in poverty in this country as the invisible poor. It is no less certain that the problems of the poor which a lawyer can help solve are so far outside the experience of most of us that they are invisible problems. But for the poor person, living in helplessness, they are overpowering."

3. One of the present difficulties caused by the fact that the legal problems of the poor have been "invisible" is that there has been little statistical or analytical study of the extent to which they exist or vary with particular segments of the poverty class. Sociolegal scholarship is just beginning to enter this field. A reasonable assumption, however, is that multilegal problems increase in frequency in concert with the collection of adverse living circumstances.

4. The specific legal problems used as examples throughout the

paper are primarily those peculiar to the urban poor. It is believed, however, that the basic fact of exclusion from the legal process is equally applicable to the rural poor and is an aspect of the "essential similarity in life styles of urban and rural multi-problem families" to which Thomas Gladwin refers in "The Anthropologist's View of Poverty," *The Social Welfare Forum* (New York: Columbia Univ. Press, 1961), p. 73.

5. New York, The Free Press, 1963, esp. pp. 32–48. A study of 464 families in low-income housing projects in New York City, where the median income was about $3300, revealed the following: 95 per cent owned at least one television set; more than 3 in every 5 owned a phonograph; more than 2 in every 5 owned a sewing machine; more than 2 in every 5 owned an automatic washing machine; more than a quarter owned a vacuum cleaner; 1 in every 7 families owned an automobile. The typical family bought sets of furniture for at least two rooms when it moved into the project.

6. Where not otherwise indicated, the case examples referred to in the paper are from the files of the author and other volunteer legal-aid lawyers in the District of Columbia.

7. *Williams* v. *Walker Thomas Furniture Company*, U.S. Court of Appeals, No. 18,604 (D.C. Circuit 1965—appeal pending).

8. Caplovitz, *op. cit.*, Chapter 6.

9. *See* Consumer Credit Symposium: *Developments in the Law, Northwestern University Law Review,* **55** (1960), p. 301.

10. Similar practices of shady used car dealers were the subject of a Pulitzer-Prize-winning series by Miriam Ottenberg in *The Washington Star,* Nov. 1–7, 1959,

11. Caplovitz, *op. cit.*, p. 158.

12. The unpublished files of the Washington Planning and Housing Association, in the District of Columbia, reveal that other onerous conditions are frequently inserted in slum leases. A provision, for example, that the tenant is to provide all the heat and hot water for a rented apartment, is common. While some lawyers think such un-usual provisions might not be legally binding, a precedent-making test case has yet to be brought. Washington Planning and Housing Association's experience has been that slum tenants are reluctant to bring such test cases at the risk of being evicted.

13. Nancy LeBlanc, "Why Tenants Need Lawyers," paper presented at the Conference on the Extension of Legal Services to the Poor, sponsored by the Department of Health, Education, and Welfare, Washington, D.C., November 12, 1964, p. 6. "Sewer service" occurs with respect to other kinds of legal actions too. Caplovitz's study (p. 160) includes the story of one woman, eager to present her case in court, but is precluded from doing so by lack of any notice of hearing: ". . . a salesman came to the door selling wrist watches. I promised my daughter I would get her one. . . . So I agreed to buy it for $60. I gave him $3 down and I got a payment book in the mail. About a month later I had the watch appraised in a 125th Street store and I found it was worth only $6.50. I called up the company and said I wouldn't pay for it and they should come and

get it. They told me I had to pay or they'd take me to court. And I said, "Fine, take me to Court, and I'll have the watch there." Next thing I know about this I get a court notice of Judgment by Default from Brooklyn Municipal Court for $69 balance, $3 interest, $5 costs by statute, $14 court costs. The total cost of the watch was $91.

14. LeBlanc, *op. cit.*, pp. 5–6.

15. *See* Earl L. Koos, *The Family and the Law* (New York: National Legal Aid and Defender Association, 1952).

16. Caplovitz, *op. cit.*, pp. 171–178.

17. Caplovitz, *op. cit.*, p. 150.

18. All tenants are told to appear at the courthouse at the same appointed hour. Landlord-tenant proceedings in specialized landlord-tenant courts proceed briskly, since there is virtually never any contest in such cases. If there is to be a contest, the case will be set for later in the day and the tenant will have to wait around until it can be heard. In other kinds of proceedings where the parties are from all income groups and there are arguments to be heard, each person told to show up at 9:30 in the morning must wait around all day for his case to be heard. For the poor woman who has arranged for an older child to stay out of school and watch the younger ones until she returns, or the poor man who has obtained a few hours leave from his job and is being docked for each hour's absence, the wait is particularly aggravating. Sometimes it develops that the case can't be heard or concluded on the day set at all. Indeed, in some instances, when the poor person without a lawyer arrives at the court, he is told for the first time that his case has been postponed to another date.

19. There is, of course, no hard-and-fast line between middle class and poor. The near-poor and the average-income earner too may at times experience inequality before the law and be faced with legal problems with which they have difficulty coping and for which they cannot afford competent help. While not in any way minimizing the importance of such problems, the point to be made here is simply that the greater the aggregate of favorable living circumstances, the easier it is to derive maximum benefit from the use of the legal process and to suffer the least from its inconveniences and inequities. Thus, while recognizing that middle-class participation in the legal process varies widely, with those closest to the poverty level sharing more of the difficulties faced by the poor, all those who are not within what is commonly understood to be the "poverty" group will in this paper simply be referred to as "middle class" or "persons of means."

20. LeBlanc, *op. cit.*, p. 10. The author noted that in at least one other state that she was aware of, Connecticut, and possibly many others, similar laws exist but, as in New York prior to the rent strikes, are virtually unknown and unused.

21. *Ibid.*, p. 7.

22. *Ibid.*, p. 8.

23. Indigent defendants in divorce, separation, and paternity suits also have difficulty obtaining legal representation.

24. Chief Justice Earl Warren in a speech at Boston University Law School recently said: "The defense of persons accused of crime

has been downgraded to a point where it is considered by most lawyers not to be respectable to represent unpopular defendants regardless of the merits of their cases. As a result each year thousands of indigent defendants are being shuffled off to penitentiaries without the benefit of any legal advice whatsoever." Reported in *The Washington Post*, Oct. 30, 1964, p. A4.

25. *See* the Allen Committee Report to the Attorney General, *Poverty and the Administration of Federal Criminal Justice* (1963), which was the impetus for the recently passed Criminal Justice Act (providing counsel fees to lawyers representing indigent defendants in the federal courts). *See also* Arnold S. Trebach, *The Rationing of Justice* (Rutgers: Rutgers Univ. Press, 1964), a study of the administration of criminal justice including a survey of such unlawful police practices as arrests for suspicion, police brutality, coerced confessions, unlawful detentions, and mass arrests.

26. *Gideon* v. *Wainwright*, 372 U.S. 335 (1963). The way that the case reached the Supreme Court is a dramatic one. Clarence Gideon was accused of breaking into a pool room. Gideon, who had only a few grades of formal education, read law books in his cell at night, and drafted a hand-written petition to the court. Following the reversal of his case, he was retried, this time with the counsel of a lawyer. The lawyer discovered a new witness, weakened the prosecution's case, and pointed out the weakness to the jury, with the result that Gideon was acquitted. For a complete and very readable account, *see* Anthony Lewis, *Gideon's Trumpet* (New York: Random House, Inc., 1964).

27. Former Attorney General Robert F. Kennedy in his Law Day address of last year asked: "The fundamental question remains: should there ever have been a need for a Gideon decision? Did we need a constitutional determination to tell us our professional responsibilities?"

28. *Powell* v. *Alabama*, 287 U.S. 46, 68 (1932). The *Powell* case was subsequently interpreted to require state-provided counsel only in capital cases.

29. Erwin Griswold, Dean of Harvard Law School, wrote as follows: "Under our present system, no provision whatever is made for counsel in post conviction proceedings, unless the case gets into court, attracts the attention of the court and results in the assignment of counsel. Yet there are an appreciable number of these cases which have merit, and which should be handled by counsel." Dean's Report, 1963–1964, Harvard Law School, p. 9.

30. Two Supreme Court cases have held, however, that where a preliminary hearing or arraignment is a critical part of the proceedings against an accused in a capital case, the defendant is entitled to be represented by counsel under the *Powell* v. *Alabama* doctrine. *Hamilton* v. *Alabama*, 368 U.S. 52 (1961); *White* v. *Maryland*, 373 U.S. 59 (1963).

31. *See* Emanuel Celler, "Federal Legislative Proposals to Supply Paid Counsel to Indigent Persons Accused of Crime," *Minnesota Law Review*, **45** (April 1961), p. 697.

32. Trebach, *op. cit.*, p. 116.

33. J. Edward Lumbard, "Better Lawyers for Our Criminal Courts," *The Atlantic Monthly*, **86** (June 1964), p. 88. *See* Trebach, *op. cit.*, Chapter 5.

34. Our adversary system can be contrasted with some European countries where an active judge attempts to dig out the truth through his own investigation. See comments on the comparative merits of the adversary system by Monrad Paulson, "Equal Justice for the Poor Man," Public Affairs Pamphlet No. 367, Nov. 1964.

35. In the federal courts, an indigent defendant may have witnesses subpoenaed without the payment of a fee, but only if he first submits an affidavit indicating the substance of the expected testimony. The effect of this rule, of course, is to require him to disclose his case in advance, a requirement which is not made of the person who can afford to pay the subpoena fees. Moreover, the affidavit may then be used to impeach his credibility at his trial. *Smith* v. *United States*, 312 F. 2d 867 (D.C. Cir. 1962).

36. Arthur Goldberg, "Equality and Governmental Action," *New York University Law Review*, **39** (April 1964), p. 205. In a recently publicized New York case, George Grosso pleaded guilty to petit larceny and was sentenced to a year in jail plus $500 or 500 days. Naturally enough, he had not earned $500 during his year's stay in jail so he faced the prospect of another 500 days' imprisonment. At the intervention of a lawyer employed by the Vera Foundation, the district attorney agreed to consent to the remission of the fine. Grosso was subsequently released, although he had already served three additional months for failure to pay the fine. See an account of the case in *The New York Times*, Dec. 6, 1964.

37. A chemical engineer visiting a detention prison one day was appalled with the bail situation and established a nonprofit foundation, the Vera Foundation, to study the problem. As a result of the study, several localities have experimented with procedures that release defendants on their own recognizance. One such experiment in Manhattan revealed that only 1 per cent released on their own recognizance failed to appear compared to 3 per cent released on bail. *See* New York City Bar Association Report on Bail, 1963. *Also see* the discussion of the bail problem in the Allen Committee Report, Poverty and the Administration of Federal Criminal Justice, *op. cit.* Also, a book on bail by Ronald Goldfarb is to be published by Harper & Row in the fall of 1965.

38. P. Freed and D. Wald, *Bail in the United States—1964*, a report to the National Conference on Bail and Criminal Justice under the cosponsorship of the Department of Justice and the Vera Foundation, Washington, D.C., May 1964.

39. The Freed and Wald report notes that jail also takes its personal toll on the defendant—"The man who goes to jail for failure to make bond is treated by almost every jurisdiction much like the convicted criminal serving a sentence. . . . Some jurisdictions even impose more stringent conditions on the detained than on convicted offenders." *Ibid.*, pp. 43–44.

40. *Ibid.*, pp. 45–48. The report concludes (p. 48): "With mount-

ing evidence the conclusion is forming that the man who is jailed for want of bail is less likely to get equal treatment in court."

41. G. Dubin and R. Robinson, "The Vagrancy Concept Reconsidered: Problems and Abuses of Status Criminality," *New York University Law Review,* **37** (Jan. 1962), p. 102; William O. Douglas, "Vagrancy and Arrest on Suspicion, *Yale Law Journal,* **70** (Nov. 1960), p. 1. Also, for an excellent in-depth study of vagrancy law enforcement, see Caleb Foote's "Vagrancy Type Law and its Administration," *University of Pennsylvania Law Review,* **104** (1956), p. 603. Justice Douglas notes that persons arrested for vagrancy "are not the sons of bankers, industrialists, lawyers or other professional people. They . . . come from other strata of society, or from minority groups who are not sufficiently vocal to protect themselves and who do not have the prestige to prevent an easy laying-on of hands by the police."

42. For a general discussion of the use of banishment, particularly in vagrancy cases, see Michael Armstrong, "Banishment: Cruel and Unusual Punishment," *University of Pennsylvania Law Review,* **111** (April 1963), p. 758, and Foote, *op. cit.*

43. Goldberg, *op. cit.,* p. 219. Justice Goldberg's written paper contains a footnote as follows: "An example of this practice, now happily abandoned in the Capital City, occurred a few years ago. A waitress had been robbed by someone whom she described in very general terms. The police immediately conducted a dragnet roundup in the second precinct, which is populated primarily by poor people. Within a few hours 90 young men, including 25 juveniles were arrested for questioning. Sixty-three of them were held overnight and released only after the victim did not identify any of them as her assailant. Many of those held overnight were forced to miss work the following day. Another man, not among those picked up in the dragnet, was ultimately charged with the crime. *See Washington Daily News,* Jan. 21, 1958, p. 5; *Washington Evening Star,* March 3, 1958, p. B1."

44. See similar comments by Harriet F. Pilpel, "Sex vs. the Law: a Study in Hypocrisy," *Harper's Magazine,* Jan. 1965, p. 35.

45. Monrad Paulson, "The Legal Needs of the Poor in Family Law," paper presented at the Conference on the Extension of Legal Services to the Poor, *op. cit.,* pp. 3–4.

46. Elizabeth Wickenden, "Poverty and the Law," National Social Welfare Assembly, New York, March 25, 1963. The memorandum notes that in many instances resentment against the unwed mother (and her children) on the public-assistance rolls is aggravated by the fact that "this group typically includes a disproportionate number of persons of minority status. Poverty, discriminatory employment practices, inadequate education, traditional culture patterns, social isolation and lack of access to such legal processes as divorce make disproportionate numbers of Negroes on assistance rolls an inevitable consequence of discrimination as *An American Dilemma* predicted in 1944."

47. Charles Reich, "The New Property," *Yale Law Journal,* **73** (April 1964), p. 731.

48. Edward Sparer, "The New Public Law: The Relation of State Administration to the Legal Problems of the Poor," paper presented at the Conference on the Extension of Legal Services to the Poor, *op. cit.*, p. 2.

49. William Stringfellow, who has represented the poor for several years in East Harlem, related in his book, *My People Is the Enemy* (New York: Holt, Rinehart & Winston, 1964), p. 75: "I had one case in which an investigator climbed a tree at 2:00 o'clock in the morning in order to perch there and spy into the window of a project apartment of a welfare family waiting to see or hear something that would be used against the family to disqualify them from further assistance."

A report on the Aid to Dependent Children Program in Chicago, gives the following account: "Because the casework staff does not have an opportunity to learn enough about their cases, a special investigation unit is used, primarily for the purpose of ferreting out fraud through surprise visits made to the homes of the recipients either on Sunday morning or after midnight. In ADC it appears that the primary function of this unit is to find men in the home where they [sic] are not supposed to be any, especially fathers, step-fathers or acting fathers who are alleged to be absent.

"In the sample of active cases studied some instances were reported in which the special investigation teams in a surprise visit in the middle of the night pushed past the one who answered the door and looked in the closets and under the bed for evidence of male occupancy. One family interviewed in this study complained of repeated harassment of this kind. . . .

"In another case the mother complained of the special investigator arriving one evening while she was taking a bath. He pushed past her nine year old daughter who answered the door—looked in the bedroom, all closets and the bathroom searching for a man or evidence of male occupancy. He had no warrant. He did find a suit in a closet belonging to the mother's boy friend, who visited on weekends and about whom the department had been fully informed. Nevertheless assistance was discontinued on the assumption a man was living full time with the family and that they could look to him for support—support which the part-time boy friend could not provide. The mother and daughter appeared destitute and malnourished at the time of the interview. Also, they had been so frightened by the visit and the attitude of the special investigator that they were almost immobilized with fear." Greenleigh Associates, Inc., *Facts, Fallacies and the Future, A Study of the Aid to Dependent Children Program of Cook County, Illinois,* **64** (1960).

50. One such raid was the widely publicized one in Alameda County, California, conducted in a single night on 500 mothers receiving public assistance. One social worker, Benny Parish, was discharged by the Alameda County Welfare Department for his refusal to take part in the raid, on the ground that the raid was unconstitutional. His suit for reinstatement is currently pending in the courts.

51. But see *Note 50,* above. Mr. Parish's suit for reinstatement

may, though it is not clear, result in a ruling on the constitutional question of the validity of the raid itself.

52. C. Reich, "Midnight Welfare Searches and the Social Security Act," *Yale Law Journal,* **72** (1963), p. 1347.

53. *People* v. *LaFountain,* App. Div., 3d. Dept. (New York) No. 6513, May 19, 1964. One rather novel legal argument urged by the ACLU, as a ground for reversal, but not ruled upon by the court, was that the state's action was in violation of the thirteenth amendment forbidding slavery!

54. The above examples, as well as other national items, were summarized and discussed by Edwin J. Lucas in a paper entitled, "The Rights of the Poor—In What Ways Are Civil Rights of the Poor Safeguarded or Infringed on by Social Work Practices," presented at the Alumni Conference of the Columbia School of Social Work, April 18, 1964.

55. See Murray Kempton, "When You Mobilize the Poor," *The New Republic,* Dec. 5, 1964. Sparer's own account is set forth in his paper, *op. cit.,* pp. 18–24.

56. Unpublished study by Z. F. Hostetler, *The Need for Staff Legal Counsel,* Report to Family and Child Services Agency, Washington, D.C.

57. Sparer, *op. cit.*

58. Hostetler, *op. cit.*

59. It is interesting to note that in communities statistically studied a much larger percentage of families with income below the commonly accepted poverty level are living in the community than are on the public-assistance rolls. A recent study in Westchester County, New York, for example, revealed that only one-fifth of the families living in "abject poverty" received public aid. *See The New York Times,* Oct. 29, 1964.

60. *The Washington Post,* Dec. 26, 1964.

61. The Moreland Commission Report on Public Welfare in the State of New York (1963) stated, p. 68: "When cases are closed, are reasons given? Again, not always. In one county, for example, 35.7 per cent of those interviewed claimed they were not told why assistance was cut off and the case records failed to indicate that the former recipient had been given a reason."

62. A Washington, D.C., study of the District's welfare program noted that it is a "tenaciously held official view that a mother who deviates from the social code thereby somehow acquires funds to feed, clothe, house and nurture her children." The report continues that "it is especially inapplicable for the Department of Public Welfare to require a non-husband to assume responsibility for the support of children he did not sire—support of such children is the legal responsibility of their father until a court, not an administrative agency, rules otherwise." *The Public Welfare Crisis in the Nation's Capital,* study by the Metropolitan Washington Chapter, National Association of Social Workers and the Commission on Human Resources (Washington, D.C.: The Washington Center for Metropolitan Studies, 1963).

63. See Justice Sutherland's famous statement regarding the skill of the average man in dealing with legal issues, cited supra, p. 91.

64. In many instances welfare-department workers, of whom there is a high turnover rate, do not even know their own departmental regulations. The regulations are often contradictory, interpretations vary from department to department, and from caseworker to caseworker, and even policy decisions or court rulings are not communicated. Thus legal precedent is virtually unknown in welfare administration.

65. Kempton, op. cit. The article discusses the unhappiness of New York welfare authorities with Edward Sparer's vigorous advocacy on behalf of his poor clients under the Welfare Abuses Act (discussed above, p. 198).

66. Sparer, op. cit., p. 2.

67. Allanson Willcox, General Counsel of the Department of Health, Education, and Welfare, in an address before the Virginia State Bar Association candidly noted what everyone in his audience already knew: "The fact that a citizen can retain you to represent him goes a long way towards assuring that he will receive the treatment to which he is entitled at the hands of a government agency." Mr. Willcox continued as follows: "I say this despite my conviction that the officials who administer local, state and federal programs would stand toward the top in competence and dedication to duty. But no one would deny that administrative agencies can and do make mistakes; as with any group, no official is infallible, and some are more fallible than others. And not infrequently a lawyer can bring out facts or considerations that the administrator with the best will in the world would otherwise overlook."

68. E. Wickenden, "The Legal Needs of the Poor—From the Viewpoint of Public Welfare Policy," paper presented at the Conference on the Extension of Legal Services to the Poor, op. cit.

69. Edgar and Jean Cahn, "The War on Poverty: A Civilian Perspective," Yale Law Journal, 73 (July 1964), p. 1317.

70. Various descriptions of the ombudsman appear in the following articles: Stephan Hurwitz, "Denmark's Ombudsman: The Parliamentary Commissioner for Civil and Military Government Administration," Wisconsin Law Review (March 1961), p. 169; K. C. Christensen, "The Danish Ombudsman," University of Pennsylvania Law Review, 109 (1961), p. 1100); B. Davis, "Ombudsmen in America: Officers to Criticize Administrative Action," University of Pennsylvania Law Review, 109 (1961), p. 1057; Ronald Goldfarb, "Declaring a War on Injustice," The New Republic, Jan. 16, 1965, p. 15.

71. See Mildred Zucker, "Citizen's Advice Bureaus," paper presented at the Conference on the Extension of Legal Services to the Poor, op. cit.; Goldfarb, op. cit.

72. A pilot information and referral service program similar to the English Citizen's Advice Bureau has recently been inaugurated in the Capital Hill Section of Washington by volunteers of the Lutheran Church of the Reformation under the leadership of Bessie Lee Athey.

73. Address given to the Conference on the Extension of Legal Services to the Poor, op. cit.

74. Grosser, "Neighborhood Legal Service: A Strategy to Meet Human Need," Conference on the Extension of Legal Services to the Poor, op. cit. Mr. Grosser comments that if the inconvenience and impersonal atmosphere are difficult and bothersome for articulate and knowledgeable middle-class persons, they are overwhelming to the lower class, so much so, in fact, that large-scale private service organizations have suffered a common experience: alienation and self-selection have occurred, with the result that they are serving a disproportionate portion of persons in the lowest income groups.

75. A 1963 study revealed that one woman was refused public assistance on four separate occasions because she could not get the father of her three youngest children (she had four) to come to the welfare department for the interview. "The Ineligibles, a Study of Fifty Families Terminated or Ineligible for Public Assistance," (Washington, D.C.: Bureau of Social Science Research, Inc., Aug. 1963), p. 59.

76. "The Ineligibles," Ibid., p. 62, reports the following case: "In October 1962 Mrs. E received from the welfare department the following 'Notice of Ineligibility': 'On the basis of information available to us, we find that you are no longer eligible to receive assistance because:

"On September 21, 1962, your son . . . said he would give you $15 per month starting Sept. 26, 1962. You say he has given you nothing. He will have to come with you to the office to discuss this if he cannot give it to you. . . .'"

With this notice, Mrs. E's monthly income dropped from $144 to $64 [received as Social Security]. Her son, because he has a family of his own to support, has been unable to give her the monthly $15 ordered by the Welfare Department.

Among the hardships she endures is living in a third-floor room of a boarding house. She moved to this room after assistance was terminated in order to reduce her rent. She is eligible for surplus food but . . . [i]t is very difficult for her to carry her allotment home and she frequently lacks the carfare to go get it.

77. Until this past year, surplus food in the District was distributed only at one main depot. No transportation was provided to help carry the 53 pounds of groceries back home. Moreover, if a woman welfare recipient showed up with a man friend to assist her, this was a fact that under the welfare department's regulations could be taken as evidence that she had someone capable of supporting her, thus making her ineligible for welfare payments. See The Public Welfare Crisis in the Nation's Capital, op. cit., pp. 39–40.

78. The average five-weeks' delay that a family must wait before receiving emergency public assistance in any case, whether because of illness, loss of work, absence of a husband, or other reason, was the subject of a Washington Post editorial "First Aid," April 29, 1964. The Post noted that the only reason children don't starve to death during the waiting period is because they are fed by voluntary agencies. The editorial suggested that the department have a special

fund "not controlled by the usual abundance of regulations, to assist families that cannot wait five weeks for a routine clearance."

79. When the woman's lawyer asks for too large a percentage of the man's earnings, and it is awarded by the court, she may be precluded from any welfare payments if the amount ordered by the court (whether or not paid) is deemed sufficient for the family's needs under the agency's standards.

80. In the District, as is the case in many jurisdictions, welfare standards of income necessary for sufficiency are based on outdated cost estimates—rent allowances, for example, are based on 1953 rent figures; food allowances on 1957 food costs. In addition, the payments for each additional child to a family of three children or more are reduced on the unverified assumption that large families live more cheaply. See The Public Welfare Crisis in the Nation's Capital, op. cit., pp. 14, 29.

81. Sometimes the husband is given a suspended sentence on the condition that he begin to make monthly support payments plus an additional sum toward the arrearage due under the earlier court order to support the family. When this happens, the welfare department frequently reduces the public assistance check to the family in a sum which is equivalent to the amount of support payments ordered plus the amount ordered in payment of the arrearage.

82. A report on the Aid to Dependent Children Program in Chicago noted: "The climate in the department which places such emphasis on denying assistance and the lack of consistent application of . . . policies in the Aid to Dependent Children program is damaging to the applicant or recipient and serves to prolong and perpetuate dependency. Some of the staff treat the families with consideration and decency and try to be helpful and understanding while at the same time adhering strictly to policy. Others are rigid and punitive, with little regard for human dignity. Their attitudes are destructive of personality, ambition and self respect—and intensify existing problems." Greenleigh Associates, Inc., op. cit.

A study of the public assistance program in New York State reached a similar conclusion: "An applicant becomes eligible for assistance when he exhausts his money, gives a lien of his property to the welfare department, turns in the license plates of his car and takes legal action against his legally responsible relatives. When he is stripped of all material resources, when he 'proves' his dependency, then and only then is he eligible. Welfare policies tend to cast the recipient in the role of the propertyless, shiftless pauper. This implies he is incompetent and inadequate to meet the demands of competitive life. He is then regarded as if he had little or no feelings, aspirations or normal sensibilities. This process of proving and maintaining eligibility in combination with the literal adherence to regulations and procedures tends to produce a self-perpetuating system of dependency and dehumanization." Report to the Moreland Commission on Welfare of Findings of the Study of the Public Assistance Program and Operations of the State of New York (Nov. 1962), p. 78.

83. To a great extent, of course, the problem of the urban poor involves the problem of the urban racial minority. More study needs

to be made of the extent to which the attitude of the poor toward the law varies in degree as the particular persons concerned are of differing racial and ethnic groups. Jim Finney, who has represented Negroes in Harlem, finds that there "the attitude of cynicism about the law and the fairness of its administration is related to the Negro struggle, impatience with the progress of that struggle, and with the pace of that progress." Finney, "Neighborhood Legal Assistance Program: The Harlem Experience," paper presented at the Conference on the Extension of Legal Services to the Poor, *op. cit.*, p. 2.

84. The quotation is from a review by Nat Hentoff of the newly released set of records: Woodie Guthrie: Library of Congress Recordings, *The Reporter*, Jan. 14, 1965, p. 48.

85. *See* O. Lewis, *Children of Sanchez* (New York: Random House, Inc., 1961); Gladwin, *op. cit.*; Harrington, *op. cit.*; E. Herzog, "Some Assumptions About the Poor," *The Social Service Review*, Dec. 1963, pp. 389–402. The latter article cautions, however, that the culture concept is a useful one only if it is recognized that a vast range of individual differences coexist with the prevailing patterns of thought, feeling, and behavior that make up what might be called "culture character."

86. A few of the leaders in the bar who have for years urged greater representation of the poor include Mayer C. Goldman, author of *The Public Defender*, New York: G. P. Putnam Sons, 1917; Reginald Heber Smith, who wrote the landmark *Justice and the Poor* (New York: Carnegie Institute for the Advancement of Teaching, 1929); Emery Brownell, author of *Legal Aid in the United States*, Rochester: Lawyers' Coop, 1951; and Elliott Cheatham of Columbia University, who recently wrote *A Lawyer When Needed* (New York: Columbia Univ. Press, 1964).

87. C. Ares, "Legal Education and the Problems of the Poor," paper presented at the Conference on the Extension of Legal Services to the Poor, *op. cit.*

88. *Ibid.*

89. Edward Bennet Williams, in an interview for the Center for the Study of Democratic Institutions, noted that he had been a guest lecturer at some twenty-five law schools. "I quickly discovered that most of the law students have as their professional goal the securing of a position with a large law firm, preferably in New York, San Francisco, or Los Angeles, and that they want to work in the field of antitrust, or corporate law, or in the taxation field. . . . They are preparing for professional fields wholly concerned with problems affecting property rights. The facets of the law dealing with the human freedoms and individual liberties safeguarded by the Bill of Rights hold their interest only in an academic way." Quoted in *The Law* (Dec. 1962), pp. 3–4.

90. Erwin Griswold, dean of Harvard Law School, contends that the problem of inadequate representation for indigent defendants is essentially a political failure to establish a well-financed public-defender program.

"The difficulty has not come from lack of professional leadership but from the failure of the political leadership in our legislatures, state and federal, to take appropriate action. . . . The scarcity of persons interested in the practice of criminal law is directly traceable to this lack of publicly recognized responsibility." Dean's Report 1963–1964, Harvard Law School, pp. 5, 7.

91. In the state of Virginia, for example, National Legal Aid and Defender statistics reveal that only three cities had legal aid organizations providing help in civil matters. Two of the cities were set up by local bar associations and one through a social agency. Each agency had only about $4000 financial support (less than eight-tenths of a cent per person) and handled less than 200 new cases during the year. Statistics of Legal Aid Work in the United States and Canada, National Legal Aid and Defender Association, for 1963. In the criminal area, public-defender agencies exist in only 184 out of the 3100 counties in the country, according to Trebach, *op. cit.*, p. 111, who was until recently Administrator of the Defender Project of the National Legal Aid and Defender Association.

92. In response to charges that free legal aid is subject to abuse, the Junior Bar Section of the Bar Association of the District of Columbia undertook a study of the matter. It issued a report based on close examination of the cases of about 100 criminal defendants in the District court who had posted bail prior to arraignment but had been assigned appointed counsel for their trials because they claimed "indigency." After reviewing its detailed findings, the committee concluded that "virtually *all* of the defendants . . . would, under any reasonable standard, be considered sufficiently impoverished to require free legal counsel." (Emphasis added.) Report of the Committee on Standards of Indigency, Bar Association of the District of Columbia, Jr. Bar Section, Aug. 1, 1963, p. 31.

93. See the report of the Commission on Legal Aid of the Bar Association of the District of Columbia, 1958, one of the most comprehensive studies made of legal aid service as it commonly exists. Commenting on the deficiencies of volunteer legal service, the report states: "Time consuming litigation may be shunned even though litigation is warranted; time consuming research is eschewed even though extensive research is essential to resolution of the problem." (pp. 140–41).

94. Charles Parker, a leading member of the Connecticut Bar and President of the Board of Directors of a Ford Foundation sponsored legal-aid program, has described legal-aid history in New Haven as follows: "In common with other traditional social agencies, public and private, neither legal aid nor the public defender in New Haven seemed to have any capability of dealing creatively with the problems of the deprived citizens at the core of the City, the multiproblem families. . . . An illusion of service for these clients has taken the place of constructive social therapy." Parker, "The New Haven Model," paper presented at Conference on the Extension of Legal Services to the Poor, *op. cit.*

95. A. P. Blaustein and C. O. Porter, *The American Lawyer* (Chicago: Univ. of Chicago Press, 1954).

96. One leading example is the Center for the Study of Law and Society at the University of California at Berkeley, established in

1961 to develop a program of research and study of the social formulations of law and legal institutions. Others include Southern
Illinois University's Center for the Study of Crime, Delinquency, and
Corrections, and Howard University's Law and Human Rights Program.

97. Georgetown University offers a graduate law degree to students who combine study with practical criminal-defense work in
the District of Columbia courts. Boston University Law School offers
a course in criminal law as a part of its regular curriculum which
includes actual representation of indigent defendants in Massachusetts courts. Such representation takes place under the supervision
of a faculty member of the Massachusetts Bar, who appears as
attorney of record in each case.

98. At its past midwinter meeting, the American Bar Association
frankly recognized that traditional methods of helping the poor were
no longer adequate and adopted without dissent a resolution to
cooperate with the Office of Economic Opportunity. The meeting was
attended and reported by Morton Mintz in a series of articles in *The
Washington Post*, Feb. 5, 8–9, 1965.

99. *NAACP* v. *Button*, 371 U.S. 415 (1963); *Brotherhood of
Railroad Trainmen* v. *Virginia State Bar*, 377 U.S. 1 (1964). In the
former case, the NAACP employed attorneys to attend various community meetings of Negroes to urge them to end discriminatory
practices through court litigation, using the professional services of
the NAACP legal staff. The court held that a state could not enforce
a state bar association condemnation of the practice on the ground
that it violated the bar's canon of professional ethics against "solicitation." In the *Brotherhood* case, the court reversed many state
decisions and held that a labor union might properly refer its members to certain private lawyers who would represent them for a
reduced fee. The court even hinted that it might be proper for the
union to employ lawyers to represent union members. The full implications of these decisions are not yet known, although it is generally acknowledged that group legal practice in which the legal
problems of an individual are handled by a lawyer employed and
paid by an organization was given a significant boost. In the past,
the organized bar has resisted most group legal practice. Following
the *NAACP* and *Brotherhood* cases, however, a special committee
of the bar of California recommended that group legal services be
allowed to expand under ethical standards set by the bar. See Report
of the Committee on Group Legal Services, State Bar of California,
July 30, 1964.

100. Perhaps the best exposition of the built-in pressures from
vested community interests which the proposed neighborhood sociolegal programs face in their attack on poverty is set forth in the
law journal article by Edgar and Jean Cahn, *op. cit.*

101. *The New York Times*, Dec. 20, 1964. The *Times* article
reported further that the Connecticut Bar Association's Committee
on Unauthorized Practice of Law would conduct an investigation of
the proposed "controversial plan to provide free legal aid to indigent
persons . . . on a neighborhood basis."

102. *See* C. E. Silberman, "Up From Apathy—The Woodlawn Experiment," *Commentary*, May 1964, p. 51; and *idem.*, *Crisis in Black and White* (New York: Random House, Inc., 1964), pp. 207–208, 308 *et seq.*

103. The necessity for incorporating the "consumer" or "civilian" perspective in legal institutions has been advocated by both the late Edmund Cahn ("The Consumers of Injustice," *New York University Law Review*, 34 (Nov. 1959), p. 1166; "Law in the Consumer Perspective, *University of Pennsylvania Law Review*, 118 (Nov. 1963), p. 1, and by his son Edgar. The latter, together with his wife Jean have recently stressed the importance of that perspective in waging the current War on Poverty: ". . . the elimination of poverty [must] be understood as comprehending spiritual as well as physical subsistence and as involving the assurance of civil as well as economic self-sufficiency. . . . It was to one aspect of the disenfranchisement of the urban poor that the Supreme Court addressed itself in the malapportionment cases. Yet the process of enfranchisement must not cease with the composition of the legislature; it must take place in all the organs of government—both public and private where law is made." Edgar and Jean Cahn, *op. cit.*, pp. 1331, 1333.

The Politics
of Poverty

ELINOR GRAHAM

In January 1964, a man familiar
to congressional surroundings delivered his first address to
a joint session of Congress in his new role as President of
the United States. As he presented his presidential program
to Congress, Lyndon Johnson called for an "unconditional
war on poverty," a government commitment "not only to
relieve the symptoms of poverty, but to cure it; and above
all, to prevent it."

The complex of ideological themes and political programs officially recognized and initiated by this address—
all under the slogan of a War on Poverty—is the topic of
this paper. The analysis developed here views this "war"
as a key ingredient in the social and political ideology
embraced by President Johnson, his administrative officials,
and his advisers. As part of an ideology, it is designed to
motivate elements in the society to political action. The
language of the War on Poverty and the form of its accompanying social-welfare programs are set within the bound-

aries of traditional social beliefs, arise from the pressure of political needs, and are molded by the nature of those groups seeking action, as well as by the official bodies from which they must receive approval.

Poverty, consequently, is now a major preoccupation of hundreds of public officials, statisticians and social planners across the nation. In less than a year it has been thrust dramatically into the center of governmental programing on local, regional, and national levels. President Johnson has called for "total victory" in a national War on Poverty—"a total commitment by the President, and this Congress, and this Nation, to pursue victory over the most ancient of mankind's enemies."[1] Joining the administration forces and local and state governments, private social-welfare organizations and institutions normally engaged in nonwelfare activities have increasingly indicated an awareness of possibilities, and a willingness, to engage their organizational resources in "extrainstitutional" activities aimed at the alleviation of poverty. Colleges, churches, and corporations have plunged into a potpourri of activities designed to provide "opportunities" for deserving members of low-income groups in forms, and to an extent, that welfare workers could previously conceive only in their wildest dreams.

Given an "understanding of the enemy" which emphasizes the special characteristics of certain low-income groups that cannot easily be integrated into the market economy, what "strategy of attack" is advocated by the national policy-makers? The "war on poverty" proposed in 1964 consisted of a ten-point attack which strikingly resembled the President's entire domestic program: income tax cuts, a civil rights bill, Appalachian regional development, urban and rural community rehabilitation, youth programs, teenage and adult vocational training and basic educational programs, and hospital insurance for the aged. A special "anti-poverty package" was introduced—the Economic Opportunity Act of 1964. The Office of Economic Opportunity created by this legislation was to be the headquarters for the new "war."

Administration of the Economic Opportunity Act and supporting programs, as well as plans for future expansion, indicate that the War on Poverty seeks to mobilize the social services of the nation along three major lines: youth education and employment programs, planned regional and community redevelopment, and vocational training and retraining under the beginnings of a national manpower policy.

Under this "strategy of attack," aid to the poor is, in theory, provided in the nature of a new and expanded "opportunity environment." Such aid is primarily directed toward the youth and employable heads of poor families; it will not reach the really critical poverty categories—the aged, female heads of families, and poor farm families— except in the form of improvements in the surrounding physical and economic environments or the administration of welfare and health services. As the Council of Economic Advisers noted in their 1964 report, the proposed programs are designed "to equip and to permit the poor of the Nation to produce and to earn . . . the American standard of living by their own efforts and contributions." Those Americans who are not in a physical or family position which allows them to earn their way out of poverty will not be immediately aided by the programs under the War on Poverty. This situation simply illustrates the difference between social needs defined in a statistical manner and a political designation of poverty. It does not indicate that the War on Poverty is a political hoax or a hollow slogan to attract votes; on the contrary, its ideology and programs respond to social and political needs of a very real, although very different, nature, than those of poverty per se.

The Sociology of Poverty Programs

It is useful to locate welfare-state programs on two scales, vertically and horizontally, in order to visualize the range and nature of programs open to government planners in formulating the War on Poverty and to understand the implications of the particular path chosen. The vertical scale of our imaginary axes indicates at one end whether the poverty-stricken are singled out of the total society as objects for special aid or, at the opposite pole, social services and income payments are provided to all as a right of citizenship. The latter method is followed in most of the Swedish welfare programs. Family payments, old-age pensions, and health services are provided for all members of the society regardless of their financial position. Most United States welfare programs, including those proposed under the War on Poverty, are located at the opposite pole: programs are focused at a particular low-income category and need must be proven in order to receive aid. The second (and horizontal) scale indicates at one end that aid may be provided in the form of direct income payments and at the other extreme through social services. The major portion of the welfare activities in the United States, and particularly those connected with the War on Poverty, are found in the service category, even though, as was argued above, the nature of American poverty in the sixties indicates an urgent need for consideration of direct income payments to critical poverty-stricken groups.

Certain important implications follow from the need-based and service-oriented nature of the War on Poverty programs. First, separation of the poor from the rest of the society by means of need requirements, increases the visibility of the low-income earners. This is a "war" *on poverty* —the very nature of such a proposal requires an exposure of "the enemy" in its human form. In addition, separation of the poor creates a donor-donee relationship whether it exists between the income-tax-paying middle and upper classes and the low-income earners, or the social worker and his client. In the context of American social philosophy, such a situation enhances the self-image of the well-to-do and places a stigma of failure and dependency upon aid recipients. Above all, it is "the American way" to approach social-welfare issues, for it places the burden of responsibility upon the individual and not upon the socioeconomic system. Social services are preferred to income payments in an ideological atmosphere which abhors "handouts."

Second, a focus upon *poverty* allows for a redefinition of the racial clash into the politically understandable and useful terms of a conflict between the "haves" and the "have-nots." The donor-donee relationship, sharply cast into relief by the poverty label, reasserts and stabilizes the power of the political elite, whose positions have been threatened by enfranchisement of the Negro.

Third, the social-service orientation, particularly the stress upon the "reorganization" and "total mobilization" of existing programs, is strongly supported by the nature of the experimental programs started during the Kennedy years. These programs and, of more importance, the ideas and "method of attack" which they initiated, are vigorously advocated by a well-organized and sophisticated lobby within the administrative branch.

Fourth, the social-service orientation of the War on Poverty is *activity-* and *job*-creating for the middle and upper classes. Provision of social services, as opposed to income payments, requires the formation of new organizations and institutions which in turn are the source of activities and income-paying roles for the nation's expanding number of college-educated individuals. The War on Poverty, its programs and ideology, are a response to the demands of an educated "new class": it provides a legitimate outlet for the energies of a group that poses a greater threat to the political system and moral fabric of the society than the inadequately educated poor who are the official objects of aid.

Ideology and Poverty

A nation which confidently points to its unparalleled level of wealth, the "magnificent abundance" of the American way of life, has been suddenly and surprisingly engaged in the public unveiling of the impoverished degradation of one-fifth of its population. Affluence and poverty confront each other, and the shock of the encounter is reflected in the phrase that acknowledges the "stranger's" presence: a "paradox"—the "paradox of poverty in the midst of plenty." This mysterious stranger is apparently inconsistent with the nation's vision of itself and particularly with its moral notions of equality.

One supposes that there is an element of honest surprise and, with many, disbelief, for they *know* that if you work hard and take advantage of all of the opportunities available, you *can* climb out of poverty and reach the top—well, perhaps not *the* top, but certainly a comfortable level of living. It is axiomatic. Numerous individuals will tediously cite their own life experiences as examples of this general law of dynamics of American society. The following account was provided by a retired educator who sought to establish his qualification to talk about poverty in the sixties:

> . . . I was born in a homestead on the lowland swamps of Louisiana. There were no schools. We lived off the land. And, since I have viewed the very sections of the underprivileged and poor people in the Appalachian highland, I decided I must have been very poor, because those children there have much more now than I had. We lived from game, and we had no electric lights. We got food if there were plenty of ducks and geese and rabbits . . . I was a drop-in at school when they finally got a little one- or two-room school. I mean, I dropped in when there were no potatoes to plant or corn to pull, or something of that sort. I have three college degrees from standard universities, and I never spent a day on a college campus during regular session. I belong to the old school. I took correspondence; I did some summer terms, and I did extension work, traveling sometimes a hundred miles each weekend to take it. So I think I know what it means to get an education the hard way. . . . I understand the phase in our help to the underprivileged.[2]

Everyone who is over thirty will say that they know what it is like to be poor because they lived during the Great Depression; that is taken as automatic qualification. When attacked by his Democratic "bretheren" for a lack of understanding of the complexities of the problem, Representative

Griffin (R.-Mich.) responded with, "my father worked most of his life in a plant; and I worked my way through school, and I believe I do know a little bit about poverty."[3] Without denying the achievements of the poor boy from the swamps of Louisiana who is now a distinguished educator, or the son of a worker holding the office of U.S. congressman, such accounts and their implications for the "struggling young men" from present-day poor families reflect a general confusion of the income and social-class mobility of an individual with a rising national standard of living. The American dream is substituted for the American reality and evidence drawn from the second is said to be proof of the first.

President Johnson intertwined the two concepts when he declared in his 1964 War on Poverty message that:

> With the growth of our country has come opportunity for our people—opportunity to educate our children, to use our energies in productive work, to increase our leisure—opportunity for almost every American to hope that through work and talent he could create a better life for himself and his family.[4]

Traditional themes of the bright boy attaining entrance to the world of wealth through "work and talent" are intermingled with the profit figures of economic growth. In suggesting that the benefits of a rising standard of living include increased opportunity for bettering income and even social-class position, two distinct and different concepts are equated for ideological purposes.

Fusion of dream and actuality in the national vision has been strongly influenced by the American business creed and its image of the relationship between the economic system and the individual. Benefits derived from the economic growth of the nation are not conceived as social products. The idealized "free-enterprise" system produces the national wealth through the efforts of atomized individuals operating within a "free competitive market system with individual freedom." A guarantee of the rights of the individual to insure his freedom and free opportunity are thus essential. Since mythology need not correspond to reality (particularly if believed in strongly enough), equality of opportunity is assumed and is "proved" through the individual success stories which abound in the popular literature. Such "proof" is, however, subject to a great deal of doubt. Citing several sociological studies, the authors of *The American Business Creed* observe that a survey of the overall statistical situation "might well lead to more tempered conclusions about American freedom of opportunity."[5]

With an image of itself that denies the possibility of widespread poverty, a nation bent on "recognizing realities" must squeeze the poor in through the basement window. We are told that we are not faced with extensive conditions of poverty (as are other less fortunate nations). Poverty in the United States is "grinding poverty," found only in "pockets of poverty" and has defied all laws of genetics to acquire an hereditary quality exhibited in the "ruthless pattern" and "cycle of poverty." This is not a case of good old-fashioned poverty, it is a special and uniquely American—1964 brand.

A particularly vivid exposition of this version of poverty can be found in the explanation of the Economic Opportunity Act prepared by Sargent Shriver's office for the first congressional hearings.[6] Much of the credit for the modern version of poverty expounded within its covers must go to the influence of John Kenneth Galbraith's writings. He broke the poor into two groups—those afflicted with *case* poverty and those who are victims of *insular* poverty. Characteristics of the individual afflicted with case poverty prevent him from mastering his environment, while the environment proves to be the handicapping factor for those living in "islands of poverty." In both situations an hereditary factor is introduced either in fact (as a physical tendency toward poor health or mental deficiency) or in effect through the deficiencies of the social environment (as with poor schools, lack of job opportunities, lack of motivation and direction from parents).[7] Whether or not such a view corresponds to reality, it should be recognized that when one maintains that the society is affluent, poverty can hardly be tolerated as a widespread phenomenon and must be of a very special and individual variety. With such a thesis, one is not likely to observe that an average American family with an income of $5665—the median for all families in 1960—may not feel particularly affluent at this "modest but adequate" level.

Where, then, are the roots of poverty in an affluent society? Few combatants in the war of ideologies argue that the fault underlies the American landscape and may be lodged in the economic system. The principle according to which the wealth of the society is divided is left unscathed. On official levels, voices do not openly suggest that a system which distributes economic goods solely upon the basis of the individual's present or past functional role within the economy may be at the source of American poverty now and increasingly so in the future. Although not reflecting official opinion, the statement of the Ad Hoc Committee on the Triple Revolution was a notable exception. This group of distinguished educators, labor leaders, economists, and critics suggested in part that:

> The economy of abundance can sustain all citizens in comfort and economic security whether or not they engage in what is commonly reckoned as work. . . . We urge, therefore, that society through its appropriate legal and governmental institutions undertake an unqualified commitment to provide every individual in every family with an adequate income as a matter of right.[8]

Right-wing reaction is clear and quite predictable when the legitimacy of the American economic system is questioned in any context. There was no doubt in the mind of Representative Martin (R.-Neb.) that the suggestions of the committee were of "the same kind of plan worked out in Communist nations."[9] Such a reaction hardly leaves room for political debate.

Where questions regarding "the system" are taboo, those focusing upon the individual are welcome and quite com-

prehensible to the political protagonists. In acceptable
political circles, the causes of poverty are sought in the
process through which individuals acquire qualities enabling
them to succeed and share in the national wealth. Conservatives argue that the fault lies with the poor for being
lazy or stupid and not taking advantage of opportunities
to obtain education, good health, a marketable skill, and a
stable family life. "The fact is that most people who have
no skill, have had no education for the same reason—low
intelligence or low ambition!" says Barry Goldwater.[10] On
the other hand, liberals maintain that something is wrong
with the present means provided for individuals to obtain
these desirable attributes—in short, the society is at fault:
the poor are the "have-not people of America. They are
denied, deprived, disadvantaged, and they are discriminated
against," argues Walter Reuther of the United Auto Workers.[11] President Johnson and Sargent Shriver, commander
of the poverty forces, bow to both groups. They maintain
that it is first necessary to change the attitudes of the poor
—to give them achievement motivations by changing "indifference to interest, ignorance to awareness, resignation
to ambition, and an attitude of withdrawal to one of participation."[12] At the same time, present education, social-
welfare, and job-training programs sponsored at all levels
of government and in both the public and private sectors of
society, must be coordinated, consolidated and expanded to
provide a new "opportunity environment" for the poor.

The emphasis is upon the process by which Americans
attain the attributes necessary to achieve economic success
rather than the legitimacy of the system to distribute the
national wealth. This view is enhanced by the assumption
that Americans, and poor Americans in particular, must
earn and "want to earn" any social or economic benefits
they receive. In our society, states former Senator Goldwater,
one receives rewards by "merit and not by fiat"—essentially,
you earn your keep or you get out (or stay out):

> I strongly believe that all people are entitled to an oppor-
> tunity . . . to get an education and to earn a living *in*

keeping with the value of their work [emphasis supplied].
. . . But I do not believe that the mere fact of having little
money entitles everybody, regardless of circumstance, to be
permanently maintained by the taxpayers at an average or
comfortable standard of living.[13]

Conservatives make no effort to conceal their reliance
on this basic assumption; they quite frankly do not want to
change the present distribution of wealth, or potential
advantages they may have in gaining a greater future share.
They are successful because they deserve to be successful,
while others are poor because they are innately incapable
of doing any better. This assumption about human nature
is an integral part of the business creed, for the idealized
economic system is dependent upon the "achievement motivations" of the individual. These crucial motivations could
easily be destroyed if people became dependent upon government doles. If this happened, the greatest welfare system
of all, the "free-enterprise system," would be destroyed. As
the witness from the Chamber of Commerce explained to
Representative Edith Green during the House antipoverty
hearings, the Chamber does not support "programs for
people" because:

. . . economic measures to improve the efficiency of production and thus to get a larger output for our people from the
same input of materials and manpower and capital goods is
one of the greatest contributions to wealth that has ever been
discovered in the history of mankind and the United States
excels among all nations of the world in providing this kind
of welfare.[14]

Despite conservative denunciations, President Johnson
eagerly reserves a benevolent role for the federal government, and particularly on an ideological level. He counters
conservative views by adding a second act to the drama of
the poor struggling young man working his way to the top
in the "free-enterprise system." A magnanimous millionaire,
glowing with compassion and wisdom, stretches out a benevolent helping hand to enable "Ragged Dick" to make good in
the final panel of the American dream. Evoking an image of

a goddess of peace and plenty rather than lanky Uncle Sam, Johnson declares that both at home and abroad, "We will extend the helping hand of a just nation to the poor and helpless and the oppressed."[15] In the American reality, however, "we" take care to see that the "helping hand" doesn't contain money or tangible goods—just opportunities to earn a better way of life and opportunities *to learn* to "want to earn" in the American way.

Such a sense of *noblesse oblige* is not inherent in the actual programs and techniques proposed in the War on Poverty, but it plays a part in the language which is inevitably used to describe them (and which is perhaps latent within our "progressive" attitudes toward social welfare). It is also the result of the effective control and administration of the government by the affluent and educated classes. In short, the official government attitude toward poverty should be expected to reflect the views arising from the life-situations of those who have formulated it. In speaking of poverty, no one bothers to deny or to hide the fact that the federal government is an instrumentality of the successful classes. This is assumed. The poor are recognized as not having a significant political voice. The entire War on Poverty was created, inspired, and will be carried out by the affluent. Action by the upper classes and all superior groups is urged on moral grounds, because it is right, because, as Senator Robert Kennedy stated simply, "those of us who are better off, who do not have that problem have a responsibility to our fellow citizens who do."[16]

Without an economic crisis which affects the upper-income groups as well as the poor, the social philosophy of the federal antipoverty programs will necessarily contain this strong moral emphasis. Caught between the language of American social mythology and the attitudes generated by the existing social and political realities of a wealthy nation ruled by a distinct class of successful men, the public debate generated by the proposed "war" can only reveal our poverty of ideology. Conservatives balk at action because the poor are "getting what they deserve," and liberals can-

not seem to act without assuming the "white man's burden."
The militants of the new "war" look for the enemy and find
him all too often in the personal attributes of the poor. The
remedy offered for poverty amounts to a middle-class success formula (and, perhaps it *is* the route to success in
American society): education, a stable family life, and
above all, the proper attitudes. In short, there appears to be
justification for the charge that the War on Poverty can be
more accurately characterized as a "war on the poor."[17]

The Politics of Poverty and Race

Confronted with a social ideology which easily obscures
the existence of poverty, and lacking a thunderous economic crisis that directly threatens the middle and upper
classes, the public concern with poverty of a traditionally
reactive government is most remarkable. Why did poverty
become a politically important issue in 1964?

When asked the reasons for a War on Poverty, President
Johnson and Sargent Shriver presented themselves as pup-
pets of the American people who "are interested in the
Government and in themselves making a focused or concentrated effort to attack poverty."[18] A public demand for
the elimination of poverty, did not, however, exist before it
was deliberately made into an issue by the Johnson Administration in 1964. Government programs were not a
response to public protests against conditions of poverty
for one-fifth of a nation. (An exception to this was perhaps
the March on Washington in the summer of 1963, which
came close to protesting poverty directly with demands for
more jobs; but the publicity impact of this event was chan-
neled into exclusive concern with civil rights.)

After President Johnson announced his War on Poverty
in his State of the Union address on January 8, 1964, the
nation was deluged with vivid descriptions of the life of the
poor, statistical accounts of their number and characteristics, and details of their geographic location. Poverty became such a "problem" that, by the time Shriver testified

at the congressional hearings, there was a degree of truth to his statement. The power of the presidency to stimulate the news media into undertaking a massive effort to increase public awareness, if not to generate actual demands for government action, was dramatically demonstrated. This achievement should not, however, obscure the fact that demands for action directly focused upon poverty did not exist prior to the time that the administration began to produce its new policy line.

Political power-needs, rather than an articulated public demand, were at the source of the sudden resolution to recognize poverty in 1964. Briefly, the most plausible occasion for the urgency and publicity devoted to poverty by the Executive Office can be found in the political and emotionally disrupting effects of the civil-rights movement, especially in regard to white morality and the white power structure. Emotionally, the nation needed to redefine the racial conflict as a conflict between the "haves" and the "have-nots." Politically, a transmutation of the civil-rights movement secured the threatened power position of whites as whites, and further eased the agonies of the slow political death of the south. The latter, with its implications for the composition of the national political parties, has held special meaning for Johnson in his struggle to unify the Democratic Party and attain congressional compliance with presidential programs. In practical terms, the War on Poverty and its implications for opening a new field of jobs and social status, is the means by which American society will expand to accommodate the Negroes' demands for integration.

For over four years, white America has been forced into a state of acute consciousness of its prejudices and unexamined beliefs. In a white man's world, however, Negroes from the time of their early years live with a racial awareness. They must know and understand this world in a very practical sense in order to survive. But whites "experience race" at a more mature age—they are not "born" with it—and in the past they gained their experience somewhat at

their own convenience. Suddenly in the sixties, the Negro
has become a political power; he has become a "new" Negro
who won't fit into the old images. This forced racial confrontation has caught the white off-guard. He does not possess a cultural reservoir that would allow him to interact
—or avoid interaction—easily and unemotionally. Political
protests, in short, have resulted in a social dislocation of
the Negro and have created a necessity for both races to
become aware of themselves and their inter-projective
images. Politically, this awareness and the knowledge it
can bring, is both necessary and beneficial. But this is an
inconvenience for the white, an inconvenience requiring
extra effort that may result in heightened tension as well as
awareness.

The task of knowing is greatly simplified for the white
American if he substitutes "poverty" for "race." He can
more easily understand the frustrations of job hunting or
unemployment than what it means to possess a black skin.
"Poverty" has a comfortable sound to it, it makes "sense"
and is not emotionally upsetting. Politically speaking, to
redefine race and civil rights as a manifestation of conditions of poverty, opens a path for action. Where race and
nationalism are vivid, emotion-based issues, not easily re-
solved through reason and logic, conflict between the "haves"
and the "have-nots" is well understood. The Western world
has a supply of practical tools and intellectual theories with
which this persistent enemy can be explained and controlled.
Marxian ideology, liberal benevolence, or a religious morality all allow for practical political action that is denied
when confronted by race in and of itself. Whether or not
the civil-rights movement dramatized existing conditions of
poverty, white Americans had to raise the poverty issue to
relieve the emotional tension and political impasse created
by the racial confrontation. The dollar costs of a War on
Poverty are exchanged for the high emotional price-tag at-
tached to race.

Aside from this exchange of emotion for practicality,
poverty redefines civil rights in a manner that secures the

power positions of white public leaders and places them in control of a movement which frequently has attempted to exclude them, on racial grounds, from exercising a directing influence. Three groups are the principal beneficiaries of this effect: the white liberal "sympathetic" to the Negro cause, public officials in the large urban centers, and the southern politician.

The white liberal has found himself increasingly excluded from policy-making positions in the civil-rights movement. He has been told that he could contribute his warm body and little else in a revolution which was felt to express legitimately only the suffering of the American Negro. However, when the "movement" is placed in the context of a battle between the wealthy and the poor, between the "power-lords" and the "exploited underdog," it is possible to carve out a legitimate place for whites within a dynamic and powerful social movement. Such a recasting of the Negro struggle cuts across racial boundaries to transform it into a fight for "all humanity." A new struggle is created which has a great potential for rallying sustained activities within accepted political channels. But, also, it may push the Negro to the background once again, for he does not have the same priority for a leading role in the new antipoverty struggle. Professional and respectable, social revolutionaries assume directing positions in a poverty war whereas indigenous leadership was beginning to develop out of the civil-rights struggle.

Public officials in the large urban centers have also found their authority threatened and severely shaken by a ground swell which they had to appease in order to survive. Something had to be offered the angry Negro segment of the populace. They couldn't offer to make a Negro white, or at least they couldn't overtly approach the racial question in this manner, although such an objective may underlie the antipoverty programs offered the Negro, with their emphasis upon instilling white middle-class motivations and values. They could, however, offer to train him, to educate him, and perhaps give him a little more *hope* of obtaining solid employment. In other words, the Negro must be viewed as "poor," as deprived of services which the government apparatus can provide, in order to engage him in political bargaining. The demonstrators are taken off the streets and placed in the hands of the welfare bureaucracies and the new "antipoverty" programs which can placate demands more quickly than the courts. (And, hopefully, in a more substantial and lasting manner.) This need exists on the national level, but in its War on Poverty the federal government has left the distribution of public goods and services to the local political leaders, whose positions are most immediately threatened by the volatile protest and developing political power of the Negro.

Reaction to the race riots of previous summers provides ample illustration of the ideological function of an antipoverty slogan and the practical role of its accompanying programs. Immediately after the 1964 riots in New York City, Wagner made a special trip to Washington to see if more antipoverty projects and other federal money could be directed toward the slum areas of the city. As *The New York Times* interpreted the visit:

> It would be highly surprising if Mr. Wagner—Mayor of the city where the present epidemic of racial disturbances began —did not mean, as part of his mission, to remind members of the House of the intimate connection between the battle against poverty and the battle against riots. . . . The antipoverty bill, in the new perspective given by the disturbances of this long, hot summer, is also an anti-riot bill. The members of the House of Representatives will do well to bear that in mind when the time comes for a vote.[19]

The fact that Wagner's trip produced few promises for programs and less cash was not as important as the public assurance that something could and would be done. Fortunately, the city had initiated its own antipoverty planning in the spring and could point to several programs already underway. Both large federal juvenile-delinquency programs, Mobilization for Youth and Haryou-Act, as well as the city's own program, Job Opportunities in Neighborhoods, were paraded before public view. In addition, the city signed a contract providing a $223,225 grant for Youth in Action, Inc., to develop an antipoverty program for youth in Brooklyn's Bedford-Stuyvesant area. A job-finding project for semiskilled and unskilled youngsters was accelerated. Programs of training and basic education conducted under MDTA received personal inspections from the mayor, with attendant publicity.

Not only has the President's War on Poverty provided evidence of sincere efforts to alleviate some of the needs of the low-income Negro ghettos, but it also provided white society with a defense against charges of overt racism. Poverty and racism have joined hands to create the Negro's hell—the effects of one cannot be separated easily from the other. When given the choice, however, white society prefers to attribute the source of Negro resentment and protests to poverty. *The New York Times* employed this defense when it maintained that the race riots were "as much demonstrations against Negro poverty as against discrimination and what some call 'police brutality'."[20] In this respect, we should note the extent to which right-wing politicians ignore the racial aspect of the Negro protest and refer to it almost exclusively as a conflict between the "haves" and the "have-nots." They simply make it clear that they are on the side of the "haves." Morally there may be something wrong with denying privileges on the basis of race, but within the right-wing ideology, there is "nothing wrong" with defending your own property and privileges from someone who is not as successful.

For reasons of a less than morally commendable nature, white America has responded to the Negroes' demands for an integrated society with an antipoverty movement: a response slow in coming and pitifully inadequate at first, but still a response. In terms of realistic social dynamics, integration is not, and will not be, an interpenetration of the old by the new, but will be a process of *expansion* and then assimilation. Societies expand and contract; they do not bend except with passing of generations, and that cannot even be predicted with assurance. Those who are within the socioeconomic structure will not give up their positions to Negroes seeking entrance. New roles must be added to the job structure and new status rungs created in the social ladder.

Such is the function of the War on Poverty. As was pointed out, it is a service-oriented welfare measure. The activity- and job-creating nature of its programs are presently opening and shaping new fields in the social services, a process that is certain to increase its range in the future. New professional positions in community organization and social planning, as well as the clerical and blue-collar jobs created to staff the research institutions and service organizations of the "antipoverty" projects, are particularly accessible to the Negro. This is true, above all, for the now small but increasing ranks of the college educated and professionally trained Negro. The politically dangerous energies of the Negro elite can be molded into socially legitimate channels through the creation of roles in an entirely new area of the nation's job structure.

The Negro asks for integration and receives a War on Poverty: it is perhaps not exactly what he ordered nor in the form he imagined, but it is the first step American society is capable of providing. And it is a step that can lead potentially through jobs and social status toward the dignity and justice he desires.

NOTES

1. President's Message on Poverty to the Congress, March 16, 1964.

2. House Hearings, *Economic Opportunity Act of 1964,* Subcommittee on the War on Poverty Program of the Committee on Education and Labor, House of Representatives, 88th Congress, 2nd Session, Part II, pp. 1120–1121, "Statement of Joseph J. Vincent, Superintendent of Schools, South Park Independent School District, Beaumont, Texas."

3. *Ibid.,* pp. 854–855.

4. Special Message on Poverty to the United States Congress, March 16, 1964.

5. F. X. Sutton *et al.*, *The American Business Creed* (Cambridge: Harvard Univ. Press, 1956), p. 26.

6. *The War on Poverty, A Congressional Presentation*, Office of Economic Opportunity, March 17, 1964.

7. John Kenneth Galbraith, *The Affluent Society* (Boston: Houghton Mifflin Co., 1958), p. 251 ff.

8. Report of the Ad Hoc Committee on the Triple Revolution, April 1964.

9. House Hearings, *op. cit.*, p. 747.

10. *The New York Times*, Jan. 16, 1964.

11. House Hearings, *op. cit.*, Part I, p. 429.

12. *The War on Poverty, A Congressional Presentation*, *op. cit.*, p. 43.

13. *The New York Times*, Jan. 16, 1964.

14. House Hearings, *op. cit.*, Part I, p. 707.

15. *The New York Times*, Sept. 23, 1964.

16. House Hearings, *op. cit.*, p. 330.

17. "Johnson vs. Poverty," Christopher Jencks, *New Republic*, March 28, 1964.

18. House Hearings, *op. cit.*, p. 99.

19. *The New York Times*, editorial, "Riots and Poverty," Aug. 4, 1964.

20. *Ibid.*

Poverty and the
Legislative Process

ELINOR GRAHAM

Enactment of the Economic
Opportunity Act of 1964, provides an illuminating case
study in the strategy of compromise required to achieve congressional approval. As a manufactured policy not produced
as the result of overt public or political pressures, the outlines of the EOA were plotted by the administration with
the objections of its principal adversary, Congress, in mind.
The obstructionist role which Congress often assumes
within our governing structure allows it to deal two blows
to presidential policy: first in the anticipatory and planning
stages of drafting carried out by administrative officials, and
then again within the halls of Congress.

If one is sufficiently familiar with the objections and the
objectors, it appears possible to "play" Congress like a game
of croquet. One simply applies the correct pressure to go
through the proper wickets in the right order. As an old

hand at the game, President Johnson creates a compelling impression that he has not forgotten the rules. Credit for his legislative prowess should, however, be tempered with an appraisal of the political situation; 1964 was an election year, and legislative returns to the congressional district or state gain votes in November. In considering the President's political technique, one is tempted to attribute his success (always contrasted to Kennedy's "dismal failure") to a "greater respect" for the role of Congress and particularly the sensitivities of the conservative power structure. His soothing language and energetic efforts to avoid dissent are reflected in each public utterance, and tend to focus attention upon his technique and the "tone" of his political method. To a certain extent, his ideological maneuvering is simply verbiage; but with party realignment an emerging reality, it serves to create a tone for a "bipartisan" Johnson Administration—a political philosophy which will prove comfortable to both "liberal" Republicans and southern Democrats. Thus the presidential political sales campaigns are quite functional.

Three arguments or issues are deemed important by Congress in exercising its veto power. Its natural preoccupation with the main source of power, control over the pursestrings, makes *economy* in government administration a prime consideration, particularly in the House. This issue also encompasses efficiency in administration and the avoidance of duplication of activities. Second, a program must do something for "the people"—and mostly for "the people back home." Better yet, there should be some public need or demand, for after all ours is a government "responsive to the people." Third, it must fit within the "historic principles of American democracy." Objectively, this requirement could well mean that the legislation must not violate basic constitutional principles; however, in congressional terms, such a maxim in fact requires that legislation not violate an array of dogma dealing with everything from the nature of the American character to the proper balance of federal, state, and local governmental power.

In preparing the way for congressional presentation of his War on Poverty, President Johnson took care to pay obeisance to each of these issues. The President did not gain or sway votes for his key programs simply by meeting these "arguments." Rather, he faced a situation containing a degree of uncertainty and flexibility. By supplying effective counters to negativism, and counters in congressional language, the President provided support for congressmen shifting to new positions. The presidential publicity efforts were simply there to be used, if desired, or ignored, if more suitable.

The Presidential Posture

Almost as soon as he assumed office, the President's major concern was completion of the 1965 budget to be presented to Congress in mid-January. Immediately, the White House began to stress economy and frugality, with efficient, effective and *un*-expensive administration upheld as the ideal of ideals. The military was the first department spotlighted. In his initial White House Conference with the Joint Chiefs of Staff on November twenty-ninth, Johnson emphasized that "he expected their cooperation in redeeming his pledge to get a dollar's value for each military dollar spent."[1] Finding similar sentiments in Secretary of Defense McNamara, Johnson engaged him in a campaign to cut defense production costs. Letters urging cost reductions were sent to 7500 defense contractors by both McNamara and Johnson. They stressed the President's desire to attain "the utmost of thrift and frugality."[2] On December twelfth, their program was furthered a step when McNamara announced plans to close thirty-five military bases by October 1966.

Shifting the focus of his economy plan to other federal departments, Johnson called for a general federal job curb. He told department heads that he would not approve new personnel requests unless absolutely necessary. He further warned: "Nine out of ten Government employees do a full day's work for a day's pay, but I want the tenth man to measure up also."[3] To emphasize his point, he personally turned out the lights in the White House.

In addition to their ideological value, the defense cutbacks and other economy measures apparently served a functional role. The President maintained that the one-billion-dollar cut in the defense budget announced at the end of December provided the funds for the initial phase of the poverty attack. He termed this allocation of defense savings a form of "redistribution of the wealth" which would "come from those who have it, to those who don't have it."[4] It was a harmless variety of reallocation which could be tolerated since it did not include expansion beyond the bounds of present government spending.

Having wrapped the administrative programs and War on Poverty in an economy-drive ribbon, the White House embarked upon an overwhelming publicity campaign in preparation for congressional presentation. Undoubtedly the aim was to bring conditions of human deprivation to the surface of public conscience and to create an acute awareness of unmet social needs. It was designed, in short, to create a public constituency to support passage of the President's antipoverty programs.

The President signaled the beginning of his battle for the public mind and its moral sentiments by echoing the oratory of Franklin Delano Roosevelt. Proposing both a half-billion-dollar budget cut and a War on Poverty, Johnson gave his first State of the Union address a theme which James Reston aptly termed the "Franklin Delano Hoover twist . . . the New Deal revisited with emphasis on the forgotten Forgotten Man and flashes of Roosevelt in a three-inch Hoover collar."[5] With phrases sounding misdated to contemporary ears, Johnson presented the all embracing "battle cry" of his Administration. In the months to come, each new legislative proposal would be flown under the banner of a War on Poverty, while the President waged a vigorous campaign to assure public support and passage through Congress.[6]

Political, social, and economic organizations enlisted in the ranks of those endorsing the presidential "war." No one was spared. Like an enterprising businessman, Johnson went to "the people" and their representatives seeking endorsements for his product. Help was asked of everyone from the Daughters of the American Revolution to the Socialist Party. The United Auto Workers called for a "Citizen's Drive on Poverty"; the Urban League announced its own "war on poverty" with a major reorganization directed toward combating "poverty and despair among Negroes." Thousands of letters, it was reported, were flooding the White House and the new antipoverty headquarters. Concerned Americans of all ages and occupations were offering to donate their time and talents to this new effort—or, so read the press releases.

A popular public figure, Sargent Shriver, was chosen as Special Assistant to the President to head up the planning stages and drafting of the antipoverty legislation. Shriver's background, his service in business and local government, association with the Kennedy family, and success in directing and developing the Peace Corps program, was an important asset in rallying popular support and confidence.

Personal visits to poverty-stricken regions by the Johnson family were utilized to highlight conditions and remind congressmen of their obligations to their constituents. The only regions deemed important enough for such favors were found in Appalachia rather than the big city slums. Early in the campaign, Mrs. Johnson made a visit to the "poverty pocket" coal towns in the Wilkes-Barre and Scranton areas of Pennsylvania. Later, in April, when the Appalachian Regional Development Bill was ready for Congress and it appeared that the original antipoverty package, the Economic Opportunity Act, might be delayed in committee sessions, President Johnson made a whirlwind tour through the Appalachian region to visit five states in one day. "We must get rid of poverty, I need your help," roared the President to the crowds that greeted him. In eastern Kentucky, he advised Tom Fletcher, an unemployed sawmill worker and father of eight children, "to keep those kids in school."[7] He apparently enjoyed the trip, for he repeated it not long afterward in the company of one of his daughters.

As cities and states prepared for their own "war on poverty," President Johnson found it convenient to promise them federal aid as soon as the legislation was passed. City governments were quick to respond, for money was to be distributed on a first-come, first-serve basis. Many, like Mayor Wagner of New York, hoped that the initiation of planning "will put us ahead of many other localities in pressing for allocations under the President's program."[8] According to the mayor, the city hoped to collect $125 to $150 million of the $1 billion under the EOA. Apparently some funds were promised, for a week later, in a letter to Governor Rockefeller requesting a $50 million state appropriation in the drive against poverty, the mayor "said that the Federal Government has made known its intention to make a 'major appropriation' to the City."[9] When the Democrats on the House Committee on Education and Labor could not reach agreement on the EOA and delayed meeting the Republicans in executive session to "mark up" the bill, the committee chairman, Harlem Representative Adam Clayton Powell, received a none-too-subtle reminder of his duties. A one-million-dollar federal grant to a major Harlem juvenile delinquency program, Haryou, was announced which, according to *Times* reporter Samuel Kaplan, would in part "be contingent upon passage of the Administration's anti-poverty programs."[10]

Congress and the Program

An opportunity for the expression of the administration-created "public support" was provided by the House Hearings of the War on Poverty program conducted by the

House Committee on Education and Labor. Of the eighty-five witnesses who were able to testify in the twenty days of hearings, only nine opposed enactment of the bill. Of those opposing, three represented the Chamber of Commerce, one was from a state manufacturers' association, and another from the Farm Bureau Federation—lobbies whose opposition to any form of government spending on social welfare or education is a basic ritual performed whenever such proposals are made. Two of the remaining four were Republican members of the Joint Economic Committee whose minority report accused the Council of Economic Advisers of exaggerating the extent of poverty in the United States. In addition, they raised questions about the jurisdictional problems among congressional committees arising from the combination of varied programs into one "omnibus" bill. The last two objectors were educators who did not flatly state their opposition (apparently in attempts to maintain "academic neutrality") but said that the focus of the bill was misdirected and its programs unnecessary.

Of the remaining seventy-six witnesses, twelve were called in as technical advisers and took no position on the legislation.[11] Nearly half, twenty-nine in all, of the remaining sixty-four witnesses testifying in support of the bill were either members of the administration or their names were specifically listed as individuals consulted in planning and legislation.[12] The witness stand was almost exclusively occupied by these individuals for the first two weeks. They included all of the "top brass"—the Secretaries of Defense, Interior, Agriculture, Commerce, Labor, Health Education and Welfare, and the Attorney General, as well as Sargent Shriver and Walter Heller, the Chairman of the Council of Ecoonmic Advisers.

The remaining public witnesses included twelve representatives of social-welfare, civic and religious organizations, ten officials in state or local government, seven educators, four congressmen, and two businessmen. Several were individuals who had previously endorsed the War on Poverty and represented groups that expected to be active participants as well as eager recipients of federal funds. Rather than dealing with the legislation, much of the testimony consisted of moral statements about the need to help the poor of the nation; or poverty was used as an excuse to discuss other issues not directly related to the legislation under question.

The War on Poverty hearings, in short, were carefully engineered and overwhelmed by a well-organized administrative lobby. They appeared to fit the condemning words of a disillusioned congressman: "All a hearing does is give an opportunity to the vested interests to beat the drum and get letters out on their side of the issue."[13]

With so many administration witnesses and an opposition of insignificant size reciting the lines of a stale script, a congressional hearing becomes little more than a well-rehearsed parade of anticipated platitudes. Functionally, it provided for a public presentation of the right phrases of the officially approved social philosophy toward poverty and the proposed legislation. In this respect, the proceedings were strikingly similar to the report of the social process of defining "happiness" in Red China, as viewed through the eyes of a Western reporter. Letters suggesting that "happiness" was not unrelated to material comforts were "planted" in several large newspapers. Letters in reply and editorials by the papers soundly denounced this suggestion and reasserted the official government line—that happiness is labor.[14] In a similar manner, Walter Reuther was rebuked by Republican committee members for suggesting a redistribution of the wealth (even if he didn't *really* mean it) and the Chamber of Commerce representatives were thoroughly scolded by Democrats for suggesting that the bill would undermine the American character. Representative Griffin (R.-Mich.) was angrily castigated by the Democrats when he made remarks which could be construed to mean that Negroes were a mentally inferior race. The proper philosophy, "the philosophy behind the Economic Opportunity Act of 1964," wrote the committee majority, "is not that existing wealth should be redistributed but that the poor people can and must be provided with opportunities to earn a decent living and maintain their families on a comfortable living standard."[15]

Because the proceedings of the public hearing had so little to do with the content of the proposed legislation, it was continually necessary to reassert the mythical essentials of working congressmen drafting and revising legislation on the basis of the suggestions and criticisms of the witnesses. Each witness was thanked for his "very constructive suggestions" by the congressmen who favored his position and told that "when we commence to mark up the bill, many of your suggestions may be followed." At one point an extended analogy—to elaborate the myth—was provided by a department store president who noticed a similarity between the role of a merchandise buyer and that of the congressmen in drafting the legislation. He termed the representatives "specialists in government" who were filling the nation's order for an antipoverty program.[16]

Few probing questions were asked, and with reliance upon ideological arguments relating to the need for, and administration of, federal social-welfare programs, a rational line of reasoning could not proceed very far. The frustration encountered by a Chicago businessman at the hands of Peter Frelinghuysen, the ranking Republican on the committee and most outspoken antagonist of the bill, is recorded:

MR. MARTIN: . . . again I want to go back to this residential revolution that I talked about earlier, Congressman, I think you are talking essentially about a problem that many of the communities have inherited from a national situation and not necessarily generated locally.

MR. FRELINGHUYSEN: I do not know what local problems you feel have been inherited from the national situation, Mr. Martin.

MR. MARTIN: I think the tremendous mobility of population

that we are talking about, the tremendous mobility of population in the northern cities.
MR. FRELINGHUYSEN: But the Federal Government is not responsible for the mobility of the population.
MR. MARTIN: I did not say this. I said it is a national problem and not a local problem. I did not say the Federal
Government was the cause of national problems. I said that
there is a national problem. This is different than Federal.[17]

Thus, a businessman from Chicago learned that Republicans believe all national problems are caused by the federal government—no matter what their nature. Normally,
the dialogue did not reach this level of relevance, but was
grounded on platitudes of agreement or attacks on the political principles of individuals testifying and the "enemy"
groups they represented. If the witnesses were not easily
subject to abuse, the congressmen of the opposing party
were always available to fill the role. In short, as one congressman participating in the Brookings seminars stated,
"on most issues members are looking for things to bolster
the decision they already have reached."[18]

Why is this so? Perhaps because it is easier to rely upon
"principle" than to study the legislation; and besides, it
doesn't "pay off" to be a serious legislator. Members find
they have "little time" to spend studying legislation, because
it appears to be of little importance in the evaluation of
their performance by the people back home, the people who
determine their political future. The congressmen participating in the Brookings seminars were unanimous in their
agreement that effective, conscientious work on legislation
did not "pay off" in the district. Support of the right legislation was more important than a role in shaping it, bringing
home "the goods" more important than forming national
policy. According to Clapp, realization of this fact leads
many congressmen "to decreased interest in the hard often
boring, legislative work and concentration on the publicity-
seeking accomplishments or devices."[19]

Undoubtedly a great deal of the irrelevance of the dialogue at the public hearing and the sharp partisan antag-

onisms which developed can be attributed to the fact that the congressmen weren't asked to draft legislation but simply to approve a finished product. The bill was drawn up solely by the administration and was labeled an important Johnson program—"to be passed." Before Powell became chairman, the committee had suffered from extreme partisanship; in the past two or three years, however, it had achieved a reputation as a key "working committee." A bipartisan approach was followed in drafting the Manpower Development and Training Act and the Vocational Education Act—both of which were drawn up in close coordination with the administering departments.[20] In addition, certain congressmen put a great deal of effort into the formation of the Juvenile Delinquency Act and legislation under the National Defense Education Act. The execution and operation of these projects, particularly the "community-action" programs under the juvenile delinquency legislation, were closely watched and checked for their effectiveness.[21]

The bill offered as an antipoverty program was largely an extension of the legislation just cited, but put into special forms. Not only had the committee previously considered the basic legislation, but they had also reviewed several of these "new" forms. The youth programs under Title I included a Job Corps and Work-Training Program, both of which were part of the Youth Employment Opportunities Bill passed by the Senate and the House Committee and left to expire in the deep recesses of the House Rules Committee. A third provision under Title I, the work-study programs for college students, was considered under the NDEA a year previously, but was dropped because it did not receive warm support from educators who testified at that time.

The "community-action" approach of Title II, considered to be the real "essence" of the bill by the administration and the majority of the witnesses who testified, was drawn from experience with the Juvenile Delinquency Program. This "social-problem" approach views the social ills of a community as interrelated and city or community-wide in dimension. The problems of juvenile delinquency, the aged, poverty, unemployment, housing, education, and so forth, are approached through a central planning and research operation which analyzes the problems and designs and supervises the action programs. The attack is focused on specific neighborhoods (a geographic as distinguished from a functional approach) in an attempt to decentralize and facilitate the administration of a wide variety of social services. It is a high-powered, professional approach which places emphasis upon planning and control; it results in the reorganization and expansion of the existing community welfare programs, as well as an integration of public and private services. As previously noted, several of the committee members had serious reservations in respect to the effectiveness of this new method and were particularly concerned about an apparent by-passing of the local authorities and city-government officials and facilities.

Title III contained provisions for grants and loans to small farmers, as well as a "land-reform" proposal under which large parcels of land were to be bought by a government corporation and resold in family-size farms at less than cost to marginal farmers. Farmer's cooperatives were also mentioned and could have been extended to production since they were not specifically limited to the sale of merchandise. With little background in agricultural legislation, the committee largely ignored this section; specific hearings dealing with it were conducted by the House Committee on Agriculture.

Two loan plans for business were contained in Title IV. The first was designed to increase employment opportunities for the long-term unemployed and members of low-income families (to be conducted by the Area Redevelopment Administration), and the second authorized low-interest loans to small business concerns (to be administered under the Small Business Administration). Both loan programs were to be conducted only in coordination with the community-action programs of Title II. Again, the committee had little experience in this area and largely ignored these programs in the public hearings.

Ambitiously titled "Family Unity Through Jobs," Title V provided funds for demonstration projects to train welfare recipients for jobs under the Social Security Act. In addition to establishing the administrative office, Title VI contained a provision for a "Domestic Peace Corps," termed Volunteers for America—known as the National Service Corps in previous administration proposals. The committee had both considered the National Service Corps under past legislation and approved a grant in 1961 to establish a Domestic Peace Corps and Adult Volunteer Service Corps for Powell's Harlem district.

And, of course, one should not forget that all of this was offered at the bargain price of only $962.5 million—about $25 for every man, woman, and child living at income levels below the official poverty line.

To summarize, the committee had previously considered most of the legislative proposals contained within the not-so-new War on Poverty program, and in several instances they had reason not to look upon them in an especially favorable light. Yet Democrats who had reservations publicly held their tongues and battled the Republicans who denounced the entire proceedings as a political hoax.

Poverty and the Community

What was the major attraction of the proposal to "eliminate poverty in America"? According to the administrative designers, it was the new *comprehensive, coordinated,* and *focused* approach. This method was to be followed on two levels—the federal and the local. On the federal level, the new Office of Economic Opportunity became a managerial arm for the President which could cut across cabinet lines to facilitate the coordination of programs. A revealing statement about the purpose of this form of structure and the authority given to the director was made by Shriver when he said, "This is an authority which the President wants because he wants to be at the focal point with respect to this aspect of our domestic effort."[22] Republican congressmen on the committee found it difficult to accept the notion that such an arrangement would be satisfactory to the department secretaries who were *supposed* to guard jealously their jurisdictional rights. Yet, each of the cabinet officers stated that "No, he didn't foresee any difficulties in the coordination of the various programs . . ." The administration offices were just one big happy family!

Secretary of Labor Willard Wirtz emphasized that when he said "us," he did not mean the Department of Labor, he was talking "about the United States; namely, the administration as it is right now."[23] When Representative Frelinghuysen suggested that Wirtz and his fellow department heads would become the subordinates of a tyrannical "poverty-czar," the following noncommunication took place:

> SEC. WIRTZ: When you talk about master-and-servant relationship and subordination, frankly the point is so completely contrary to any thinking that I have on the subject that I can't helpfully comment on it. There is no master and servant.
> MR. FRELINGHUYSEN: I do not know what that means.
> SEC. WIRTZ: That means if your reference to master and servant is a statement of your own view on it, I respect that as I always do. If it is part of a question to me, I can't answer it because it is not responsive to anything I understand in the situation.
> MR. FRELINGHUYSEN: You do not understand my question and I do not understand your answer.
> SEC. WIRTZ: I am not sure either of those is right.[24]

Whether or not an "understanding" occurred between the two gentlemen, it is quite clear that they do not view the dynamics of federal government administration in the same manner. Frelinghuysen tends to view it in terms of rigid power relationships and lines of authority, concepts

which are foreign to Wirtz's modern managerial view dealing in images of "teamwork" and "cooperation." The administrative structure formed by the establishment of the Office
of Economic Opportunity is consonant with this managerial
approach. It is a modern managerial tool and, to a certain
extent, a form of administrative reorganization.

Franklin D. Roosevelt, whose administration Johnson
tends to emulate, successfully practiced a high degree of
flexibility in managing the administrative branch.[25] With
the Executive Reorganization Act of 1939, he promoted the
cause of scientific management and established the tools for
a national governing body in initiating changes recommended by his Committee on Administrative Management.
This report, issued in 1937, has provided a blueprint for
further executive reorganization. One of the central points
made by the committee was the need to install coordinating
"managerial arms" for the President in the areas of personnel, fiscal policy, and national planning. They were to be
distinguished from the operating administrative departments of the government and were to be on a level between
the executive and the cabinet.[26] To a large extent, such a
coordinating and managerial function in social planning
describes the role of the Office of Economic Opportunity as
it was sold to the public. Whether or not it will develop fully
in this direction will depend upon Johnson and the degree
and kind of control he desires to exercise over domestic programs, as well as whether or not the coordination of business, labor, and government required to achieve the "great
society" becomes a reality.

"Community action" is the second and local level of the
comprehensive, coordinated, and focused approach—and,
immediately, it is the most potent form. Originally, "community action" referred to a fairly sophisticated concept of
social work. The ideal was found in the organization of the
members of a low-income locality into a working group
that could provide its own social services and economic opportunities, and/or have the power to obtain them from the

local authorities. The dynamic and potentially explosive energies underlying life in slum neighborhoods were to be harnessed into constructive collective efforts. It was hoped that through actually confronting their environment, individuals would be able to overcome the frustration and alienation that were at the source of previous apathy. Saul Alinsky's work in the "Back of the Yards" district and more recently in the Woodlawn section of Chicago, cases of community organization initiated by SNCC workers in the south, and the idealized version of the work of Peace Corps volunteers, are all classic examples of this technique. Its basic method and aims have been incorporated into several of the large youth programs financed under the President's Committee on Juvenile Delinquency, notably, Mobilization for Youth and Haryou in New York City.

With the full-scale adoption, by the federal government, of the "community action" approach, it has acquired another meaning more in line with the concept of "the community" held by its new advocates. To middle-class political scientists and social planners, "the community" is the local government apparatus of the city or county *plus* the influential civic and business leaders. "Community action" in this context means the "reorganization" of the total community power structure in a manner which will focus both public and private resources on combined activities designed to eliminate juvenile delinquency, poverty, or some other undesirable social problem. All of the public and private social service agencies and organizations within the community are expected to join together and coordinate their programs in a comprehensive, planned attack. (There is a tendency to assume that the methods they will employ will be somewhat consistent with the original meaning of "community action" of the professional social worker.)

According to the language contained in the original version of the bill, the planning and execution of this "attack" was to be carried out by a "community action organization" which was "broadly representative of the community." Only if the planning was sufficient, the program comprehensive, the full utilization of community resources demonstrated, and the program "developed, conducted, and administered with the maximum feasible participation of residents of the areas" under attack, would federal funds be granted. Individual projects could be financed "even though a community has not completed and put into effect its community action program, if the director determined that there was a representative group engaged in developing such a program in the community," and the specific projects would not run counter to the final "community action program."[27] (Notice the effect: before the War on Poverty, no one would have thought to ask the federal government's permission to eliminate juvenile delinquency or eradicate poverty! On the other hand, too few were making the attempt—federal "permission" or not.)

The term "community action" had little appeal to congressional ears. Some, like Representative Perkins (D.-Ken.), who continually referred to Title II as "the community facilities provision," were lost in memories of the public-works programs of the New Deal and never grasped the nature of the new proposal. Others, like Representative Griffin (R.-Mich.), appeared to get the idea all too clearly. In fact, with Secretary Wirtz's candid answers, he couldn't miss the potential shaping power of the new approach:

> MR. GRIFFIN: I would suspect that every nonprofit organization in every community and all the local governmental units which can get additional hands to work by putting up to 10 per cent of salary will be flooding your office with applications and you are going to have to pick and choose.
> SEC. WIRTZ: I think that is right.
> MR. GRIFFIN: How the decision is made can have an important—and sometimes a frightening—influence upon the direction that our communities can take.
> SEC. WIRTZ: That is one problem I love to look forward to.[28]

When one proposes to "redistribute" or "reshape" or just plain "change" anything in American society, one doesn't get very far with Congress. Particularly not when that body's existence, in its present form, is based upon the prevention of change. The potential for toppling personal power structures found in a proposal to reorganize local community services and institutions could hardly be expected to receive ready acceptance. Consequently, by the time the bill returned to the White House to be signed into law, the concept of "community action" had been quietly emasculated—on paper.

The idea of a single "community-action program" executed by a "community-action organization" was dropped. All references to a "community-action organization'" were eliminated, as was the requirement that the agency receiving funds be "broadly representative of the community." The relevant clause in the proposed statute was revised to allow for grants to "components of a community-action program" without reference to the concurrent planning of a single comprehensive plan. In short, the component parts were substituted for the single, carefully planned, community-wide program. By a simple deletion, "pork-barrel" legislation was produced that no longer made local grants contingent upon the creation of a community-wide administering and planning agency or the formation of an overall development program. To Congress, "community action" in an abbreviated form was more useful than the potentially disruptive shape of the original.

Furthermore, to insure that the program directors would be responsible to local authorities rather than federal planners, the state governors were given veto power over any proposals. An allotment system was devised for the distribution of the funds in order to establish allotments by need to all of the states. Grants for "general aid" to education were forbidden, although "special remedial and other noncurricular educational" forms of assistance were permitted. In addition, blueprints of the "preferred" types of "community-action program" were inserted in the form of an Adult Basic Education Program to be administered by the states, and a Voluntary Assistance Program for Needy Children which would "allow individual Americans to participate in a personal way in the War on Poverty. . . ."

Changes in other sections of the bill included a state allotment system for distribution of funds under Title I and a veto for state governors over the installation of Job Corps camps. Title III was expanded to include migrant agricultural workers, but the direct grants proposed were eliminated as were the "land-reform" measures. The "pink" tone of the provision for farm cooperatives was also found objectionable, and they were forbidden aid if organized for "the production of agricultural commodities or for manufacturing purposes." For no apparent reason, a program of indemnity payments was provided for farmers who had to remove their milk from the commercial market "because it contained residues of chemicals registered and approved for use by the Federal Government at the time of such use." Slight rewordings were made in Title IV, and the ambitious Title V was toned down to read simply, "Work Experience Programs." Since Volunteers of America was the name of an evangelist group, the "Domestic Peace Corps" was termed Volunteers in Service to America, or VISTA. The final gratuitous touch inserted the requirement that any individual employed under any programs receiving federal funds must file "an affidavit that he does not believe in, and is not a member of and does not support any organization that believes in or teaches, the overthrow of the United States Government by force of violence or by any illegal or unconstitutional methods." Thus Congress added its own contribution to the shape of the War on Poverty.

NOTES

1. *The New York Times*, Nov. 30, 1963.
2. *The New York Times*, Dec. 2, 1963, text of letter.
3. *The New York Times*, Dec. 12, 1963.

4. *The New York Times*, March 16, 1964, from a TV interview.

5. *The New York Times*, Jan. 9, 1964, p. 17.

6. Press commentators and critics have not failed to grasp the campaign tone of all of Johnson's activities. However, they repeatedly linked this to the elections rather than grasping the extent to which it was an integral part of Johnson's presidential style. He *will* run the presidency like a political campaign whether elections are one, two, or four years away. Basically, it is the style of the congressional leader who organizes divergent factions and puts all of the votes in line to defeat or carry through someone else's proposal. All of the emphasis is upon the vote-getting campaign rather than the content of the legislation. This style obtains results of a sort, but it provides little comfort to those who are interested in seeing the formation of coherent and comprehensive national policy.

7. *The New York Times*, April 25, 1964. It was *eleven* children by the time the President made a speech at the convention of the Amalgamated Clothing Workers in New York City two weeks later. (*See* transcript of address, *The New York Times*, May 10).

8. *The New York Times*, March 24, 1964.

9. *The New York Times*, April 5, 1964.

10. *The New York Times*, May 7, 1964. President Johnson personally announced the grant on May tenth in a speech at the New York World's Fair.

11. They represented government statistical services from the Bureau of the Census, the Bureau of Labor Statistics, and the Welfare Administration. Their testimony was devoted to census definitions and the reliability of the data rather than the merits of the proposed legislative programs.

12. The list is found in House Hearings, *op. cit.*, p. 23.

13. Charles L. Clapp, *The Congressman: His Work As He Sees It* (Washington, D.C.: The Brookings Institution, 1963), p. 265; referred to in the text as "the Brookings seminars."

14. *The New York Times Magazine*, Sept. 27, 1964.

15. Report on the Economic Opportunity Act of 1964 by the Committee on Education and Labor, June 3, 1964, p. 2.

16. House Hearings, *op. cit.*, p. 842.

17. Statement of Virgil Martin, President, Carson-Pirie-Scott Co., Chicago, Illinois. *Ibid.*, p. 847.

18. Clapp, *op. cit.*, p. 269.

19. *Ibid.*

20. Representative Albert Quie (R.-Minn.) in a seminar on education conducted by the Institute for Policy Studies, May 11, 1964.

21. Representative Edith Green (D.-Ore.) made a special trip to Cleveland on April 18, 1964, to hold hearings on the operation of the Juvenile Delinquency Program in that city. They proved to be disastrous. Amid charges that local citizens had been ignored in the planning of programs which were not yet in operation, the director of the project resigned and its future appeared most uncertain. This episode, plus her previous experience with Washington Action for Youth in its disputes with the District of Columbia Superintendent

of Schools over the experimental Cardozo High School program, left Representative Green in doubt about the effectiveness of the "community-action" approach.

22. House Hearings, *op. cit.*, p. 97.

23. *Ibid.*, p. 201.

24. *Ibid.*, p. 200.

25. For example, under the Emergency Relief Appropriation Act, F.D.R. was given a lump sum which he had the authority to administer. A system, known as the "five ring circus," was set up under which applications were sent to a Division of Applications where they were examined by an advisory committee which made recommendations to the President. Execution of the work was coordinated by Harry Hopkins and the W.P.A. Secretary Morgenthau set up disbursing and accounting facilities, and control of funds for administrative expenses was handled by Budget Director Bell. For further information on the Roosevelt administration and its significance for the development of the Executive Office, *see* Barry Dean Karl, *Executive Reorganization and Reform in the New Deal* (Cambridge: Harvard University Press, 1963).

26. President's Committee on Administrative Management, *Administrative Management in the Government of the United States* (Washington, D.C.: U.S. Government Printing Office, 1937).

27. Section 204, (c) of the original bill.

28. House Hearings, *op. cit.*, p. 212.

The War on Poverty: Perspectives and Prospects[1]

S. M. MILLER AND MARTIN REIN

Perspectives: Fundamentalism and Incrementalism

The War on Poverty has been greeted by sharp criticism from those on the political right as well as those on the left. It has been described as "too small and too limited to cope effectively with the problem" (*The New York Times* editorial, November 21, 1964)—only $800 million had been appropriated for its first year of operation. It has been interpreted as a war on the poor: "Under the delusion that we are pressing against poverty [we may] exert pressure against poor people" (Alvin Schorr, "Equal Opportunity All"). It has been thought of as a "hodge podge" of programs . . . a curious combination of the techniques made famous by the phrase "Madison Avenue" and "the Wizard of Oz" . . . designed to achieve the single objective of securing votes (minority views of the Senate

Committee on Labor and Public Welfare). It has been described as "a mockery," "a deliberate fraud," and "a conservative embracing of the status quo" (David Komatsu). It has been characterized as a dangerous gimmick designed to show that poverty can be eliminated without changing the structure of society (Richard Titmuss).

Its supporters, on the other hand, defend it as an effort that at least begins to deal with the problems of the poor; it is the best that could be carried through Congress, they say, considering other pressing requirements (such as keeping federal expenditures to less than $100 billion); it is one program with some chance of success and it is likely to improve and expand over the years. Defenders are concerned with the pragmatics of political possibility, not with the fundamentals of long-run necessity.

Fundamentalism and incrementalism—the clashing claims of large-scale, sweeping changes and of small, gradual movement arising from the reduction of dissensus —are the fulcrums on which policy is evaluated. Fundamentalists and pragmatists talk past each other and become principled, conscientious objectors to each other's contrasting visions. One states the case in terms of long-term developments, the other in terms of political feasibility. Pragmatists tend to tailor their analysis of long-term developments to what is possible today. But it is a delusion to think that the image of the future can be remade to meet the needs of today. The analysis of what is needed should be based on an understanding of the problem, rather than on political feasibility. Analysis can be modified to encourage action, but it should not be stunted in its development, for then it becomes an apologetic for previously determined policy. Contrariwise, the fundamentalists cannot have the rich advantage of criticizing everything because it is insufficient. They must also consider how to move from what seems possible today to what seems necessary tomorrow.

Present-day social criticism in the United States lacks a middleground, a "skeptical idealism," which bridges the concern with the long-term drift of society and the pragmatic possibilities of politics.[2] If we assign George Meany as the symbol of the latter and Paul Goodman as the symbol of the former, most social analysis is presently pre-empted by the Meany and Goodman schools of thought. We lack a middle-range social and policy analysis, informed by an understanding of the trends of society and relevant to, but not bound by, present-day policies and programs. We lack an *incremental idealism* which has a vision of the future and a strategy for intervention to effect change at critical points in our present society.[3]

We think the poverty program must be discussed in the larger context of economic and welfare policy. We have done so in the first draft of this paper, but space limitations have forced us to narrow our analysis to some limited aspects of the work-training and educational programs. We deal broadly with sections of Title I and II of the Economic Opportunity Act, but we will not deal, as we would have liked, with the policy issues of the community-action program. Other neglected areas are:

> The needed expansion of jobs and the application of diverse methods for achieving this goal in today's affluent society.
> The extension and improvement of Social Security and other direct income-maintenance programs.

Highlights of the Economic Opportunity Act

The act contains seven Titles:

Title I involves youth programs and contains three sections.

IA *The Job Corps.* Provides for rural conservation camps and urban residential training centers.

IB *Work-Training Programs.* To provide work experience and training for school dropouts and those continuing in school. This program is operated by the Department of Labor and is referred to as the Neighborhood Youth Corps.

IC *Work-Study Program.* To provide part-time employment, with a maximum of 15 hours a week when classes are held, for students in institutions of higher education.

Title II covers the Urban and Rural Community Action Programs.

IIA *General Community Action Program.* The act defines a community-action program broadly to include "services, assistance and other activities of sufficient scope and size to give promise of eliminating poverty." Illustrative examples of such programs are employment, job-training and counseling, health, vocational rehabilitation, housing, home management, welfare, and special remedial and noncurricular educational programs. One-half of the expenditure will probably go for educational programs. The focus is on the mobilization of public resources to be administered by a single agency which is required to submit a broad plan of action. The act encourages "maximum feasible participation of the residents of the areas and members of the groups served."

IIB *Adult Basic Education Programs.* A program of literacy training for adults over eighteen years of age.

IIC *A Voluntary Assistance Program for Needy Children.* This program appears to call for the creation by OEO of a program similar to *The New York Times* annual appeal for needy families. It seeks to provide for individual participation on a personal basis in assisting in the support of one or more needy children.

Title III *Special Programs to Combat Poverty in Rural Areas.*

IIIA Authority to make grants and loans.

IIIB Assistance for migrants and other seasonally employed, agricultural workers and their families.

Title IV *Employment and Investment Incentives.* Assistance in establishing, preserving, and strengthening small business concerns and to improve managerial skills of its employees.

Title V *Work-Experience Programs.* Experimental and

pilot projects for those on welfare to secure or retain employment, self-support or personal independence.

Title VI *Administration and Coordination*. This title creates the Office of Economic Opportunity and VISTA (Volunteers in Service to America).

Title VII *Treatment of Income for Certain Public-Assistance Purposes*. This proposes disregarding income (first $85 + half of the excess per month) earned under Title I or II in determining need of individuals applying for public assistance and other programs under the Social Security Act.

The Setting—A Battle Without Supporters

The War on Poverty begins at a time of unprecedented prosperity, with Gross National Product approaching two-thirds of a trillion dollars. It is aimed at helping a minority of the population, not the majority. Indeed, it is hard to see why the year 1964 saw a declaration of "war on poverty." Of course, there is President Johnson's avowed desire to have a liberal program which he could claim as his own; no doubt liberal intellectuals' questioning of the course of our economy had some influence. And it must be recognized that the civil-rights demonstrations were probably the most important political events propelling interest in helping the poor. Yet, the bulk (70 to 80 per cent, depending on the measure) of the poor in the United States are white, and the bulk of the funds for many programs will probably benefit the white rather than the Negro poor. Nor is sizable unemployment, exacerbated by a rapidly expanding young labor force, sufficient to explain the inauguration of a war on poverty. Indeed, one of the most striking features of the antipoverty campaign is its development *without* the support of strong interest groups which usually initiate and promote such legislation. If the war were to falter, it would not be clear where its supporters could be found.

The War on Poverty was not propelled by the organization of the poor in rural areas and in large cities demanding their "economic rights." Nor do the prospective political demands of the poor seem to be great enough to "require" that a "war on poverty" be launched in 1964. If there had not been such a movement in 1964, it is doubtful whether there would have been mass pressures for such activity in that year or in the succeeding one. We suspect that nothing succeeds like success—if the program succeeds, it will develop supporters. If it fails, it will be disclaimed by those who are already critical of its mission.

The War on Poverty is an advance of the political pressures of the day. This is the achievement of the war; this is its weakness.[4] The absence of a strong, organized, well-directed movement demanding more effective measures for the poor has resulted in the formulation of a weak bill and in its further weakening during the journey through Congress. One may be disappointed that a talking horse prevaricates when it says that it won the Kentucky Derby or one may be astonished that we have found a horse that talks! While the astonishment should not eliminate the need for judgment of what is done with the unusual capacity, it should not be ignored in the race for assessment of performance. We make these remarks because we feel that much of the strong criticism of the poverty legislation, unfortunately accurate, overlooks the possibilities of the legislation and the need for understanding how it might be moved in more useful directions.

The War on Poverty can be a sop to the poor, to discourage them from asking for more effective programs. That is its danger. Its hope, despite its severe limitations and the probably unnecessarily truncated vision of its program, is that the war is a beginning, that it may lead to increasingly more effective measures to help the poor. To move in these directions requires the development of a political constituency that pushes for more appropriate programs and the clarification of the vision of what it is that will help the poor.

What is significant, then, about the War on Poverty is not the present program. Rather, it is in *the acceptance of*

a public commitment to help the poor.[5] This commitment
has to be enlarged, shaped and carried out. New goals and
successive programs will have to emerge. While we shall
deal with the strategy of building a political constituency
that can strengthen the commitment, primarily we shall be
concerned with an analysis of the improvement, expansion,
and redirection which the present programs require.

Perspectives

The War on Poverty is not just the New Deal in different
dress. True, it takes over old New Deal programs like the
CCC (Civilian Conservation Corps) and the NYA (National
Youth Administration). True, it does not initiate great inno-
vations (for the United States) like Social Security and the
unemployment insurance programs of Roosevelt. Nonetheless, *taken at its potential best,* it moves in new and very
significant directions. The New Deal was aimed at the provision of essential social services which would relieve want
and distress; it provided a floor of security, whether in terms
of minimum wages or old-age pensions. The War on Poverty
is aimed at expanding choices (of jobs and education) and
thereby enlarging human freedoms. Its goal is not the construction of a floor but the opening up of doors into the main
edifice of our economy. The preamble of the Economic Opportunity Act states the goals of the program: to open "to
everyone the opportunity for education and training, the
opportunity to work, the opportuniy to live in decency and
dignity."

Poverty within affluence and economic boom requires
different programs than poverty within scarcity and national economic failure. The social-service state, with its
concerns for securing basic minimums for all and thereby
relieving want, is possibly supplanted by the welfare state,
directed to increasing opportunity to break into the affluent
sectors. This perspective represents a dramatic and bold
departure from the welfare policies which enjoined our legislation in the past decades.[6]

The call for the extension of opportunity goes beyond the established consensus and consequently contributes to the great range of criticism with which the War on Poverty has been greeted. The conservatives fear not only the expenditures, but the possibility that the expansion of choice for all will reduce the freedom of some. The role of government is expanded, and the possibility of structural changes reducing the advantages of some of the advantaged, at least in the short run, is enhanced.

While the rhetoric of the act promises a new and bold departure from past policies, important historical continuities in the act must be examined, not only in the limited sense that it embodies the legislation of the Kennedy Administration which was not passed by Congress—the Domestic Peace Corps, the Youth Employment Program, the Work-Study Program—but in the more fundamental sense of the philosophical assumptions which underpin the act. These historical continuities, as Titmuss has suggested, can be traced back to England's New Poor Law of 1834. The goal of welfare policy then was the reduction of pauperism (the receipt of public funds) and not the elimination of poverty. Pauperism was seen as a condition of individuals. Poverty, a condition of society, was not discovered until the turn of the nineteenth century when Charles Booth revealed that a third of the city of London lived in poverty. Given the goal of reducing pauperism, the strategy devised was that of inculcating proper work habits among the able-bodied poor through the elimination of outdoor relief and the use of the work or almshouse. This overarching preoccupation with a small sector of the poor, the able-bodied poor who are not motivated to work, is a recurrent theme in social-welfare policy. It can be found in the English legislation of 1911 and in the poverty program of today.

But this approach neglects the 60 per cent of the poor (defined as having a family income under $4000) who are employed but do not earn sufficient income to meet their needs; it neglects, also, the 25 per cent of the poor who are aged and who have presumably earned their right to retire from work if they so desire. The poverty program of today is not directed at these groups, which constitute the bulk of those in poverty. It is directed at the present and future pauper (today the more polite term is "dependent"). President Johnson has graphically stated the issue—the program seeks to convert tax-eaters into taxpayers.

The single most striking aspect of the present War on Poverty, in addition to its historical continuities, is that it has little to do with poverty in the sense of income deficiency. Indeed, the program makes no pretense about addressing itself directly to the matter of income. The act does make a step forward in providing that income earned in the training and work programs is not to be calculated as family income in applying for or staying on public assistance. But discounting income can hardly be described as a major plank in the program or as a major strategy of providing income to the poor. As Ida Merriam has suggested, any attempt at comparing the billion spent for the war on poverty with the $11 billion needed to bring all families up to a $3000 level is irrelevant. The program essentially does not provide direct income for the poor, although it does provide some limited funds for those who work. The absence of direct income support to the poor accounts for much sarcasm and derision about the small scale of the program, and the possibilities of benefits accruing to highly demanded but scarce middle-class professionals, rather than to the poor.

The assumptions underlining the act cripple the possibilities of accomplishing its mission of expanding opportunity. We shall examine seven sets of assumptions which involve: (1) the concept of poverty; (2) the fixing of a poverty line; (3) the use of characteristics as causes; (4) the comprehensiveness of the programs; (5) the concentration on youth; (6) education as the opportunity vehicle; and (7) inviolate institutions and violate man.

THE CONCEPT OF POVERTY

Poverty is assumed to be a short-run phenomenon. The task is seen as eventually bringing everyone above a poverty line; this line is relatively fixed, even if adjusted for price and other minor changes. *It is important today to shed this fixed-line orientation in defining poverty.* As John Kenneth Galbraith has declared: "The poor are those who have fallen behind the rest of society. In this view, the poverty line is always relative to time, place and possibilities."[7] As the conditions of society change, so does the concept of poverty:

> No matter what standard is selected and what phrases are used to describe it—maintenance, health and decency, modest, but adequate, comfort—the specific goods and services that comprise that level of living change over time.[8]

In the family budgets of city workers, more than half of the increased costs between 1951 and 1959 can be traced to increases in the general standard of living.

The casualties of the affluent society are not accidents; they are produced by their unprotected and unrewarded structural relationship to the affluent society. They are not placed in positions in society that lead to their advance with the rest of society. Thus, we have new groups recruited into poverty as new conditions emerge. Most striking today are the new, aged poor, those who were not poor during their working lives but are poor in their "retirements." Our very rough calculations, based on cross-sectional age data rather than more reliable longitudinal data, suggest that perhaps half of the aged poor are newly poor. If the fears of the Triple Revolution analysts are realized, then cybernation will lead to another group of poor—formerly well-off workers displaced into long-term unemployment by productive servomechanisms.[9]

It will not avail us much if we believe that to bring everybody up to a particular level is enough, for such a notion implies that all of society will stand still while we achieve this improvement. Obviously, this is a myth. As society and the economy change, as new demands and expectations emerge, the poverty line will shift. Those not poor today may be poor in tomorrow's circumstances, though they have not suffered any absolute decline in their conditions. For example, as more jobs provide better vacations and adequate old-age pensions, then those in decreasingly attractive jobs, which do not provide these benefits, are falling behind. The poverty line cannot be fixed, because it is in an escalator position, moving with society. Groups once protected against insecurity and poverty become vulnerable as society changes. It must be acknowledged that the War on Poverty is not based on protecting those who are vulnerable today (like the aged, female-headed families, and such), nor on building escalator improvements into the conditions of various groups so that they improve as society advances.

Beyond poverty, stand the issues of inequality. They are ignored in the War on Poverty. By inequality we refer to the disproportionate slices of the economic pie that are received by different income groupings. There is considerable evidence that inequalities in the distribution of income, wealth, and social services are growing in the United States.[10] The suction power of World War II produced a social revolution, bringing greater equalities of income and wealth. This power has been assaulted by a rising tide of inequalities. The poverty programs, even taken most broadly, make no effort to reduce such inequalities.

The orientation of these programs is quite different. They ignore issues of inequality. In their analysis of poverty they attempt to exhibit a modern anthropologist's sophistication by regarding poverty not only as inadequate income, but, perhaps more centrally, as inadequate motivation, resulting in a poverty cycle. In this view, as Peter Marris has observed, deprivation in one generation leads, through cultural impoverishment, family breakdowns, parental indifference or misunderstanding of their children's educational needs, to deprivation in the next generation. One can break one poverty cycle by entering at many points. The danger in this cyclical theory is that it is difficult to assign priorities. It is not clear from this perspective which intervention is likely to produce the most payoff at a given time with a given group. Also disturbing is the fact that the thrust of this view

is to ignore economic, demographic, and other changes. When taken in the extreme position, this perspective suggests that a growth in aspiration, without an extension of income, will lead to the reclassification of people as "unpoor." The attempt to have a cultural rather than a psychological view of poverty, then, results in a formulation of the poverty cycle in intrafamilial and intergenerational terms, rather than in intrapsychic language. It nevertheless seeks to change the poor and not their social situations. Consequently, structural changes are ignored and neglected.

THE POVERTY LINE

Despite the inadequacies of interpreting poverty in terms of a fixed-income line, the latter is necessary for measurement of present-day need and assessment of the adequacy of policies. The question then becomes: what is the appropriate point at which to place the poverty line? The Council of Economic Advisers opted for a solitary line despite the diversity in family size and in living costs in the United States. With present-day statistical sophistication[11] and the wealth of basic data, this decision seems unfortunate. It opens the War on Poverty to the criticism that farm families of two are not necessarily poor if they have incomes of $3000 and removes the possibility of educating us to the existence of poverty among families with four or more children and incomes above $3000.

But if we did need a single figure, why $3000? Available budget estimates show that $3000 family income is much too low. Careful economists like Morgan have used a higher base, adjusted for family size. The Council of Economic Advisers justifies the use of a $3000 standard by the assumption that setting the poverty line higher or lower would only affect the size and not the character of the problem. The 1964 report states: "But the analysis of the sources of poverty, and the programs needed to cope with it, would remain substantially unchanged."[12] This assertion is inaccurate. The resort to the $3000 line underestimates the scope of urban poverty, overestimates rural poverty, and encourages the view that poverty is a short-run phenomenon that can be handled by a temporary and fairly modest injection of funds and training.[13]

CHARACTERISTICS AND CAUSES

The analysis of the nature and causes of poverty has been prepared by the Council of Economic Advisers, utilizing data drawn up by the Census Bureau and other governmental agencies. The 1964 Economic Report of the President, which presents the Council's analysis, discusses poverty mainly in terms of the characteristics of the poor. What is done is to examine the incidence and composition[14] of poverty in terms of variables such as age, educational level, sex of household head, race, and so on. This approach is useful because it underlines the diversity of the poor and the need for varied programs to deal with their differing needs and possibilities. But it is only a partial analysis without an explanatory theory. The analysis is not effectively linked to economic and other structural elements.

Frequently, official poverty discussions carry the refrain that the culture, motivation, and attitudes of the poor are the essential elements in the production and maintenance of poverty. The concentration on youth in the War on Poverty makes this approach plausible but hardly adequate in attempting to understand the multidimensions of poverty today. In fact, the analysis of the characteristics of the poor amounts frequently to little more than psychologizing the causes of poverty, making the problem one of individual rehabilitation rather than social change. In depicting vulnerable risk groups, analyses have ignored why these groups tend to be vulnerable. Little attention is paid to the fact that over half of the poor are in the labor force and employed, but making insufficient income. True, the nonlabor-force poor—the aged, the female-headed families—are growing, but their plights have to be related to the character of our economic and social-welfare institutions.

In contrast, Elizabeth Wickenden's analysis[15] emphasizes the relationship of various groups to the labor market. She talks about those groups that are employed but getting low wages and other groups that are actively interested in work but are unable to secure it. In her discussion of the categories of the poor, the constant, underlying theme is the relationship of particular groupings to the economy. But this, too, is not entirely accurate since her analysis stresses status in the labor market and, on this basis, then devises various kinds of poverty groupings.

To treat the characteristics of the poor as an ætiology can be dangerous. It is difficult to know what is consequence and what is cause.[16] To what extent does living in poverty tend to encourage the development of a protective subculture, which is then labeled with those characteristics of the poor that produce poverty?[17] We thus blame the poor for their poverty. More fundamental, perhaps, than this criticism, is the fact that it does not give us a basis for thinking about the problems of poverty in terms of the economic and social structure of the United States.

We hasten to add that an emphasis on structural changes does not mean that the immediate relief of suffering cannot be achieved if basic forces are neglected. Rather, the danger is that dealing only at the level of characteristics of the poor may lull us into contentment with some immediate gains and thus delay the formulation of more comprehensive and searching programs which are based on modifications of structure.

Perhaps we are reading too much into the theoretical perspective which underlies the War on Poverty, but we do not believe so: those who think of characteristics as poverty causes and "the culture of poverty" as the main barrier to escaping from poverty are much more likely to be sanguine about the beginning course of the War on Poverty than are those who emphasize economic and social-welfare programs as the main levers of advance. Furthermore, assumptions about poverty have consequences in the choice and conduct of programs.

For example, the one-half of the poor who are in the

labor force are likely to be employed in occupations and industries which pay low wages. It is very common today to explain low wages as due to low productivity—the poor are unskilled, poorly educated, poorly motivated, and, therefore, poorly paid. Such an analysis implies that we must upgrade the skill and educational levels of the poor while leaving the economy untouched. But, as Gabriel Kolko suggests, a more probing account of the prevalence of low wages must recognize that wages are also a function of an industry's competitive position in the economy, the capital investment required to enter business, and the proportion of total costs which must go to wages. Textile industries may be unable to pay high wages, while the automotive and the steel industries can. This kind of analysis suggests solutions dramatically different from merely reeducating and retraining the poor.

In emphasizing the characteristics of the poor, we neglect those problems of poverty which are functions of our economic and social structure. We are thus less likely to turn to the problems of social change and reconstruction—of reducing inequalities—when we talk about poverty in personal and individual terms of the characteristics of the poor than when we discuss poverty in terms of the characteristics of the economy which produce the poor. Highlighting structural imbalances is important, not just because we have a certain number of poor today—more than we are now willing to countenance, though we were willing to countenance a higher percentage yesterday—but also because our society is undergoing change. We have to overhaul a number of institutions and develop others if we are to deal effectively with these new issues.

THE NONCOMPREHENSIVE WAR

The War on Poverty, even in its broadest terms, does not provide the wide coverage pledged in the preamble to the Economic Opportunity Act. This may be seen when we review the different groups that make up the poor. S. M. Miller, linking cultural, family, and economic variables, has outlined four categories of the poor: the "stable poor," who are somewhat below the poverty line and have a stable family unit; the "copers" or the "strained," who are in economically painful circumstances but have a stable family condition; the "skidders," who are close to the economic level of the stable poor but suffer a good deal of internal family conflict; and the "unstable poor," who are in great economic and family difficulty.[18]

The War on Poverty, despite the concern with the characteristics of the poor, has not sensed the diversity of their condition and the need for varied programs. Rather, the initial thrust is toward those who are disaffected from work, as though this were the bulk of the problem of poverty in the United States. (And, as we shall see, the programs tend to select those most interested in working.) Many of the poor do not suffer from lack of job motivation but from the inadequate provision of jobs. This is especially true of those who are among the stable poor and the strained. The War on Poverty, at least initially, pays inadequate attention to these sizable groups, and the tax cut—the primary employment measure—is inadequate for the task of adequate job creation. The emphasis on increasing employability rather than assuring employment is insufficient for today's poor.

The categories of the stable poor and the copers contain many aged; presumably Medicare, when enacted, will be part of the poverty war and will help the aged poor. But there is little attention to the overhauling of the Social Security system so that it will provide a decent floor for the aged, automatically adjusted as economic conditions change.

The 23 per cent of the poor who are in welfare are sprinkled through all four categories, but they are more likely to be in the strained and unstable groupings (the aged, welfare poor are probably among the stable poor). The War on Poverty has only the most limited of programs to deal with those on welfare. These provisions are extensions of the philosophy embodied in the 1962 amendments to the Social Security Act, which take as their underlying assumption that increasing professionalization of personnel in local welfare departments and the provision of services (usually interpreted as casework services) would help attenuate the problems of the welfare poor and reduce the number of cases. We doubt that this is true. Benefit levels in many states are fantastically low; the average grant for each dependent child is slightly over a dollar a day. Grants must be raised, at least to the state's own definition of budgetary need. Stigma must be erased and the "right" to welfare assured if welfare is not to be a debilitating experience. Activities to promote self-help should be separated from the provision of financial aid, so that they will not serve as instruments of social control or infringements of rights.

The poverty war has a narrow scope. Perhaps it will reach out in more effective directions to deal with the variety of the poor, but its initial perspective is stunted.

THE CONCENTRATION ON YOUTH

The Economic Opportunity Act focuses almost exclusively on youth. In contrast, the British have emphasized providing a floor for the aged. Our emphasis probably arose from the American emphasis on "education," and from the continuing fears of juvenile delinquency and the search for more effective means of social control. Such "poverty" measures seem to obtain congressional approval more easily. But there are dangers in the heavy reliance on youth poverty. Such concentration encourages the feeling that the problems of poverty are easily solvable, that we can relatively quickly train youth out of poverty and into existing or expanded niches in society. Consequently, we are less likely to think in terms of structural changes which are needed if we are to reduce the number of our present and future poor.

Where programs are seen as beginning programs, perhaps inadequate in dealing with their tasks, one criterion of their usefulness is whether they unfold and sharpen our vision of the larger and more complicated task. The emphasis on youth poverty may, we fear, hide rather than clarify the further tasks of a War on Poverty. By emphasizing youth, it is easier to perpetuate the myth that most poor are misfits, unwilling or unable to work. This orientation supports the underemphasis of the War on Poverty (1) on insuring the availability of jobs for those who want to work (the bulk, we suspect, of the nonaged, male poor) and (2) on those who do work, but earn low wages or only obtain part-time employment.

The emphasis on youth has its attractive side—to rescue the young before they have fallen into apathy and despair; to provide new life for this rising generation and the generation which they will father. The question is how well will it work? Can the young be "rescued" at age sixteen? To speak of the importance of "the culture of poverty" and then to be optimistic about small programs changing the outlook and life-prospects of the youth of this culture implies that one does not believe in the analysis. We cannot have it both ways: that the culture of poverty is the problem, and that hope can be injected into the situation with relative ease through a training program (even of high quality with an obvious payoff, two conditions which we shall discuss later). The culture-of-poverty theme is overplayed while under-believed.

We think there is some importance in changing the conditions of groups as a whole, rather than providing "a career open to the talented few" of an impoverished group. Would increasing the income of a poor family do as much to increase the children's interest in further advance as would specific training programs? We are not confident that the results of a study of these alternative ways of spending poverty funds would support a training program, separate from improving the economic conditions of families and neighborhoods. True, *some* youth would escape from poverty more easily than before, but would the greater number of youth? Economic and social change may have to precede the call for individual responsibility and adjustment.

EDUCATION—THE OPPORTUNITY VEHICLE

The firmest element in the American consensus is the emphasis on the central role of education in pulling people out of poverty or in maintaining them above the poverty line. Today education is the major route to social mobility. This thought underlies much of the antipoverty analysis; for example, we are frequently shown the greater incidence of poverty among families whose heads have had less than a grammar-school education (eight years of education) than in higher-educated families. Despite the accurate emphasis on the importance of education in a highly industrial society, the poverty analysis has failed to make clear a number of important points about educational achievement levels and expenditures.

Our thinking is mired in an older era and is not sufficiently attuned to emerging trends. We are shooting to get drop-outs to become high-school graduates, as the latter increasingly suffer economically, especially relative to college and graduate school alumni. It is likely that in the high-education society, toward which we are moving, high-school graduates will increasingly fall behind college graduates in income and security[19] and will be prey to many of the vicissitudes now occurring among drop-outs. Our educational aim should be to increase substantially the number of college graduates (and to increase employment opportunities for them, especially in the social services).

President Johnson's speeches during the 1964 presidential campaign were very hopeful, speaking of guaranteeing everyone as much education as he can use. But the War on Poverty does not reflect any sense of preparation for emerging educational trends. The amounts spent on education are not very great, though current expenditures in diverse educational programs are considerable. The question is not only as to the total amount spent on education, but on whom it is spent. While the poor have a fifth of the children, they probably receive as little as one-tenth of the $28 billion spent on education in the United States. Morgan reports that children in the lowest income families attend schools where the expenditure per child is 13 per cent below the national average.[20] This is a conservative estimate, since it is based on the questionable assumption that average local expenditures are a useful estimate of educational expenditures for all individuals who live in the community, regardless of income level.

As in many other realms of American life, a redistribution of expenditures is needed so that the poor benefit *more* than other groups. If the educational level of the poor advances at the same rate as, or less rapidly than, the more advantaged groups, they will achieve at best only marginal gains in their ability to compete in the labor market. Despite the increase in educational expenditures, it is not at all clear that the low-income groups are gaining relative to others. We cannot make a definitive statement on this question because we do not have adequate data, but it is the impression of many that the overall increase in educational expenditures in the United States has not meant that a higher percentage of the outlays benefits low-income groups who need the help most. This impression may be inaccurate, but what is significant today is not only the total level of expenditures on education but the share that goes to the poor. Expanding educational expenditures will undoubtedly help them, but the contribution may not be substantial.

And—let us face the sad fact—giving more money to financially starved educational institutions will not be sufficient. True, they desperately need money, but many close observers of the American educational scene are increasingly pessimistic that the great changes needed in the conduct of education—changes which do not depend primarily on funds, but on goals, selection, organization, pedagogy—can be attained. Consequently, it is not enough to give money to school systems, but it must be given in ways that improve the quality of education. This has partly occurred in the Vocational Education Act of 1963, which aims to support and redirect vocational education away from home economics and farming. It is implicit in President Johnson's new legislative proposals for education, but much remains to be done in reorganizing the fabric of our educational system. The proliferation of the educational system, rather than the reform of old institutions, may only serve to complicate and elaborate an already unwieldy structure.

INVIOLATE INSTITUTIONS AND VIOLATE MEN

The primary thrust of the War on Poverty is to affect the opportunities of the poor by changing them as individuals, rather than by changing the institutions which impinge upon them. The beginning programs in the work-training field are largely rehabilitative programs; the underlying assumption is that if the poor are further trained, motivated, and remotivated, they will be able to increase their chances to reach the main economy. The employing institutions are not major targets of change, whether through subsidies, direct governmental expenditures, or investments to ensure the employment of the poor.

The great distance from the theme of social change is also revealed in the willingness to give funds to institutions that have already failed with the poor. Educational systems, employment services, social agencies—many, if not most of them, have a sorry record of inadequate and low-quality service to the poor (and frequently, to the nonpoor as well). Providing additional funds to financially starved institutions may improve their services, but not drastically. The need is for change—in goals, in organization, in selection of personnel, in practices. Money helps achieve some change, but it does not guarantee *qualitative* improvement.

Political issues intrude in providing funds with hooks that will lead to change in educational, employment, and social service organizations. But overcoming bureaucratic and professional encrustations is essential if we are to produce the kinds of services that will really improve the situations of the low-income population. Monitoring programs

only in terms of fiscal accountability or immediate placements will be insufficient. What is most disturbing is the
widespread feeling that money will solve most of the present
problems of the educational and social services. In truth,
the latter need to change so that they fit the people and
needs of today. Existing agencies and professions are not
geared to working effectively with the poor. Giving money
to them will only partially solve problems; they need to be
jogged, led, helped, checked, pressured into doing effective
work. New kinds of agencies will have to be developed; new
kinds of service occupations will have to emerge. We cannot
take the existing network and performance of our social
institutions as given. The War on Poverty cannot exempt
the agencies that dispense its largesse from the need to
change. If it does, even large sums will yield sterile results.

Prospects

It is extremely difficult, of course, to attempt to evaluate
the War on Poverty at its very beginning. But we know
enough about the experience on which the specific programs
are built and about their outlook to assess what problems
will be emerging. We do not expect the opening years of the
War on Poverty to produce stunning achievements. Rather,
the major contribution will be to open up issues in the
conduct of a better designed and coordinated set of activities
and programs. We think more could have been done in the
opening year, but the haste, the failure of social scientists
to develop effective, policy-relevant theory, the lack of a
thought-out approach, the bureaucratic in-fighting, and the
absence of a strong and positive political constituency have
led to limited programs.

Some who assume a fundamentalist position would question whether it might have been wiser to wait until a better
design could have been forthcoming. We doubt it, for while
the present programs are not taken as models to be strengthened, they may become models to be tested and possibly

discarded or sharply revised. The present package can contribute to policy and programs if it is used to highlight issues and trends, suggesting in which direction further lines of policy may come.

JOB TRAINING

In a success-oriented society, one tries to make sure that one is successful. In part, this can be engineered by defining success and the criteria utilized to measure performance in certain ways. Another procedure is to select subjects for programs who are of the highest caliber and who would be likely to improve or succeed without our intervention. "Selective recruiting standards" is what we mean by "creaming," that is, working with the least disadvantaged. This was the experience during the first year, at least, of the Manpower Development and Training Act, the programs of which concentrated on prime (ages twenty-five to forty-five), white males with at least a high-school diploma—that is, those easiest to locate in jobs.

We expect creaming will also be the experience of the Neighborhood Youth Corps. Consider the following projections for this program. Out of 200,000 anticipated jobs, only 15 per cent will be for full-time employment. More than half of the jobs (110,000) will be for summer employment or for quarter-time jobs. Such programs are best suited for those already in school. The drop-out is clearly neglected.[21] The paid work experience of the Neighborhood Youth Corps will likely keep out difficult youth.

President Johnson has demanded that the War on Poverty evince early success. Consequently, the pressure will be to cream, to select those youth who are most likely to "achieve" through these programs and, indeed, might have achieved without them! The Job Corps will not accept youth with physical handicaps or with *serious* delinquency records, regardless of when the delinquencies were committed.

Some are outraged at creaming, since it neglects those who are most disadvantaged. But creaming as a *short-run* tactic is not always objectionable. It may be a political necessity to win support for further legislation by evincing "success." New activities may require a tooling-up period, during which the program involves primarily those easiest to work with. Either or both reasons provide a rationale for *temporary* creaming. But creaming cannot be a permanent policy. It cannot be the basic structure of a program. There should be structural constraints against long-term creaming. After an initial period of grace—a year perhaps—all programs at the national and local level should demonstrate that they are dealing with a range of youth, and perhaps disproportionately with the most disadvantaged. This would require that reports of program performance provide the data to check on whether creaming persists. The funding agencies would have to be empowered to reduce expenditures to agencies that continue creaming.

While creaming is important, we must also examine the programs within a broader administrative context. Questions of social policy can be posed in three strategic areas: entry, continuity, and reabsorption. Together they comprise a completed cycle of social change; no stage can be neglected, for each depends on the other. The question of entry most obviously deals with those who apply for programs and are turned away. Titmuss has suggested that rejection from the Job Corps may be one of the more important sources of rejection that a person experiences in his life, for it may well imply final rejection from the world of work. It is therefore essential that we follow those who are rejected and make sure that they receive the physical and mental-health services they require. There is danger that they be written off as the forgotten youth of America's social underclass. We also need to consider those who do not apply—the invisible clientele who are unaided by the service world. They may not know how to negotiate the complex service jungle and come to reject what they cannot understand, or we may not yet have devised means to reach out to provide them with help. Youth Opportunities Centers will serve as recruiting, screening and referral sources for MDTA, the Job Corps, and the Neighborhood Youth Corps. All will play a part of this crucial role. Decentralization of their operation into neighborhoods may be essential for them to be effective, since disadvantaged youth will not travel readily.

Obviously, it is important that those who start a program, complete it. Yet one of the most persistent characteristics of all work-training programs is their low holding power: typically, attrition rates are very high. The best antidote may be the provision of *authentic* programs which lead to increased skill competence and to jobs. Programs develop a "rep" (reputation) among youth. Inauthentic programs which lead nowhere will create dejected youth, with little faith in themselves and in the programs. They will become fall-outs. Many of the CCC camps during the depression discovered that large numbers of youths were deserting the camps. Mass desertions from the Job Corps may be a real, if disturbing possibility, which should not be discounted as long as the programs permit voluntary participation.

In addition to those who are dejected, we must also consider those who will be ejected—push-outs—because they cannot adjust to the program or the program cannot adjust to them. Some efforts have been made to limit the discretion which administrators of the Job Corps have on ejecting youth. After the first several months, special permission may be needed before a camp can request that an enrollee leave.

Finally, there is the persistent dilemma of reabsorption. Low arrival rates from referring agencies is by far the typical pattern. What mechanisms will be developed to assure that those who graduate from the programs will be absorbed into the labor market, MDTA, schools, community-action programs, or established community services? Referrals will simply not be adequate unless firm assurance is provided that these youth will be given preferential treatment.

We must not neglect the question of the equitable distribution of poverty programs among disadvantaged youth.

The high reliance on summer and part-time employment in the Neighborhood Youth Corps may lead to creaming—a high proportion of white youngsters who continue in high school—while the Job Corps may recruit large numbers of Negro youth. We have been informed that 70 to 80 per cent of the Job Corps may be Negro. If this gloomy prediction is accurate, a new form of indoor and outdoor relief may have been created—Negro youth are removed from the community for periods of up to two years, whereas white youth are absorbed in the local labor force.

We must avoid the notion that the prospective participants are inadequate; the responsibility is always with the program and its administrators to provide activities that are effective. *It is not so much that individuals fail to comply or utilize established programs, as it is that programs fail to devise means for meeting the needs of individuals.* This is the essential context in which to view recruitment, the content of programs, and the high attrition rates which all programs seem to have.

CAUSES OF FAILURE

A more general point about programs is involved. It is likely that if the War on Poverty does not do well that many administrators, politicians or social commentators, will leap to the assertion that there is something wrong with our youth. They may fail to enlist in the war, or, if they do join, they may fail to see any payoff and desert in great numbers. If they fail to get decent jobs later despite their training, it may be charged that it is something about *them* that is the obstacle. This is the easy path in analyzing failure and defeats. It will be important as we encounter failure—as we will—to police ourselves so that we do not make the youth who go through or fail to go through the programs the ultimate scapegoats. If we concentrate on youth as the source of failure, then we ignore the kind of analysis which might lead to new, more effective programs. Evaluating goal and program success is more useful than impugning those who do not neatly fit into plans.

In a difficult task, failures will always occur. It is what they do to us and what we do about them that becomes significant in the longer-term picture. The great danger is in looking at failure as stemming from the inadequacies of the clientele and not in terms of the tasks of society.

THE VALIDITY OF THE "EMPLOYABILITY" GOAL

In some ways, the work programs of the Economic Opportunity Act are more sophisticated than other work programs aimed at low-income youth. Their administrators recognize that many of the jobs that graduates of such programs receive are low-grade, dead-end jobs, frequently kept for only short periods of time. The work programs are primarily oriented to increasing "employability" rather than delivering youth into presently available, low-level jobs. The hope is that those who graduate will be able to move into higher-level jobs via training programs which prepare them for better positions.

But will this occur? For example, will working on problems of conservation in the Job Corps increase urban job possibilities? Will enhancing "job motivation" open many good jobs? One necessarily raises these questions, for much of the initial scheduling of activities of the work programs is to improve work attitudes and motivation, not to provide marketable skills. The latter may be talked about, but the practice seems to be to favor attitude-improvement exercises. For example, the Neighborhood Youth Corps programs will provide funds to public and nonprofit agencies to employ youth, but there are no requirements about skill development on the job nor provisions for mandatory educational or training components. Indeed, the very goal of employability in Title IB may have been lost, as the program seems to have become converted from work-training to work-relief. The Neighborhood Youth Corps should pay for the effective supervision and training of its clients as well as for their working hours.

Today's labor market does not lead to optimism about the success of increased "work motivation." First, we believe many unemployed youth can do much better than become "remotivated"—they could develop skills. Second, motivation programs will lose youth rapidly, as the youth increasingly recognize that they do not have great job payoffs. But, most important of all, we doubt that a great many youth would be hired because they have completed a "work-motivation" program. The problem, as Cloward has so aptly put it, "lies not with the input of their motivation but with the output of competence after training."[22] True, the state employment services may be more willing to refer than previously, because the youth have been through such a program, but there just does not appear to be a million or so jobs for low-skill youth. A small number of youth in any large city can be placed through intensive job-development procedures with private employers. But we should not deceive ourselves into believing that private enterprise, un-aided, can provide jobs for low-skill youth. It will be extraordinarily disturbing if we get youths who feel that they have been given a rough time, to go through new programs of training, only to find out that they still cannot get employment. We must deliver adequate jobs, or we are perpetrating a hoax.

Mobilization for Youth, one of the more thoughtfully organized work-training programs in the United States, found that in the 14-month period after the program began in October 1962, 1700 young people applied for assistance. Approximately 25 per cent of these recruits were placed in competitive jobs as a direct result of this program. (These percentages can be inflated, as are national statistics on job placements, by calculating placements as a percentage of those who have completed the program rather than those who have enrolled.) The bulk of the 425 youth were placed in marginal occupations at low wages.[23] While follow-up

data are not available on the length of time youth held jobs
to which they were referred, some figures are available on
wages received. JOIN, another New York City program,
reports that 66 per cent of their 2410 placements earn
between $50–54 a week.[24]

Irregular and low-paid employment is not a satisfactory
outcome of programs which stress the employability theme.
Employability has to be seen as the means to decent employment, and someone in the War on Poverty—the Secretary of Labor, the Director of the Office of Economic
Opportunity—must have the responsibility and power to
see that the end, decent employment, is achieved. In the
present situation, no one has the responsibility for insuring
the final payoff—a decent job. We do not believe that the
structure of present programs can deliver adequate numbers
of worthwhile jobs; jobs will have to be created.

AMBIGUITY OF AIMS

The War on Poverty also reflects concern with juvenile
delinquency and the misdeeds of the young. The attractive-
ness of the Job Corps idea is largely based on the mystical
American belief in the purifying effect of contact with tall
trees and mountain air. We want to do "something" about
our youth. The "something" may mean that we are mainly
interested in social control, rather than helping youngsters
obtain decent jobs. The various job programs in the War on
Poverty can degenerate into devices to reduce our fears of
delinquency and rioting, to police the poor, not to develop
them. This danger persists because an underlying theme
among many connected with the War on Poverty, especially
at local levels, is that the purpose of the programs is to
provide settings which administer control over youth and to
"resocialize" them for "living in society."

Youth programs might not be considered failures if they
just take care of youth for several years in an "aging vat"
called a work camp or training program. Although one
might hope that they will be trained, as well as "aged," the

programs could be considered successes even if the youth did not later obtain jobs. If this becomes the fate of the programs, then some critics are right in charging that the War on Poverty is a cloak for a war on the poor.

We would be getting youth into programs on the presumption that their job careers would be moved along, but that would not be the real goal. And such manipulation is likely to fail. Low-income youth, much experienced with the con games of the adult, "outside" world, would soon recognize the training for what it is—control, not aid.

Some of the professionals involved may abet this tendency as they stress the therapeutic effect of work experience. They see an opportunity to sneak in a mass-therapy program as work-training. Psychotherapy will have a role with many a youth in the programs, but it should not be bootlegged in the guise of directly improving career chances. Further, the stress on counseling and group therapy is a threat, particularly since much of it will be done by those unclear about its goals and how to conduct it effectively. If it is not done well, it would be better not done at all.

A program with therapeutic effects is not necessarily one that is therapeutically oriented. We frankly believe that securing low-income youth decent jobs is the most important therapeutic agent of all. For those youth who cannot easily achieve this goal because of personality difficulties, then dealing with the internal obstacles is in order. But this situation cannot be assumed to be always present, nor can therapy, or training as therapy, function as a substitute for the availability of jobs.

What we must remember is that "motivation" is the means in these programs, not the end. If it really is the end, then the programs will fail, both in gaining jobs for youth and in "motivating" them.

CONFUSION IN PROGRAMING

Reflecting the variety of low-income youth, there is a great diversity of work programs. Some of them are *prepara-*

tion programs to develop work-motivation and literacy skills, others are *prevocational,* providing a beginning and supervised work experience that may lead to further training or a job; still others are at the level of *vocational* training in which a fair degree of skill is involved.

The availability of diverse programs is good, but there is the danger of confusion in the diversity. Sometimes work-training to provide skills is confused with work-training experience to provide motivation.[25] There is need for much greater clarity in specifying the training needs of different kinds of youth and developing the kinds of programs which are appropriate.

At the local level, especially, many agencies do not seem to have a good fix on the kinds of youth they have and want to deal with. Their programs seem frequently to be copies of programs elsewhere, with little regard to local labor market conditions and the diversity and potentials of their youth. The funding agencies will have to provide more effective leadership here.

A training program may wish to accomplish one or another of the three goals of preparation, or prevocational and vocational training. Then, the question is the appropriateness of the particular goal. The aim may be to achieve all three. Then, the issue becomes the phasing and coordination among the programs. But the starting point must always be the needs and possibilities of the youth involved.

THE RELEVANCE OF TRAINING

Successful training requires that youth be fitted for jobs that exist. To aid in achieving this goal, labor market analysis is required. The impression we have gained is that many of these analyses are not adequate. They lack adequate information about available jobs, since there is no provision for mandatory listing of job vacancies and for the projection of labor trends, a complex task, which, when performed at its best is often hastily completed and based on inadequate and incomplete data. In some cases, the analyses favor jobs which have a high rate of obsolescence. In other cases, jobs are recommended which are inappropriate for the population to be served; for instance, secretarial work is indicated as the avenue of development for youth who cannot speak English or have substantial reading retardation.

The choosing of possible employment skills is not a simple, mechanical task. It requires sensitive and far-sighted awareness of job trends; it must be related to an understanding of the youth to be trained. If training areas are not selected with the greatest of care, the programs will avail little. Perhaps the professionals who make the analyses need further training. Perhaps specialists have to be sent into at least some communities for a limited period to make the needed determination. Perhaps, too, a variety of groups have to be brought into the process of need determination. The best arrangement will probably vary from community to community. Unfortunately, this flexible orientation is difficult for a federal agency to maintain, since communities can take differential treatment to imply that one of its agencies is inferior to that of another community. Perhaps at this stage, then, bringing in experts from outside to work with the local analysts will be most efficient.

Regardless of the device used to improve the determination of training area, it must be recognized early how vital this is. We do not want to provide more obstacles to swift action, but this step of training requires the most thoughtful analysis. And many involved in programs have told us that they do not think their local agency is adequately equipped to do the job!

TRAINING AND COMMUNITY FACILITIES

In order to produce adequate training programs a variety of community services will have to be immediately available; these range from good, available, free medical and dental care to psychological services to vocational services to school programs which are effective with former drop-outs. The inadequacies of educational and social services will become glaringly apparent. Many communities do not have such services; those communities that do, usually have waiting lists. In many places the quality of service is shockingly low. We have to begin now in community after community to plan for and produce the kinds of services that are necessary. Community action programs and the variety of work programs will have to work together much more effectively than presently if we are to see a great improvement along these lines.

THE OBSTACLE COURSE

In discussing MDTA programs, Gerald G. Somers writes:

> . . . the complicated relations between the Office of Manpower, Automation, and Training, the Bureau of Employment Security, and Health, Education and Welfare—both in Washington and at the local level—have sometimes served to delay the inception of programs and impair their effective functioning.[26]

Many would consider this rebuke mild. The War on Poverty which multiplies programs and redirects old-line bureaus will worsen the tangled web of relationships. The demand in the Economic Opportunity Act, as finally enacted, for a high degree of state participation in programs makes the course of action even more unsettled and difficult to engineer. There is need for much greater authority in the Office of the Director of Economic Opportunity, and he must be willing to knock together heads of contributing and subordinate agencies—which are frequently competing with each other and uncooperative—and to gain some control over other governmental agencies involved in the War on Poverty. It is now a jungle. And perhaps the hardest part of the jungle to traverse is federal-state-local relationships. We need new kinds of relationships among these levels. If state activities are going to be expanded through federal tax allotments, then we will need even more a significant turning in the present, complicated, slow-moving interplay.

Despite the reading of reports, attendance at conferences, and discussions with administrators, we must
sheepishly report that we have the greatest difficulty in
keeping in mind the various programs that comprise the
War on Poverty. Where does the jurisdiction of the Youth
Opportunity Centers, the Neighborhood Youth Corps, the
Manpower Development and Training Program, the work-
training programs of the Community Action Program leave
off and resume? It is like listening to a fluent and idiomatic
native speaker of a language one is just learning—it has a
familiar ring but very little meaning gets through! The
decoding runs well behind the rushing verbal stimuli.

We may be defensive, but we do not believe that the
problem is one of a lack of application or a characteristic
difficulty to absorb information. The programs and their
jurisdictions—multilayered, overlapping, and fragmented—
are complicated, and they frequently change. If professionals
in ordering information are overwhelmed by the task of
understanding the independent and frequently competing
battalions engaged in the War on Poverty, what will happen
to youth dealing with them? And their task will be complicated by the need to figure out what is the best part of the
program for them.

It will soon be apparent that there is great need for
decentralized information-orientation service units. They
should be located in low-income neighborhoods; they should
be able to refer youth on-the-spot among the Job Corps, the
Neighborhood Youth Corps, training programs, educational
remedial work and social work services and to see that they
are immediately serviced. A youth should not be forced to
find his way unaided through the unmarked fields of agency
sovereignties. The unresolved dilemma remains: referral
must have an assurance of action; it must not be a means
for one agency to expel its "crocks," its undesirables, to
another agency unwilling to accept such refugees. If the
situation is enormously complicated, if referrals are meaningless, if services are not immediately provided, and if

attention is not given to the achievement of interlocked progress, then low-income youth will be expended, rather than invested, in the fight for agency aggrandizement. *The unit of the war on poverty is the youth, not the program.*

This point is especially important for youth who have been in one program and then need a different kind of program. For example, a boy who has improved his basic reading and writing in the Job Corps may now need specific skill training which his camp cannot provide. If he has to go to a city to get this training, will the further training, under, say, the jurisdiction of a community-action program be carefully and explicitly arranged? *Continuity of services must be assured.*

The logical place for such a central service is in the community-action programs. The Youth Opportunity Centers of the state employment services, administered through the federal Bureau of Employment and Security, hope to provide some central referral and screening services in the manpower field. Whether the state employment services, which have a poor record with low-income youth, can be adequately revamped to do this new (for them) manpower job and to go beyond that is uncertain. Undoubtedly, the agency under which such decentralized service centers should be provided might well differ from one community to another, though we see the strongest case for the community-action programs. The most important thing is the provision of easy and *effective* entrance to the battlefields of the War on Poverty; otherwise, much of the good will of youth may be spent in traveling from one sector of the front to another, only intermittently getting action, and becoming disillusioned veterans of rear-guard "snafus" and interagency squabbles.

THE MEASUREMENT OF PROGRESS

The mode of evaluation of a program is not only a technical issue but a question of values, that is, a public policy issue. Good programs require useful criteria of evaluation.

A serious War on Poverty requires both long-term and short-term goals and means of measuring the degree of achievement of these goals.

We suggest below two approaches to the evaluation of programs. One set of criteria involves the fairly immediate impact of the training programs on securing jobs for trainees; here both quantity and *quality* of jobs are important. The other set of criteria utilizes changing income profiles as a measure of the success of the War on Poverty.

In judging the effectiveness of the work programs and the possible need for strengthening or changing them, we must be clear about the ultimate goal—a "decent" job. A "decent" job is one which comes close to prevailing standards in terms of pay and security. It should have high likelihood of leading to a better job and/or withstanding the immediate pressure for obsolescence and eradication. In short, the job must provide not only a decent floor, but offer advancement or longer-run security. To be trained for a job that will soon disappear is an advance over unemployment, but not a continuing one if unemployment is likely to recur.

Experience with the hiring of difficult-to-place youngsters underlines the importance of length of time on a job. A great many placements are soon ended; youngsters are pushed out or drift off a job in a matter of weeks. The training agency may produce a good record of placements when, in actuality, many of its graduates are unemployed.

In evaluating training programs, questions like these must be pursued: What kind of jobs did the trainees get? How long did they keep them? What occupational futures do they have? What has happened to those unplaced? Are youths' opportunities to get decent, secure jobs actually enhanced to any considerable extent? This should be the overarching theme of the evaluations and reports.

It will not be possible to evaluate failures among the Job Corps in a short period of time, and definitive answers may not be forthcoming even later because of the complexities of conducting research on action programs. To rely solely on research findings may delay necessary changes. Some changes can be proposed even at this point. For example, one might question on moral grounds the present requirement that youth sign a loyalty oath to qualify for the benefits of the programs.

Since one of the goals of the work programs is to increase drop-outs' return to school, a comment is necessary here. It is frequently not realized that a high proportion of drop-outs—perhaps 10 to 25 per cent do return to school without any special school or community effort to get them to return. But most of them drop out again.[27] For example, President Kennedy's crash program in the summer of 1963 to get drop-outs to return to school did lead quite a number to resume their education. But, in many cities, they soon left again. The schools had not changed in ways that would permit them to deal more adequately with youth who had earlier school difficulties. *Consequently, it will not be enough to say that youth have returned to school without checking whether or not they graduate.* Reports should also indicate the number who enter a program as distinct from those who complete it. Many placement performances are inflated by neglecting those who start but do not finish the programs. Information on drop-outs from programs can reveal much about possible creaming.

The income criteria of evaluation can follow the lead of the Council of Economic Advisers. In the realm of economic policy, the council has utilized the concept of "frictional unemployment," the minimal amount of unemployment that would occur in a dynamic economy. Unemployment above the frictional level of 2 to 4 per cent is a signal that the economy is not successfully dealing with unemployment and that action is needed to reduce the rate. Thus, the frictional rate provides a goal for the federal government—to strive to reduce the rate to this level.

A similar kind of goal measurement, as Bertram Gross has suggested, may be useful in conducting antipoverty programs. We can establish the poverty equivalent of "fric-

tional unemployment," that is, "frictional poverty." The goal
of public policy would be to reduce poverty to this level in
some stipulated time period. Once we achieve the frictional
poverty level, we strive to prevent the poverty rate from
rising. Further, the poor should constitute a fluid group. If
"frictional poverty" is made up only of those who are long-
term poor, then we are failing to develop programs which
deal with the forces that have produced poverty in selected
groups of the population. Those who are poor should be only
temporarily so. If this is not true, current programs are
failing in their objectives of helping the poor. The intent is
to reduce poverty to a transitional level, to be eliminated as
the appropriate program emerges. Frictional or transitional
poverty, then, should affect a small percentage of the population: those who are poor are temporarily so, not a long-
term poor for whom society has failed to develop programs
to deal with their problems. A figure of 5 per cent, we suggest,
might be the target goal of frictional poverty. Above that
level, immediate action is called for.

Since poverty is many-sided, multiple indicators are
needed. Not only do we need indicators of income poverty,
but also indicators of asset poverty (particularly important
as people age), educational poverty, health poverty, and
the like. We should strive to reduce poverty in all these area,
not just in the income area. Improvement in one dimension
does not automatically produce improvements in others.
Policies may vary in order to be effective with the different
dimensions of poverty. For example, income poverty may be
reduced by transfer payments through social insurance,
while health poverty would probably require investments in
public health measures as well as the reorganization and
refunding of medical care. While we have written mainly
of income poverty, the other dimensions cannot be ignored.

The speed with which we move to achieve the 5-per-cent
rate is a political one. We would suggest that in five years
the rate of poverty be reduced to the 5-per-cent level; this
would mean a rate of reduction in poverty of less than 3

per cent per year. This requires speeding-up the long-term rate of reduction as calculated by Robert J. Lampman.[28] If we fail to move at this rate, then the poverty programs should be carefully assessed and redirected so that the rate of progress can be accelerated.

In setting out goals and measuring performance, it is important not to become a prisoner of a fixed poverty line. If we do, we may be solving the old poverty, but not the new. As average income goes up in society, so does the poverty line. Consequently, the line which defines who is poor should be moving up as income increases. The poverty line should be adjusted for cost-of-living changes and for the annual average increase in income or productivity or some such measure of changing conditions in the general society. Otherwise, we can reduce the number of poor only to discover that we have a new poor, who are above the outmoded poverty line, but below the new standards established by society.

SOCIAL REPORT

The impetus of the War on Poverty might be utilized for the introduction of a *Social Report*.[29] The Employment Act of 1946 gave rise to the important and influential *Economic Report* of the President and Council of Economic Advisers. The Manpower Development and Training Act provides the useful *Manpower Report* of the Secretary of Labor, outlining statistics and issues in the utilization of manpower. Today, we need the introduction of an annual "Social Report" which will highlight changing conditions in the United States. Issued by the Office of Economic Opportunities, it might not only report the performance of its various programs (for instance, the number of youths placed in what level of jobs for what length of time as a result of training programs), but also analyze the larger issues. It might well include statistics on morbidity and mortality rates for various income levels and groups in the United States (it would shock many congressmen to learn that the country is not among the first ten nations in low infant-mortality rates, or that the older a reservation-Indian youth gets, the more his chances of longevity fall behind that of the rest of the population); on the quality and quantity of housing; on the level of education attained by various income groups; on the adequacy of benefits received under welfare and Social Security schemes; on indicators of social unrest; and so on. True, many such items appear in periodicals like *Welfare in Review* and the *Social Security Bulletin* and in annual summary tabulations issued by the Department of Health, Education, and Welfare. But the systematic annual summation in one place of these data, a vast expanse of the indicators of social life, and an assessment of their implications for economic and social policy appear extremely urgent. It would place the antipoverty programs in the widest possible context.

Together with the *Economic Report* and the *Manpower Report*, the *Social Report* would provide the basic information and continuing analysis necessary for the development and monitoring of programs that deal with the emerging issues of American society.

MONITORING THE PROGRAMS

At the beginning of this paper we discussed the absence of a firm political pressure propelling the War on Poverty. If the poverty program is to move in more productive channels, it will undoubtedly require the monitoring support and active pressure of diverse groups.

Outside organizations can play a most important role in monitoring programs, studying what is going on, evaluating the effectiveness of the programs, pressuring to upgrade quality and appropriateness of programs, and the like. Well-informed groups, such as civil-rights organizations, can be pushing the programs into more effective channels. This pressure will be particularly important in communities where professionalism on the part of staff must be overcome (for example, emphasizing selection tests of students to near-exclusion of placement on jobs), or where community-business reluctance to employ minority or poorly schooled youth is great. At the national level, support will be needed to move the programs into broader lines.

The role of the intellectual, the scholar, and the informed citizen will be great in watching over the progress of the programs, developing standards of accountability, and spreading their findings. It is important to have wide public understanding of the progress made (or the lack of it). Social criticism will be an important device for promoting goal success. Social scientists have an especially important role as informed, independent analysts and critics.

If the criticisms of newspapers (see *The Village Voice,* November 19, 1964, on *The New York Times*) to the effect that they no longer develop their own reportage and increasingly are dependent on public-relations releases are valid (as they seem to be), then interest groups must do the basic news-collection job that the press once did. By building effective links with newspapers, this information and analysis could then get attention.

The monitoring of the antipoverty programs should (and we believe will) become one of the major activities of civil-rights groups. Less and less will these groups be met with an out-and-out unwillingness to improve the conditions of the downtrodden. Increasingly, a variety of programs will be proffered to ameliorate the situation. The task of the civil-rights groups will then be to pressure for more effective programs and to monitor and criticize the performance of programs that are initiated or expanded.

Some of those in the civil-rights movement are offering a catastrophic view of the shoals and reefs threatening the American economy if it is to navigate to the shore of high production and high employment. They demand far-reaching programs of planning that are unlikely to generate much political strength today. Whether or not their analyses are correct, they must develop a strategy to deal with the programs that are emerging today. They can reject them totally as "tokenism" and inadequate; or they can use them to open up important issues. We see no politically useful alternative to the latter course.

To assess poverty programs adequately so that new issues can be raised and weak programs supplanted by more effective ones requires detailed knowledge of what the programs do and what happens to those who have been through them. Some technical competence is needed here, but not very much. More important is a stern and steady eye to the sparrow—the actual opportunities of those who have been in touch with the program. Where do they stand now?

What is required is to ask the right questions. For example, are youth getting the fullest protection that our society is already offering to other citizens? Why not press for unemployment insurance for successful graduates of the programs who fail to secure a job or who are placed in jobs that have only limited tenure and then are unable to find another job?

It is also important to make sure that the answers which are given are valid. This may require some spot-checking of those who have graduated, but this has been done by some civil-rights groups. It is in the tradition of checking to see, for example, whether a stated change in personnel practices has actually led to the employment of large numbers of minority members. The technical questions in monitoring are not grave, and many liberal social scientists would be eager to help.

GAINING A CONSTITUENCY

The civil-rights groups, thus, form a crucial part of the constituency of the antipoverty programs. They will be pressuring for broader, better funded, more effective programs. Their pressure alone will probably win considerable legislative extensions of the programs over the years.

Whether their pressure will be enough to win programs that will lead to structural changes (for instance, more progressive tax structure to increase redistributive effects) in the economy is less certain. It seems likely that other groups must be brought into central concern with the poverty programs if the latter are to move in new directions. Here, two lines of action have been suggested: coalition of the white and Negro poor; coalition of civil-rights and liberal groups.

Some in the civil-rights movement are thinking of encouraging political mobilization among the white poor, both in the big cities and in Appalachia. With many concerns similar to those of the minority poor, the white poor might be willing to join the latter in political campaigns to strengthen and expand the antipoverty programs. Two steps are involved: the political mobilization of all the poor, especially the white poor who have lagged behind Negroes in expressing their unrest and in seeking improvement in their conditions; and bringing together on specific issues or on a wider basis the variety of groups of the poor.[30] They would seek the election of those who would represent the amalgamated poor and be *accountable* to them because they owe their political fortunes to them. Whether the black and white poor will move together will depend on the issues that emerge, the skill of organization, and the like. The key, though, is the mobilization of many groups of the poor.

The community action programs of the War on Poverty can help to stimulate the poor to organize. If we are genuinely interested in having Americans self-determining— providing opportunity, not a dole—then mobilization of the poor is significant. Providing services without involving the poor in decisions and in operations perpetuates dependency and apathy. The theme of community participation in the Economic Opportunity Act should not mean only elite citizen participation, as it has in the administration of urban renewal. An effort must be made to overcome "social-work colonialism" in all the programs, for this props the poor but does not encourage community self-governance.

The attacks on Mobilization for Youth are symptomatic of the reluctance to permit community self-direction. But the movement toward political activity is important for the effective conduct of the programs and for their development in more penetrating directions. The community-participation provisions can serve as a Wagner Act for community organizations, not only legitimating them but requiring their active participation in the negotiations which determine the fate of their localities.[31]

Thus, the War on Poverty may make its major contribution in legitimating the grievances of the poor. By paying attention to poverty and accepting a governmental responsibility for at least some action, the poverty war may encourage more of the poor to feel that they have a right to protest when their conditions do not improve rapidly. They may then organize to express their views. Yet this is a possibility that many believe to be very unlikely today. Gunnar Myrdal and many American social scientists have emphasized the apathy of the poor in the United States. Certainly, the poor and the unemployed are not currently an active, pressing political force.[32] We should not, however, assume that the absence of militant behavior is necessarily a permanent condition. Similar comments were made about Negroes just a short time ago. Under some conditions a long-time, poverty-stricken, and politically inactive group emerges into political aggressiveness. Frequently, this happens when its conditions are improving, for then it acquires hope and gains the feeling of new, legitimate claims on society. The inadequate meeting of hopes and claims stirs discontent even though conditions may be improving. Rising expectations rather than ever-increasing debasement are more productive of political anger.

The War on Poverty may encourage new expectations and claims which will energize the poor. In doing so, the poverty war may produce the political pressures which will make possible more effective programs to eliminate poverty in the semi-affluent society. The second line of strategy is to move outside the poor in building support for the improvement of antipoverty legislation. Here, labor unions and members of the middle classes must be increasingly brought into support. They are already supporting the general outlines of the poverty program, but they would have to put these activities on a higher priority level.

If the poverty programs are an enclave separate from other attempts to improve the conditions of Americans, their general support will probably be limited, permitting weak programs to continue. But if their scope is comprehensive, and if they enlarge economic demand to preserve and expand prosperity and to improve the housing, mass transportation, civic amenities, and the like of the nonpoor as well as the poor, then the possibility of building a broad constituency will grow.

Conclusion

Some critics are treating the antipoverty programs with distaste and prophesying disaster. We think this overstresses the inadequacies of the programs. Others are blithely convinced of assured successes to come. We think this view ignores the stunted character of the programs and their faulty engineering and organization. We would have liked to have seen a better-designed and more far-reaching set of proposals and a more coordinated administration. But, to paraphrase President Johnson, this is the only War on Poverty that we have. We have to learn what directions are more effective and how to move in those directions. We would have liked another beginning, but this is it. There is no guarantee of how far or how fast the War on Poverty will move to alleviate the plight of the poor. Informed social analysis and increased political pressure will be needed to move the poverty campaign into more effective channels. High optimism curbs analysis; high pessimism cuts the involvement that will produce pressure. A strategy of analysis and change is the urgency of the day.

NOTES

1. We are indebted to Bertram M. Gross, whose comments have affected the texture of much of the analysis. The preparation of this paper has been aided by grants to S. M. Miller from the Stern Family Fund and the Ford Foundation for study of the distribution of income, wealth, and social services. The authors alone are responsible for the paper. Many have aided us by their criticism and comments: Ben B. Seligman, Richard Titmuss, Adrian Sinfield, Ida Merriam, Kurt Reichard, Sar Levitan, Harry Kranz and Robert Schrank. Fern Freel made the paper possible by translating scribbles into type pages.

2. Bertram M. Gross has expressed the issue well in his discussion of "skeptical idealism": It would be intellectual blindness not to see all these negative potentialities. Our eyes can be opened and our eyesight cleared only by the searing frankness of skepticism.

But skepticism alone is only part of realism. The other part is idealism, the vigorous formulation of positive potentialities in careful, flexible sequence from the present to the near future and onward to the distant future.

This is no simple matter of a choice between the two. Either one without the other is self-defeating. *The Managing of Organizations* (New York: The Free Press, 1964), Vol. II, p. 837.

3. Middle-range social analysis is further discussed in S. M. Miller, "Prospects: The Applied Sociology of the Center-City," in Alvin W. Gouldner and S. M. Miller, eds., *Applied Sociology* (New York: The Free Press, 1965).

4. Bertram Gross has forcefully argued that a perceived crisis is a necessary though not a sufficient condition for the introduction or expansion of national planning. We do not believe that the civil-rights thrust and the "disinvisibilizing" of the poor by social commentators created a "crisis," goading action. See B. M. Gross, ed., *Planning Against Poverty,* forthcoming.

5. Adam Walinsky, in a thoughtful article, questions the adequacy of this formulation. He argues that the status panic of the middle classes in America today will prevent investments in raising the relative status of the poor. See "Keeping the Poor in Their Place," *New Republic,* July 1964.

6. Assistant Secretary of Labor Moynihan has asserted quite sharply this distinctive emphasis of "the War on Poverty." Daniel Patrick Moynihan, *Monthly Labor Review,* 1964.

7. This view of poverty is developed in S. M. Miller and Martin Rein, "Poverty and Social Change," *American Child,* March 1964. Reprinted in Louis Ferman, Joyce Kornbluh, and Tom Hayden, eds., *One-Third of a Nation,* forthcoming.

8. Lenore A. Epstein, "Income Security Standards in Old-Age," *Research Report No. 3*, Social Security Administration, U.S. Department of Health, Education, and Welfare, 1963, p. 4.

9. For a spirited criticism of the analysis of the Triple Revolution, see Charles E. Silberman, "The Real News About Automation," *Fortune,* January 1965. However, *see also* the response of C. C. Killingsworth in *Fortune,* March 1965, and Ben B. Seligman, "Real News and Automated Villains," *Dissent,* Spring 1965.

10. The scattered data are discussed in S. M. Miller and Martin Rein, "Poverty, Inequality and Policy," in Howard S. Becker, ed., *Social Problems* (New York: John Wiley & Sons, Inc., forthcoming). Poverty and inequality are frequently confused; in the article just mentioned we try to clarify the differences.

11. One glaring and surprising lack of sophistication appears in the current handling of statistics on poverty. The trend estimates show a decline in the percentage who are poor today compared to an earlier point, frequently 1947. The more recent year is used as the base year for price corrections. This type of index, the Paasche index, is known to lead to a high statement of the degree of fall over time. The alternative method, the Laspeyres index, which uses the early year as the base year, understates the degree of change. We do not argue that the Laspeyres index should have been used. What is singularly lacking in the trend statements is a discussion of the well-known, built-in bias of the statistical methods employed—which, in this case, leads to overstatement of the degree of decline in poverty.

Incidentally, our own calculations show a startling reversal of the findings about a reduction in the extent of poverty. If 50 per cent of average family income is used as the poverty line, the percentage falling below this line has actually increased since 1947. We do not defend this procedure—though it is an interesting one—but only wish to point out the misplaced satisfaction with a single indicator in a situation which requires multiple sights of the nature of movement.

12. *Economic Report of the President,* January 1964 (Washington, D.C.: Government Printing Office, 1964), p. 58.

13. The range of criticism of the War on Poverty is due, in part, to different assumptions about the extent of poverty in the United States. Komatsu defines the scope of the problem as coming close to 43 per cent of all American families (using a Department of Labor Family Budget standard), while the Minority Report of the Senate Committee on Labor and Public Welfare defines the scope of the problem as closer to 13 per cent of American families (using for its definition a study by Herman Miller which defines poverty as the proportion of families living below the prevailing public-assistance standards of eligibility in each state).

14. The "incidence" of poverty refers to the percentage of a group, for example, the aged, who are poor. "Composition" refers to the percentage of the poor who have a given characteristic, for instance, old-age. These distinctions are important because it is possible, for example, for a group having a high incidence rate of poverty to constitute only a small percentage of the poor. This is true of Negroes. Many of the writings on poverty—though little of the work of the Council of Economic Advisers—make this error.

15. Elizabeth Wickenden, in a mimeographed paper prepared for the National Social Welfare Assembly, 1964.

16. Leon Keyserling's discussion of the interplay of "cause" and "consequence" is very important. *Poverty and Deprivation in the United States* (Washington, D.C.: Conference of Economic Progress, 1962).

17. We hasten to add that we do believe that attitudes are important in keeping some in poverty, and that the attitudes of the poor have to be considered in the development of programs. We question whether attitudes are always the prime issue and whether they can be changed drastically in the absence of actual advances into the main society.

18. S. M. Miller, "The American Lower Class: A Typological Approach," *Social Research*, Spring 1964; reprinted in Reprint Series, Syracuse University Youth Development Center; in Arthur Shostak and William Gomberg, eds., *Blue Collar World* (Engelwood Cliffs: Prentice-Hall, Inc., 1964; in Frank Riessman, Jerome Cohen, and Arthur Pearl, eds., *Mental Health of the Poor* (New York: The Free Press, 1964).

19. Clearly, the income differential between high school and college graduates is widening. At the same time, the advantage of a high-school diploma over noncompletion of high school is not always clear and decisive. See S. M. Miller, "The Outlook of Working-Class Youth" in Shostak and Gomberg, *op. cit.*

20. The basic data are from James N. Morgan *et al.*, *Income and Welfare in the United States* (New York: McGraw-Hill Book Co., 1963), p. 306. The analysis of the data is in an extraordinarily useful paper by Robert J. Lampman, "Prognosis for Poverty," presented at the meetings of the National Tax Association, September 15, 1964.

21. Harry Kranz, "Washington Charts a Course," *American Child*, January 1965.

22. Richard Cloward and Robert Ontell, "Our Delusions about Training," *Ibid.*

23. *Ibid.*

24. *The New York Times*, December 14, 1964.

25. Many programs have added to the confusion by giving new meanings to old jargon. Some of the new terminology may well have been introduced as a conscious subterfuge, a device to bypass the archaic vocational-education system. The result is a new and growing vocabulary which includes "work readiness," "work preparation," "work orientation," and "basic skills," to mention but a few. This terminology makes analysis difficult, since many of these programs actually attempt to teach reading as well as vocational skills.

26. Gerald G. Somers' discussion is a cogent and informative criticism of MDTA, in Arthur M. Ross, ed., *Unemployment and the American Economy* (New York: John Wiley & Sons, Inc., 1964), pp. 83–84.

27. *See* Betty L. Saleem and S. M. Miller, *The Neglected Dropout: The Returnee* (Syracuse: Syracuse University Youth Development Center, 1963).

28. Robert J. Lampman, *op. cit.*

29. The most promising analysis along these lines is Bertram M. Gross, "Towards National Social Accounting," prepared for the committee on Space Efforts and Society of the American Academy of Arts and Sciences, 1964. Similar suggestions have been made by Daniel Patrick Moynihan and Harvey S. Perloff.

30. We recognize that Negro-rights organizations are not largely organizations of the poor. But their major impact increasingly will be to improve the lot of the poor and to engage the poor in some of their organizations. See S. M. Miller, "Politics, Race and Poverty," in Irving L. Horowitz, *The New Sociology* (New York: Oxford Univ. Press, Inc., 1964), p. 290 ff.

31. Warren Haggstrom of the Syracuse University Youth Development Center has suggested to us the Wagner Act aspect of community participation of the Economic Opportunity Act.

32. Bertram Gross has suggested that this is because welfare-state measures of unemployment insurance and welfare allotments provide an income floor, cutting the edge of discontent.

Job Opportunities
and Poverty

GARDINER C. MEANS

In recent discussions of unemployment there has been a major controversy over whether the present relatively high unemployment rate is structural or due to insufficient demand. The proponents of the structural argument have held that the present unemployment rate is largely the result of the wrong people being in the wrong places. They emphasize lack of skills, geographical disadvantage, pockets of unemployment, and cultures of poverty. The proponents of demand unemployment hold that the aggregate demand for goods is not sufficient to absorb all the manpower that is practically available. They emphasize fiscal and monetary policies to stimulate spending, such as the recent tax cut or a more rapid increase in the money supply.

This controversy has its application to the problems of poverty. If practically all of the present unemployment is structural, then a part of the War on Poverty must be to reduce the structural difficulties, and increasing aggregate demand is more likely to work itself out in inflation than in greater employment. If it is primarily a result of insufficient demand, a part of the War on Poverty must aim to increase aggregate demand.

I am convinced that part of the unemployment problem is structural. But I am also convinced that a part of it is a result of inadequate demand and that much of the present unemployment would disappear with a sufficient increase in demand. In this paper I am primarily concerned with the latter.

In order to discuss the effect of ample job opportunities on poverty, I am going to make two bold assumptions and consider their effect. The first is that, through fiscal and monetary measures, we can increase aggregate demand to whatever extent we desire. The second is that an increase in aggregate demand will increase job opportunities.

The basic question is, therefore: *What would be the effect on poverty of an increase in aggregate demand which produced ample job opportunities?* Just what do we mean by ample job opportunities?

At the end of 1963, we had roughly 4 million persons actively looking for jobs and not employed. We had 2 million persons who worked part time and wanted to work full time, making the equivalent of perhaps another million workers. If there were ample job opportunities there would probably be another million persons who would want jobs, but are not now looking for work. And there would be perhaps a half-million persons who would leave farming for nonfarm jobs. If we had ample job opportunities we would thus have a pool of potential labor not now used equivalent to 6 million full-time persons.

Even with ample job opportunities we could not expect that all of this manpower would be absorbed. There are three major reasons for this: first, when a person leaves a job there is likely to be a delay before he or she enters a new job, and when a new worker enters the labor market there may be some time required in looking for a job. In both cases, the individual would be recorded as unemployed. Such unemployment would be reduced by ample jobs but could not and should not be eliminated. Second, some persons would be looking for work but as a practical matter are incapable of holding down any job likely to open up in business. Ample job opportunities alone will not absorb such people, and their problem lies mostly outside of the normal labor market. Third, there are many persons who would be able to find jobs if given retraining and assistance in relocation (such as Sweden provides for its unemployed workers) but are not now given that assistance.

The Committee for Economic Development (CED) once suggested that unemployment of 4 per cent of the labor force, or about 3 million, would correspond to full employment, and the Council of Economic Advisers has adopted this figure as an *interim* goal. I believe these figures are too high. After the Korean War, the remnants of price control were eliminated early in 1953 and for the year as a whole unemployment averaged *appreciably less* than 2 million *without any evidence of demand inflation*. Since then the labor force has grown and the corresponding figure of unemployment would be about 2 million unemployed. I believe we could go well below this figure if we used extensive measures for retraining, for relocation of both people and production, and for bringing people and jobs together. However for the purposes of the rest of this paper, I am going to use the figure of 2 million unemployed as the level that could be reached through the expansion of aggregate demand and a resulting increase in job opportunities.

This gives us at least 4 million man-years of additional labor that I believe we could bring into employment if we increased demand to the necessary extent (6 million less 2 million). I would say that we had ample job opportunities if we had 4 million more jobs in addition to those required to absorb the growing labor force and those made available by reduced structural impediments. If this manpower were effectively used, we would all be better off not only in our psychology but, as I will presently show, in our pocketbooks.

To me this unemployment is not a problem but an opportunity.

In the remainder of this analysis I am going to consider first what the employment of an extra 4 millions of manpower would mean for the economy and then consider what this would mean for the problem of poverty. What would happen to the economy if aggregate demand were increased by as much as would be needed to absorb an extra 4 millions of manpower outside agriculture? Or more precisely, what would our economy look like 2 years from today, if we expanded demand enough to absorb not only the usual increase in the labor force but an extra 4 million?

The first thing to notice is that in addition to normal growth this would require an extra demand for goods—commodities and services—of close to $35 billion at present prices, and if this extra amount of goods were produced it would mean $35 billion more in wages, return to capital, and taxes. This would amount to an addition of 5 or 6 per cent to Gross National Product.

Also, we should notice the composition of the extra demand. On the basis of some admittedly crude estimates, I come out with the conclusion that between 35 and 45 per cent of the additional demand from consumers would go into services, another 25 to 35 per cent would go for nondurables, and 15 to 20 per cent would go into consumer durables. From 6 to 10 per cent would be saved. The most important thing to notice here is the high increase in services. This includes household rent and operation, transportation services, medical care, amusements, barber and beauty shops, laundry and dry cleaning, and repair of our million-and-one consumer durable goods.

Given this extra demand, what would be its effect? The first question that is likely to be asked is: *Would a $35-billion higher demand create inflation?* If we didn't already have agricultural surpluses and extra manpower and a good deal of idle machinery available, my answer might be yes. But an extra demand for farm products would be met primarily by lower surpluses and less restrictions on farm production, not by a rise in farm prices. The extra demand for most industrial products would not mean significant price increases. Most industries could supply an extra 5 or 6 per cent more products with their present equipment and, at least in the more concentrated industries, prices are relatively insensitive to moderate changes in demand. With a vigorous campaign against arbitrary prices increases, there need be little rise in industrial prices unless wage rates increased more than productivity. We could expect a rise in the prices of some products, such as lead and zinc, and a creeping up of some prices at wholesale while other wholesale prices creep down. I believe an extra 5 to 6 per cent of aggregate demand in addition to normal growth could be satisfied without any substantial rise in wholesale prices.

I would expect that a rise in the consumer price index would continue, not because of the increased demand, but because services in which technical progress is slow constitute such an important item in that index; and if wage rates in the economy as a whole rise with productivity, price for such services must rise. But this would not be greatly stimulated by an extra 5 to 6 per cent of aggregate demand.

A second question is whether the increased demand would not be satisfied through overtime and increased automation and without any increase in employment. Experience suggests that some of the extra production would come from greater overtime, but only a small part. For example, in the first quarter of 1964 the total hours worked by production workers in manufacturing increased by 3 per cent over the same quarter in 1963, but only a sixth of the increase came from longer hours, and five-sixths came from the employment of more people. If the increase in employment were greater, an even larger proportion would be likely to come from additions to the payroll. On the other hand, automation is a very real problem and one which demands much study and action to reduce the burden of adjustment on those displaced by automation. But I do not believe that automation stands in the way of bringing about increased employment through ample job opportunities. I have two reasons for this belief. The first is the character of the extra demand. A major proportion of the extra demand would go into services in which the progress of automation is likely to be slow. The second is that more rapid automation means greater productivity and the opportunity to raise wages more rapidly without inflation. We must reduce the burden of automation on displaced workers (and, of course, one of the most effective means would be by providing ample job opportunities). But if automation and technical progress together increase national productivity by say 6 per cent a year instead of the recent 3 per cent, and wage rates are correspondingly raised, the increase in demand would have to move up to a corresponding extent. But I believe that, with increased wage rates, fiscal and monetary measures, if properly used, are capable of the necessary expansion in demand.

Support for this view is given by the developments of the last three years. The increase in aggregate demand from the last quarter of 1961 to the first quarter of 1964 lifted the real Gross National Product by 17 per cent. Nearly half of this added production resulted from the employment of 4.8 million more workers, while the increase in productivity due to technical progress, automation, and similar developments was at the annual rate of only 3 per cent a year, not much different from the long-run trend of technical progress. Clearly, the increase in aggregate demand substantially increased job opportunities.

A third question that needs to be asked concerns productivity of the newly employed. I have assumed that the employment of an extra 4 million outside of agriculture would increase aggregate production and income in proportion to the extra employment. Yet we can assume that the additional workers would on the average have much less education, be less well trained, and in other ways would be less well equipped to be productive than those already employed. Can these two positions be reconciled?

I think they can because most of the overhead work required by our economy is already being done. A considerable part of our labor force is engaged in social overhead work, including police and fire protection, the courts and other aspects of government, and such things as highway maintenance and the maintenance of public buildings. For the most part, the employment of an extra 4 million would not increase the manpower necessary for these functions. Similarly, a great deal of labor in industry is overhead, utilized for upkeep and all the things that business has to do whether or not it expands its production. This means that only a part of our employed labor force is *directly* producing commodities and services. If 4 million more were employed, most of these would go into producing directly for consumption or investment. This means that if each additional worker employed produced a smaller quantity of usable goods than the average of those already *producing* such goods, they could still produce as many usable goods as the average for all persons employed—including overhead workers as well as those actually producing such goods. In an important sense, the increase in employment would increase the "productivity" of the overhead workers already employed. Statistics support this conclusion, showing that, with a cyclical increase in employment, the taking on of less able workers does not reduce the *average* output per hour of the total employed labor force.

A fourth question likely to be asked is whether, if demand increased so that there were 4 million more job openings, would the unemployed be able to fill them? The answer to this question is almost certainly no. But that is not the problem. Let us say that the increase in demand called for a 6 per cent increase in work to be done at each level of skill and training—6 per cent more engineering work to be done, 6 per cent more mechanics required, and 6 per cent more unskilled labor. What would happen?

Two developments would go on at the same time—the upgrading of workers and the breaking down of jobs. In the upgrading of workers more assistant managers would become managers, leaving room for second assistant managers to become first assistants, and so on down the line. The same would happen for engineers and mechanics. Inexperienced engineers would be pushed ahead faster, and more mechanics helpers would be given the responsibilities of full mechanics. All along the line this upgrading could be expected and would leave more room both at the bottom and along the way for unemployed persons who had no skills or insufficient skills for higher level jobs.

Also, the breaking down of jobs would help to absorb less skilled or unskilled. We are already familiar with the way doctors at hospitals have been delegating more of the routine activity to nurses. Less-trained nurses' assistants have made it possible for one nurse to give her trained services to more patients. The same process goes on in industry, with particular jobs being broken down to fit the available labor supply more closely.

Of course, if the increase in aggregate demand were very sudden, these adjustments could not be made. But if it occurred over say a 2-year period, there is great likelihood that jobs and workers would adjust so that the extra 4 million could be absorbed, even though their abilities were at the lower end of the ability scale. I have a high regard for the ability of industry to make-do with whatever materials and manpower are available if the demands for its products are sufficient and enough time is available to make the necessary adjustments.

There is one more question which I will just touch on because our money managers who have the power to expand aggregate demand are so vitally concerned with it. This is the question of whether expanding aggregate demand enough to absorb an extra 4 million would seriously increase our balance-of-payments difficulties.

My own opinion is that the extra demand would not significantly increase an imbalance in payments. The increase in consumer demand would undoubtedly take in small part the form of an increase in the demand for foreign commodities and services. But at the same time the increase in consumer demand would very considerably increase the investment opportunities at home and thereby reduce the export of capital. Whether the *net* effect would worsen or improve the balance of payments difficulties is not clear. But it does seem clear that it would not greatly aggravate the problem. And even if it did aggravate it, are the 4 million who *should* be working at nonfarm activities to be made the instrument for reducing the imbalance in payments?

Now we come to the heart of our discussion. How different would the poverty problem be if we had 4 million more employed today? What groups would be lifted above the arbitrary level of $3000 for a family of four which the administration has adopted? And even more important, who would remain below this level? Or more exactly, what groups would not be taken care of through expanding demand and job opportunities?

Here I will adopt the President's suggested figure of $3000 a year for a family consisting of a man, wife, and two children living in an urban community and in the age bracket (for the head of the family) of thirty-five to fifty-four. I will call this a "benchmark family" and the level of living it can achieve with a $3000 income as a "benchmark level of living."

Of course, some families would need more than $3000 to achieve such a benchmark level of living and others would require less. It has been estimated that a man, wife, and four children would require an income of nearly $4000 to attain the benchmark level of living—this reflects the need for an extra $500 for each extra child. It has also been estimated that for families with a head under thirty-five a somewhat smaller income could yield the benchmark level. This would also appear to be true for a family with a head over sixty-five. For families with a head age fifty-five to sixty-four, a somewhat larger income would be required. Finally, a smaller income would be required for farm families, particularly if the home is owned and farm produce used is not included as income. And it has been estimated that single persons living alone could achieve the $3000 benchmark level of living with an income of around $1500. More elaborate figures for different types of family have been worked out, but the figures above are sufficient for present purposes. These incomes, which would be needed to achieve the level of living of the benchmark family, will be called "benchmark incomes."

A second preliminary step is to examine the relation of the minimum wage of $1.25 an hour to the benchmark level of incomes. A single person working for $1.25 an hour for 40 hours would obtain the benchmark income with approximately 30 weeks of full time work a year; a family of two could do likewise if only one member worked and obtained the minimum wage with around 40 weeks of full-time work; and a family of three with only one worker would require around 50 full-time weeks of work. On the other hand, a family of four would require not only the equivalent of one full-time worker at the minimum wage, but also an extra $500 from overtime, moonlighting, work by a second member of the family, or from some other source. And it would take two full-time workers at the minimum wage to obtain the benchmark income for a couple with eight children.

Amount of full time work at a minimum wage of $1.25 to achieve the benchmark income:

Single individuals	30 weeks
Man and wife	40 weeks
Man, wife, and 1 child	50 weeks
Benchmark family (2 children)	60 weeks or equivalent
Man, wife, and 8 children	100 weeks or equivalent

Such figures give some idea of the amount of work that would be required to attain the benchmark income for those receiving the minimum wage of $1.25 an hour. But only about half of our wage-and-salary workers are covered by the federal Minimum Wage Law. There are many jobs that pay much less than this.

Fortunately, for our present problem, a sizable increase in the demand for labor could be expected to have a marked effect on the wage rates of the lowest paid workers. In the recovery from the Great Depression of the 1930's, the largest percentage increases in wage rates occurred for unskilled and unorganized workers and not for the skilled and well organized. I can see an increase of 4 millions in employment occurring without any significant increase in the bulk of wage rates over and above that which occurs as a result of productivity increases. But at the very low end of the wage scale, the absorption of 4 million workers could be expected to remove the competition of the unemployed with each other which now holds down the lowest wage rates. This would also make easier an expansion in the coverage of the federal Minimum Wage Law.

With this as background, I divide up the problem of poverty into five segments covering older people, farm families, and nonfarm units to give the following groups:

   1. All consumer units with the head sixty-five or over.
   2. All farm consumer units with the head under sixty-five.
   3. All unrelated nonfarm individuals under sixty-five.
   4. All unbroken nonfarm families with head under sixty-five.
   5. All broken nonfarm families with head under sixty-five.

What would be the effect of an extra 4 million jobs on each of these groups separately?

Individuals and Families with Head Sixty-five or Over

The census figures for 1962 show:

Unrelated individuals sixty-five years or over with income of less than $1500	2.6 million
Families with head sixty-five years or over with income of less than $3000	3.2 million
Total	5.8 million

Let us assume that the level of living for most of these older persons and families with older heads falls below the benchmark level. Some of them have property and are living off that. Three hundred thousand live on farms and are somewhat better off than their income data suggests. But the bulk appear to fall below the benchmark level of living. Also, assume that ample job opportunities would not greatly benefit the members of this group. Of the unrelated individuals, less than 16 per cent reported any earned income and a somewhat similar situation may well apply to the families with heads sixty-five or over, though there is the likelihood that other members of the family produce some earned income. For these older people, other means than ample job opportunities must be the chief reliance for reaching the benchmark level of living. And this group can be expected to supply only a very small proportion of the extra 4 millions of employment.

Farm Individuals and Families with Head Under Sixty-five

For the farm units with the head under sixty-five, the census figures show for 1962:

Unrelated individuals with incomes under $1500	0.3 million
Families with incomes under $3000	1.4 million
Total	1.7 million

Not all of these belong below the benchmark level of living. Farm income varies so much from year to year that a family can *average* income above the necessary level and yet fall below it in a particular year. Also for farm families, less money income is likely to be required for a given level of living than for the urban families. However, when full account is taken of such factors, the bulk of this group would appear to fall below the benchmark level.

This low-income farm group is likely to benefit greatly from the development of ample job opportunities. It is likely to supply a substantial part of the half-million workers which I have suggested would be drawn into nonfarm production. Many could be expected to get nonfarm jobs which paid the minimum wage or better. Furthermore, the rise in aggregate demand and the shift to nonfarm activity would tend to raise farm wage rates appreciably so that those farm families depending on farm wages could be expected to gain even if they continued to depend on agriculture as a source of income. I suggest that at least half of the 1.7 million in this farm category could be lifted above the benchmark level of living either by the shift to nonfarm work or through the rise in the wages for hired hands. This would by no means eliminate rural poverty, but it might well be the largest single step toward its reduction.

Nonfarm Unrelated Individuals Under Sixty-five

My third category consists of the individuals under sixty-five with incomes less than $1500 and not living on farms. The census figures indicate there were about 2 million individuals in this group in 1962. Presumably some of these were students who received some income, but mostly lived off capital or from borrowing while they completed their education. I would not class such persons as living below the benchmark level. But I presume that the bulk of the 2 million fall below the benchmark level, particularly since something like three-quarters of this group are over twenty-five years of age.

I suggest that adequate job opportunities and a rise in wage rates at low levels would lift a substantial proportion of these individuals above the benchmark level, perhaps over a million of them.

Unbroken Nonfarm Families with a Head Under Sixty-five

The census figures indicate that in 1962 there were approximately 3.4 million nonfarm families with the husband and wife living together, the husband under sixty-five, and the family income under $3000. With ample job opportunities, we could expect that, for a great many of these families, incomes would be lifted above the $3000 level partly by a rise in low wage rates and partly from greater employment or a shift to better jobs. Altogether perhaps half of this group would be able to achieve the $3000 level of income. Of course, for those with more than two children such an income would not necessarily provide the benchmark level of living, but this would seem to present a different kind of problem not directly tied to job opportunities.

Broken Nonfarm Families with Heads Under Sixty-five

Finally, there were 1.6 million broken nonfarm families with a head under sixty-five who received less than $3000 in income. Most of these families were headed by women, the husband being dead or separated. For many of these families in which the head now works, the increased demand for labor would lift wage rates appreciably and provide more work opportunities; others would find jobs. How many of this group would be lifted up to the $3000 level is hard to say. For some, a smaller income could provide the benchmark level of living, but for those with a larger number of children even the $3000 would be insufficient for the benchmark level. I am going to suggest that perhaps a third of this group would reach the benchmark income level if demand were sufficiently increased to absorb the extra 4 million.

Summary

Let me summarize the conclusions in Table 1, following, showing the estimated effect of an extra four million job opportunities on the various poverty groups.

These are conservative estimates and the figures may underestimate the reduction in poverty which would come from ample job opportunities. What they suggest is that for the 8.7 million individuals and families in the working population with incomes below the poverty level, something like 3.7 million or 40 per cent, would be lifted above this level by an expansion in demand to provide the equivalent of 4 million extra jobs. This would be an important step

Table 1—Effect of Job Opportunities on Poverty Groups

	Number with Incomes Below the Poverty Level	Number Lifted Above $3000/1500 by Employment of Extra 4 Million	Number Whose Poverty Must Be Reached Through Other Means
	(in millions)		
Over sixty-five	5.8	0.3	5.5
Farm, under sixty-five	1.7	0.5	1.2
Nonfarm individuals under sixty-five	2.0	1.0	1.0
Unbroken nonfarm families under sixty-five	3.4	1.7	1.7
Broken nonfarm families under sixty-five	1.6	0.5	1.1
Total	14.5	3.7	10.5
Under sixty-five	9.3	3.7	5.0

toward the reduction of poverty. At the same time, even with the utmost that could be accomplished through expanding demand, much of the existing poverty would remain, particularly among older people, families with low earning power and a large number of children, the mentally and physically handicapped, broken families, and in special areas. Ample job opportunities provide an important means for reducing poverty, although much poverty cannot be eliminated by means of jobs alone.

Poverty
and the Criteria
for Public Expenditures

HAROLD WOLOZIN

The Problem and Its Setting

The criteria for public expenditure have always posed both theoretical and conceptual problems for the economist, particularly in prescribing specific projects designed to serve the community. In exposing some of the limitations of current economic analysis for this purpose, we hope to point the way to research and subsequent modification of theory in directions which will make it more useful in evaluating public expenditures for such community needs as the elimination of poverty.

What guidelines can economic analysis offer for the expenditure of public monies to increase the well-being of the community? To what extent do the tools of economic analysis enable the economist to execute meaningful studies and dispense practical advice on the optimum direction and size for public expenditures?

There are a good many economic analysts who believe that the nature of the assumptions underlying most of existing economic theory render it inadequate for this complex task. There are grounds for asking, for example, whether it is realistic to treat economic rather than political man as the basic decision-making unit in this area. Economic consideration alone may be unrealistic and consequently a path to naïve policy prescription. Perhaps we ought to maintain that man's "politically-revealed preferences are 'higher' than market-exhibited ones?"[1] For example, in much of the literature on public expenditure policy the so-called compensation principle assumes an important role; yet its relevance and usefulness have been the focal point of extended debate. The issues raised are fundamental: whether it involves an "undue sanctification of the status quo," an argument objecting on ethical grounds to the nature of the implicit value judgments embodied in the principle, or whether these value judgments are "inconsistent with the possibility of rational choice by the community as a whole."[2]

The attempt to make economic analysis applicable to the public sector goes back a long way in the economic literature. In the opinion of some economists the results have been meager, not only because of the crudeness of the tools, but because of the special socioeconomic problems encountered in the pursuit of an "operational" theory. We are faced with the divergence between market and social decision-making in the allocation of resources; moreover, third-party or indirect effects of policies have to be taken into account. As far as practicable, nonmarket social goods need to be considered in the economic calculus. As Allen V. Kneese suggests, "values must be introduced into the decision-making process."[3] He argues:

> The U.S. economy generally depends upon private enterprise and market processes for the generation of values and on

private decisions to incorporate them into the economic
decision-making process in an efficient fashion. For a variety
of reasons, unregulated market processes cannot deal effi-
ciently with certain [social problems]. Consequently, there
are adequate grounds for public intervention and planning
. . . even though the general rationale for a market economy is accepted. Indeed in large measure, such intervention
can be justified by the desirability of moving actual results
more closely into line with ideal market values not arising
from market-type valuation at all.[4]

Since economic policy is rarely concerned with the
attainment of "the best of all possible worlds," it is frequently asserted that economic policy by definition seeks to
improve economic welfare *in the face of constraints*. In de-
vising a policy model, argues Otto Eckstein, the economist
must recognize and build the relevant constraints into his
analysis. How many and which ones to include present the
crucial difficulty and decision. There comes a certain point,
however, where the constraints and assumptions can be so
specific that they produce "bad economics."[5] That is, a
narrowed-down solution often is inadequate, unrealistic, or
impractical for policy purposes. But as Eckstein himself
points out, "the line between realism and bad economics"
is often hard to draw.

Planning Under Constraints

There are many types of constraints, originating in institutional or physical limitations, under which public policy
must operate. Building these into an economic study not only
makes the analysis more applicable, but gives shape to the
problem under study and determines the general nature of
the solution. Therefore, it may be useful to look at the
nature of the constraints encountered.

Physical constraints, such as the production function,
relate physical inputs to outputs. A closely related constraint
is that which limits costs to a point beyond which they will

not be accepted. Legal constraints require that a program or project fit within existing laws. But in admitting the latter, they must not be assumed as fixed, for this is an area in which the economist "is in peril of accepting *so many* constraints that he will exclude the interesting solutions." Administrative constraints reflect the capability of a sponsoring agency. They include the limits on the rate of program expansion due to personnel ceilings and shortages of administrative "know-how." Excessive centralization of decision-making, overcomplex planning needs, or too many variables also can hamper and constrain programs. Administrative constraints may also impose a fixed pattern of benefits and costs or "side conditions" of minimum benefits for different groups.

Financial or budgetary constraints set limits to the availability of funds for given projects. This is of primary importance in the way in which we go about deriving expenditure criteria; in actuality, if public monies were to be available in unlimited quantities, that is, if no rationing existed, then we would not have to expend time and effort in determining the optimum allocation of resources. Eckstein has explored this problem in detail;[6] the following gives some idea of the approach which has been devised to cope with the financial constraint:

> If there is only one constrained financial resource and one category of benefits, the criterion requires that the rate of net benefit per dollar of the constrained funds be maximized. This maximization is accomplished by computing ratios of benefit to constrained funds for each project (or smaller unit of choice where possible), ranking projects by these ratios and going down the ranked list to the point where the scarce funds are exhausted. Although the ranking is by ratios, it is not the maximization of the ratio which is the objective but rather the total net gain that is possible, given the constraint.[7]

There are, of course, many other constraints, such as the introduction of uncertainty into the situation, political realities, and the like. The problem is to identify all of the constraints involved.

Welfare Economics—the Economist's Tool Box

The question which now logically follows is: can economic analysis operate effectively under the kind of constraints we have set out, or have these constraints subtly shaped the very structure of the theory? The analytical principles designed to guide public policy can be evaluated both for their internal consistency and for their application to such programs as a "War on Poverty." Inevitably, the limitations of the conventional body of theory for determining levels and directions of expenditures of public funds will become apparent. We have already discussed one of the crucial problems, namely, the problem of constraints. In this instance what rises to the surface as an essential prerequisite for an operational theory is the need to integrate economic criteria with those implicit in other factors shaping expenditure policies, particularly social, political, and psychological. The latter signal those problems within the domain of the social psychologists (factors shaping group psychology and attitudes), for these often translate themselves into the political shaping public expenditure policy.

The economic theory most relevant to the subject matter of this paper falls under the general heading of welfare economics. Closely related to this is the evolving "theory of the public household." Although we do not wish to undertake a purely methodological exploration, it is essential that we examine the techniques of welfare economics in order to come to grips with its applicability to decision-making in specific programs (such as the diminution of poverty), whether they be undertaken by national, state, or local governmental authorities. We should be, then, in a better position to evaluate existing programs.

However, welfare economics itself has been extended as far as it can be useful for practical purposes. As I. M. D. Little so aptly puts it, "any further extension of welfare theory is unlikely to be at all valuable except as a mathematical exercise."[8] Melvin Reder has defined welfare economics as that branch of economic science which attempts to establish and apply "criteria of propriety"[9] to economic policies. Welfare economics makes "explicit" the criteria for judging public policies which were implicit in the works of the classical economists such as Smith, Mill, and Ricardo. The norm customarily adopted by welfare economists, according to Reder, is that the welfare of the community as a whole should be maximized. Now this seems unambiguous enough once the concept of welfare is adequately set forth; however, there may be numerous definitions which are then reflected in particular economic policies. Even when welfare is defined in acceptable ways, the difficulties in applying the theory are not erased, for then the problem of measurement arises. And it is this problem—what and how to measure— which eventually provides an acceptable, pragmatic solution through such techniques as systems analysis or operations research (referred to as benefit-cost analysis in the welfare area).

In economic analysis the world is starkly simplified. Production and economic organization are assumed to exist solely for the purpose of maximizing human satisfactions, and for society these are the sum of individual satisfactions. Rationality is identified with such maximization, that is, rational economic man who *knows* what is *best* for him is the decision-making unit. Kenneth Arrow observes that given these conditions ". . . the problem of achieving a social maximum derived from individual desires is precisely the problem which has been central to the field of welfare economics."[10] But this also has implied interpersonal comparisons of utility, a procedure that many economists believe to be dubious at best.

The original formulations of welfare economics reflected the simple-minded utilitarian economics of the classical economists, who were concerned principally with specifying the optimum conditions under which the total social satisfaction would be maximized. It was assumed, of course, that laissez faire insured maximum satisfaction, and even A. C. Pigou, who has been called the father of modern welfare economics, set out the argument of his *Economics of Welfare* in terms of exceptions to the rule that laissez faire ensures maximum satisfaction.[11] The fundamental theorem of classical welfare economics holds that a long-run competitive equilibrium (perfect competition is assumed) automatically ensures the best of all possible worlds—an optimum allocation of resources.

As a consequence, modern welfare economics evolved in response to fundamental criticisms of the utilitarian assumptions underlying classical economics. Thus Little abandons the idea of maximizing welfare and is satisfied only with improving it. Since satisfactions cannot be summed, it is meaningless to refer to the happiness of the community as the sum total of the happiness of individuals or to the happiness of individuals as "the sum total of their acceptance" of "utilities" or that satisfactions can only be "ordered" rather than measured. Thus, it is possible to say that one has more or less satisfaction, but not *how much*. Further, the satisfactions and happiness of different people cannot be compared objectively or scientifically. Any comparison is a value or an ethical judgment, and not an empirical one. A third criticism is that welfare economics by definition is a "normative" study, because "no change could be made without harming someone and since . . . interpersonal comparisons of satisfaction are value judgments and essential to judgments about the welfare of society, welfare economics is unavoidably ethical."[12] The foregoing is more than an academic argument, for what is involved is the nature of the social decision process and, implicitly, the nature of the constraints under which public officials move. The basic issue raised is whether "it is formally possible to construct a procedure for passing from a set of known individual tastes to a pattern of social decision making . . ."[13] An equally fundamental issue is the meaning of economic rationality assumed in the nature of economic choice which underlies much of the discussion of welfare economics. Little argues that because a welfare judgment implies that an individual is making an evaluation, whereas social decisions can be reached through the governmental process for reasons of convenience or necessity, they are, therefore, different.[14] Directing himself to this point Arrow raises issues which are at the heart of the matter:

> This distinction is well taken. I would consider that it is indeed a social decision process with which I am concerned and not, strictly speaking, a welfare judgment by any individual. That said, however, I am bound to add that in my view a social decision preserves as a proper explication for the intuitive idea of social welfare. The classical problems of formulating the social good are indeed of the metaphysical variety which modern positivism finds meaningless; but the underlying issue is real. My own viewpoint towards this and other ethical problems coincides with that expressed by Popper: "Not a few doctrines which are metaphysical, and thus certainly philosophical can be interpreted as hypostatizations of methodological rules." All the writers from Bergson on agree on avoiding the notion of a social good not defined in terms of the values of individuals. But where Bergson seeks to locate social values in welfare judgments by individuals, I prefer to locate them in the actions taken by society through its rules for making social decisions. This position is a natural extension of the ordinalist view of values; just as it identifies values and choices for the individual, so I regard social values as meaning nothing more than social choices.[15]

An alternative approach, which has by and large taken the place of the Marshallian analysis, is an Edgeworth indifference curve analysis of the behavior of the rational consumer as indicated by Pareto's "index of ophélimité." Although this analysis still assumes that the individual attempts to maximize his satisfaction, it "no longer means achieving the largest sum total of satisfaction but rather

reaching the highest level of satisfaction." Using this apparatus, the analysis then turns its attention to the needs of
the community as a whole through the so-called "compensation" principle as a principal tool for policy determination. If we assume that "welfare increases (decreases)
whenever one or more individuals become more (less) satisfied without any other individuals becoming less (more)
satisfied," then the welfare of a community is maximized
if its productive resources are used so as to make it impossible to make any person more satisfied without making at
least "one other person less satisfied." Thus, if the satisfactions of some individuals can be increased and at the same
time any others who might be adversely affected by the
process compensated for any injury, the total welfare is
thereby increased. This is the famous compensation principle first introduced by J. R. Hicks and N. Kaldor. Under
this rule a person might be made worse off by a given public
policy, but all would be righted if he were compensated.

As Eckstein points out,[16] the Kaldor-Hicks compensation criteria were subjected to considerable criticism. It was
argued, for example, that if the economic change caused
price change, the criterion might become inconsistent, since
"the gainers could compensate the losers after the change,
yet the potential losers might be able to compensate the
potential gainers prior to the change." Also, the assumption
that an individual's or family's welfare is independent of his
neighbors' was censured. Despite the theoretical difficulties
which have caused many economists to throw up their hands
in despair at the prospects for making it useful for formulating public expenditure policy, Eckstein is optimistic about
the usefulness of welfare economics. His program of action
is as follows:

> I do not insist that the economist be given the objectives in
> polished, formal manner. Rather, the economist must inter-
> pret the desires of the policy people whom he is serving and
> express them in an analytical form as an objective function.
> He then seeks to maximize this function, given the empirical

relations in the economy and the institutional constraints that may be appropriate to the analysis. In this matter, the economist can play the role of technician, of bringing his technical equipment to bear on policy problems, with maximum effectiveness. The specification of the objective function thus is not primarily meant to let the economist play omnipotent being; rather it is a device for bridging the gap between the positive quantitative research which is the main stock-in-trade of the economist, and the normative conclusions which policy requires.[17]

Yet Eckstein goes on to state that in most cases, "particularly where the analysis involves few steps such as the mere marshalling of figures," specifying an objective function would be "excess theoretical baggage." But he does feel that once the analysis takes on some complexity, an explicit objective function becomes more important if normative recommendations are to be derived. He feels that the exercise of specifying, rather than implying, a functional relationship forces the technician to state his normative assumptions. Specifying an objective function can, at its best become "a powerful analytical aid, eliminating uninteresting areas of exploration and permitting the ranking of alternatives." The advisability or feasibility of a consumer attitude survey might be evaluated on the basis of the complexity and nature of the objective function hypothesized for the project. Proposing the survey with only some vague objectives specified would be a far less helpful and perhaps a risky basis for deciding whether to undertake it or not.

Welfare Economics and the Individual Consumer

No matter what form is taken by the so-called welfare function used in the sense discussed above, it becomes clear that one of the more valuable contributions of welfare economics is that it attempts to come to grips with the problem of maximizing the welfare, however defined, of the community as a whole; and it requires the policy-maker to take into account an important set of considerations which the consumer may ignore, namely, the effects on the community around him of his consumption. These are referred to in various ways as "neighborhood effects," "spillover effects," and so on.

Now, as Kneese points out, an essential condition for an optimum use of resources through the market mechanism is that "the full costs and benefits of performing a given act fall upon the unit performing it."[18] This implies that the costs and benefits can be measured, including the neighborhood effects. Techniques for measuring these have been developed. They are lumped under the general heading of welfare "benefit-cost" analysis. Yet what about the costs or benefits which cannot be so easily valued, or are in some instances not valued by those who might be benefited by them in the opinion of *our* judgment, not theirs?

Richard Musgrave, in developing his theory of the public household, has distinguished two broad categories which call for public intervention. The first is the wide range of situations where the market mechanism brings about varying degrees of inefficiency in the allocation of resources, "inefficiencies that arise collateral to the satisfaction of private wants." The second covers situations "where the market mechanism fails altogether and where the divergence between the social and private product becomes all-inclusive."[19]

The kinds of market situations lumped under the first category include what we generally call imperfect competition and monopoly, where resource allocation "diverges from that obtained under purely or perfectly competitive market conditions." It also covers the case in which, because of decreasing unit costs, one cannot operate most profitably at the point leading to optimal resource allocation. Particularly problematical is the situation in which either external economics or diseconomies are generated by the economic actors. A relevant example is the pollution of air by industrial processes. The nuisance means a cost, often indirect as well as direct, to the community. Yet it is not a direct cost to the firm creating the pollution. In other words, the private operations "involve social costs that are not reflected in private cost calculations and, hence, are not accounted for by the market."[20] Musgrave's judgment is that wherever possible the satisfaction of this kind of want (in this case it would be relatively pure air) should be left to the market. Even if desire to prevent air pollution were required by law, the social costs would be accounted for by the market, that is, the cost could be passed on.

Yet social wants should cause public-policy planners a minimum of difficulty. They represent identifiable wants, and because consumption is widespread, they may be candidates for private production and sale. But how much does the public want them? Since they are not sold in the market, other means must be used to determine the consumer demand. Professor Alan T. Peacock, in discussing goods produced by government, such as defense and law and order, points out that because they are "indivisible" even those who are not prepared to pay for them cannot be denied their benefits. He concludes, "Escape for one means escape for all, and a pricing solution is simply not possible."[21]

The decision to spend public funds to supply a social want must be derived from "the effective preferences" of the individual members of the society. These, in turn, reflect the individual's tastes and "proper" share in national income. Musgrave's solution is, "A political process must be substituted for the market mechanism, and individuals must be made to adhere to the group decision."[22] As he points out, this approach assumes that individuals can evaluate social wants, that they want them along with the goods and services which can be purchased in the private market. Consequently, solutions to the problem of poverty become precisely such a social want. In a democratic society, it is assumed that public preferences are based upon some sort of summing of individual demands for social goods. An alternative view, in other forms of political organization, is that social wants are collective, experienced by the group as a whole or its leaders, rather than by individuals.

The most difficult category of public wants for which to determine effective public policy covers those needs which may be defined as "merit" wants. In fact, it may be a misnomer even to refer to them as "wants." They are wants met by services subject to the exclusion principle and not *satisfied* by the market—that is, acquired only by those willing, and able, to pay to get them. They become public wants if considered so meritorious that their satisfaction is provided for through the public budget, over and above what is provided by the market and paid for by private buyers.

In providing for merit wants, public policy allocates resources in a manner which ignores market consumer preferences. Consumers choose to spend their money on other things. It was not because the services were to be consumed in equal amounts, and hence could not be sold on the market, that they were provided for as social needs; the expenditures on merit goods had taken place because individual choice *was being corrected.* This is a most important distinction, and, in essence, brings out the nature of the decisions facing public planners. The spending of public funds on merit needs involves a conscious decision to interfere with the "want pattern of others," even if they are the minority.

It should now be apparent that the economics of determining public expenditure cannot be formulated without taking account of a host of social, political, and psychological factors. We have called these "constraints." Even more disturbing, to what extent is the empiricism of modern economics, like philosophic empiricism, "concealing phenomena instead of elucidating them"?[23] It is in these areas that some of the most difficult and critical problems remain. How do merit goods become social goods at some point? What is the nature of "rational choice" in such situations? What do we mean by consumer preference? Are preferences immutable? And how do they change over time?

Benefit-Cost Analysis and Public Expenditures

Whether a need be a merit or social want, once public policy has decided to provide for it, the public body is faced with the economic problem of spending its monies most effectively. But this is not so simple as it sounds. Even the situation in which the political decision to provide certain services that people want *and for which they prefer* to be taxed poses a difficult problem of valuation. But what happens where the pricing mechanism could not carry out its function even if it were desired? The dilemma is "if 'output' of government services cannot be valued, then neither can we determine with any precision how much should be produced nor what the relationship is between the change in the value of inputs and the change in the value of output."[24]

A solution, described by Roland E. McKean as but a "partial substitute" for the pricing mechanism, is benefit-cost analysis. For a number of reasons this approach, viewed narrowly, cannot be a perfect substitute for the price system. It permits only an "occasional comparison" of policies, in contrast to the day-to-day operation of the price mechanism, encouraging "frequent examination of numerous alternatives." Furthermore, although, like the price mechanism, it enables policy-makers to identify alternative courses of action, the results of benefit-cost study do not by themselves generate strong incentives to undertake the optimum project. Yet, its practitioners feel it can be an indispensable tool for economic planning:

> . . . it is extremely important at least to be able to identify preferred policies and practices. Unless we can point to the better actions, we cannot possibly expect officials to choose better rather than worse ones, nor can we devise institutional modifications that would provide incentives leading to the better policies. Indeed unless we can identify preferred actions we cannot even tell where political or administrative processes are distorting incentives of leading to poor decisions.[25]

The choice among alternatives is based upon a compilation or demonstration of the costs, or disadvantages, and the benefits, or advantages, of the various alternatives open. Although the analytical basis employed to evaluate costs and benefits is based directly upon the methods used by private firms in arriving at their policies, there is one significant difference. Benefit-cost analysis explicitly attempts to measure externalities and other divergences between private and social product. In contrast to the economic analysis of the firm, which on the assumption of profit maximization, is essentially *descriptive* with "causal" overtones, benefit-cost analysis is essentially designed, according to its proponents, to be *prescriptive*.[26]

In actual practice, many types of systematic cost-gain computations throughout the economy are very similar to benefit-cost analysis; and this has rather profound implications for the application as well as the broadening of the approach. For example, operations research, now widely used in both the public and private sectors of the economy, was originally designed to analyze alternative ways of carrying out a task or mission during World War II. It is now generally employed in industry and government for comparisons of alternative methods of operation, often with given equipment and resources. Using various statistical techniques, it is in its general framework "essentially the same" as benefit-cost analysis, for it attempts to estimate the costs or sacrifices and the gains or achievements implicit in the available courses of action.[27] "Systems analysis" compares, for the purpose of development or procurement, costs and benefits of relatively complex systems. Concerned with choices among complex systems involving investments, operating supplies, personnel, and modes of operation, systems analysis is also basically similar to benefit-cost analysis. In fact, as McKean observes, all policy oriented economic analysis "has this same general character."[28]

The evaluation of defense proposals dramatically demonstrates one of the most difficult and stubborn tasks in any benefit-cost project, namely, the estimating of external economics and diseconomics, which McKean lumps together as the "spillover effects" of any project.

> This turns out to be one of the more exacting tasks of cost-benefit analyses, for important spillovers are not always obvious or easy to measure. For example, tactical bombers and missiles, if equipped to carry A-bombs, may contribute to a different mission—that of strategic deterrence—but how much? On the other hand, if equipped only to deliver A-bombs this tactical force may well increase the likelihood of A-war, which is surely a negative contribution to strategic deterrence. As another example, the location of strategic bases near large cities may increase the difficulties of another jurisdiction, the one in charge of civil defense. (The location of installations would affect the enemy's targeting should deterrence fail, affecting the problems of civil defense and also the number of mortalities.) Or a nation's forces in N.A.T.O. may contribute to limited war capabilities elsewhere, but again, how much? Perhaps the most important spillover of all is the following. In choosing strategic defense postures a nation should be alert for spillover effects on the disarmament or weapons control mission. For two retaliatory forces may be equally effective in providing deterrent capability, but one may facilitate reaching mutually advantageous agreements on weapons control, while the other may make such agreements harder to achieve. By the same token, of course, in appraising disarmament proposals, a nation must keep a sharp lookout for, and attempt to weigh, any interim spillover on deterrent capabilities.[29]

This example clearly brings out the fact that there are certain costs or benefits which either defy measurement or at best can only be measured in units which are not comparable. McKean suggests that even in such an apparently insoluble case the benefit-cost analyst still has several courses open to him. He can calculate "efficient solutions" demonstrating relevant combinations of attainable payoffs. He also can approach the problem by indirection by calculating, for example, the value that must be assigned an intangible item in order to make it preferable to some other item.

Conclusion

Lord Robbins, the noted English economist, once stated: "There can be no doubt that throughout history economists of all schools have conceived their work as having the most intimate bearing on politics, both in the sense of the theory of political action and of the *actual practice of affairs.*"[30]

It is within such a framework that we must be clear about the nature of choices involved in the expenditure of public funds for social objectives. Given the limitations of our tools, it is in estimating the economic effects of the various alternatives that economic analysis becomes a vital part of public-policy formulation and implementation.

First of all, the treatment of social and merit needs as the unique province of public policy, as well as the distinction made between them, can serve as a realistic basis for facing up to the problem of such programs as the War on Poverty, with specific emphasis on the increased obligation of public authorities at all levels of government. Perhaps too this is an area in which efforts to enlist and educate the private sector to shoulder the burden may yield questionable returns. Secondly, the constraints which must be part of any analysis and policy prescription must be clearly identified and kept to a minimum to avoid the danger of frustrating effective action. Thirdly, economic criteria must be integrated with the social, economic, and psychological factors which are part of the total problem. Even identifying them is an ambitious blueprint for research. Quantifying them is obviously more difficult, but there is precedence, as for example in coping with water pollution.

The use of benefit-cost analysis for decision-making can be effective in determining public policy, but the difficulties and limitations point to the need for much more systematic study of the use of the technique. Measuring spillover effects is a consideration as well, for coming to grips with this problem should be viewed as of the first order of importance. Yet our tools and data present grave problems of application;

to illustrate, in some cases it does not necessarily follow that an adverse benefit-cost ratio means that a project is uneconomic or undesirable. In a poverty program, the social gains, though immeasurable, may be deemed to be worthwhile, despite the high cost in resource expenditure.

NOTES

1. Stephen A. Marglin, "The Social Rate of Discount and the Optimal Rate of Investment," *Quarterly Journal of Economics*, Feb. 1963, p. 99.
2. Kenneth J. Arrow, *Social Choice and Individual Values*, 2d ed. (New York: John Wiley & Sons, Inc., 1963), p. 45.
3. Allen V. Kneese, "Water Pollution—Economic Aspects and Research Needs" (Washington, D.C.: Resources for the Future, Inc., 1962), p. 17.
4. *Ibid.*
5. Otto Eckstein, "A Survey of the Theory of Public Expenditure Criteria," in *Public Finances: Needs, Sources, and Utilization*, A Conference of the Universities National Bureau Committee for Economic Research (Princeton: Princeton Univ. Press, 1961), p. 450.
6. *Water Resource Development* (Cambridge: Harvard Univ. Press, 1958), pp. 47–80.
7. Eckstein, "Theory of Public Expenditure," *op. cit.*, p. 452.
8. *A Critique of Welfare Economics* (New York: Oxford Univ. Press, Inc., 1957), p. 1.
9. *Studies in the Theory of Welfare Economics* (New York: Columbia Univ. Press, 1947), p. 13.
10. *Op. cit.*, p. 3.
11. Joan Robinson, *Economic Philosophy* (Chicago: Aldine Publishing Co., 1962), p. 74.
12. *Op. cit.*, pp. 13–14.
13. *Op. cit.*, p. 2.
14. I. M. D. Little, "Social Choice and Individual Values," *Journal of Political Economy*, October 1952, pp. 422–432.
15. *Op. cit.*, p. 106.
16. "Theory of Public Expenditure," *op. cit.*, p. 442.
17. *Ibid.*, pp. 445–446.
18. *Op. cit.*, p. 20.
19. *The Theory of Public Finance* (New York: McGraw-Hill Book Company, 1959), pp. 6–8.
20. *Ibid.*, p. 7.
21. "Economic Analysis and Government Expenditures," in A. T. Peacock and D. J. Robertson, *Public Expenditure* (London: Oliver & Boyd, 1963), p. 1 ff.
22. *Op. cit.*, pp. 10–11.

23. See M. Merleau-Ponty, *Phenomenology of Perception* (New York: Humanities Press, 1962), p. 21.

24. Peacock, *op. cit.*, p. 4.

25. R. N. McKean, "Cost-Benefit Analysis and British Defense Expenditure," in Peacock and Robertson, *op. cit.*, p. 17 ff.

26. J. V. Krutilla, "Welfare Aspects of Benefit-Cost Analysis," *Journal of Political Economy*, June 1961, p. 226.

27. For an excellent discussion *see* "Economics and Operations Research: A Symposium," *Review of Economics and Statistics*, 50:3 (Aug. 1958), pp. 195 ff.

28. *Op. cit.*, p. 20.

29. *Op. cit.*, p. 25.

30. *Politics and Economics* (New York: St. Martin's Press, Inc., 1963), p. 5. *Italics supplied.*

Index

Index